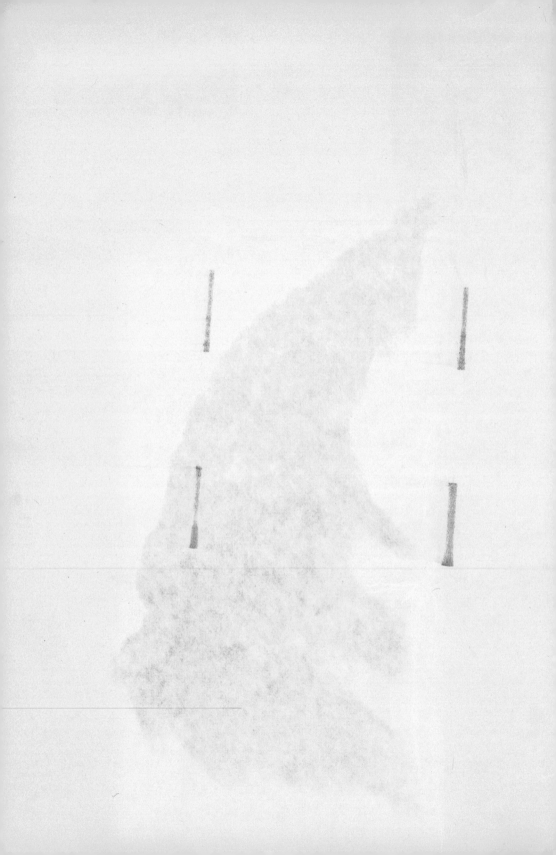

Portfolio Aspects of Corporate Capital Budgeting

Portfolio Aspects of Corporate Capital Budgeting

Methods of Analysis,
Survey of Applications,
and an Interactive
Model

E. Eugene Carter

Lexington Books
D.C. Heath and Company
Lexington, Massachusetts
Toronto   London

Library of Congress Cataloging in Publication Data

Carter, E. Eugene.
    Portfolio aspects of corporate capital budgeting.

    1. Capital investments. 2. Capital budget. 3. Capital investments—
Mathematical models. I. Title.
HG4028.C4C38   332.6'7   74-4514
ISBN 0-669-93161-6

Published simultaneously in Canada.

Printed in the United States of America.

International Standard Book Number: 0-669-93161-6

Library of Congress Catalog Card Number: 74-5414

This book is dedicated to the memory of my parents,

Marie Rowland Carter and Ernest Nick Carter

who encouraged their only child to let his mind explore.

Contents

List of Figures

List of Tables

Preface

This book analyzes a corporation manager's selection of a portfolio of projects for investment. Following a survey of the goals of corporation executives, a number of proposed models for selection of the corporate portfolio are presented. We discuss risk analysis simulation, a technique often suggested for evaluating projects, and note the difficult practical aspects of its application in a number of petroleum companies. Other models currently used by corporations in their financial and strategic planning are briefly surveyed.

We then present a model, SIFT, based on an interactive computer simulation of a portfolio of projects. This simulation allows an executive to consider risk, and to study the portfolio for a company in a variety of dimensions (sales, earnings per share, cash flow, and net present value). Later, we present the results of this model's usage with over 100 executives in a laboratory setting, and offer suggestions for implementation of the model in a corporation.

Many readers will find parts of the book hold varying degrees of appeal. The corporate manager may be interested in the survey of some corporate models and the possible application of this model in a corporation. The economist may be most curious about the values of executives in capital budgeting decisions. The professor of finance may be especially interested in the review of capital budgeting techniques and approaches to risk. With this diverse readership in mind, I have written this book with a careful discussion of the chapters and appendixes in the Introduction, Chapter 1. Hence, the specialized reader is encouraged to consult this summary in order to locate the materials of most personal interest.

This research has been supported by a National Defense Education Act Fellowship and a Ford Foundation Doctoral Dissertation Fellowship to the author at Carnegie-Mellon University's Graduate School of Industrial Administration; by a grant from the Shell Companies Foundation; and by funds from the Division of Research of the Harvard Business School. I express great appreciation for this financial support. In addition, my special thanks are due to two stimulating faculty members from Carnegie, Dean Richard M. Cyert (now President) and Professor Kalman J. Cohen (now Solomon Brothers Professor of Financial Institutions, New York University). I also acknowledge with gratitude the comments of Chris Argyris, Gordon Donaldson, Pearson Hunt, and James McKenney during several discussions of this manuscript.

My warmest personal appreciation is offered to Dr. Charlotte Boschan. Although not reared in an English-speaking household, her patience as an economist reviewing a management book was exceeded only by her thoroughness in correcting the style of a native.

The empirical results presented in Chapter 7 are from participants in the 24th session of the Program for Management Development. To these men and women and to those in the other sessions (20-23, and 26), my thanks for their being my teachers in the fullest sense of the word. My thanks, too, to Mr. Tom Flynn, Mr. Joel Glasky, and Mr. Paul Engle who completed portions of the computer programming involved in the model.

Finally, my gratitude and thanks to Mrs. Louise Peters, Miss Donna Blaisdell, and Mrs. Inez Baskerville, who with good humor and patience endured the typing of many drafts with seemingly endless ill-written corrections.

Naturally, none of these people or institutions bear responsibility for the conclusions contained herein.

List of Abbreviations
and Symbols

CV	Coefficient of Variation
CRT	Cathode Ray Tube
EPS	Earnings Per Share
$E(X)$	Expected Value, or Mean, of the Variable X
NPV	Net Present Value
NTV	Net Terminal Value
ROR	Rate of Return
S.T.	Subject To
TROR	Terminal Rate of Return
α	Alpha
Δ	Delta
ϵ	Epsilon
ρ_{ij}	Rho, the Correlation Coefficient Between i and j
$\prod_{i=1}^{n} x_i$	The Product of Variable x_i from one to n.
$\sum_{i=1}^{n} x_i$	The Sum of Variable x_i from one to n
σ	Sigma, the Standard Deviation of a Variable
σ^2	Sigma-Squared, the Variance of a Variable
σ_{ij}	The Covariance Between Variables i and j
$<, \leqslant, >, \geqslant$	Less than, Less than or Equal, Greater than, and Greater than or Equal.

Portfolio Aspects of
Corporate Capital
Budgeting

1 Introduction

True understanding comes with the realization that everything factual is, in essence, theory.

Goethe

The concept of incrementalism or marginalism, familiar to college sophomores enduring their first economics course, is often considered to have relevance toward theories of the expansion of knowledge. Thus, the work of any scientist or scholar seeking to understand odd characteristics in his field (where "odd" usually means "unexplained" or "outcomes inconsistent with predicted behavior") is considered to move by evolution from one discovery or insight to the next. Each link in this evolution is seen, not as a breakthrough, but as a logical evolution of a "world view" derived from previous developments in that field. The many instances of parallel "discoveries" in other fields (such as the nature of species and nuclear fission) by scholars working independently support this concept of evolutionary thought, as opposed to the idea of a "great person" whose contribution would have been unrealized had (s)he not lived. One might even argue that the real "breakthrough," heralded as completely novel by discoverer and observers alike is often but a subconscious evolutionary or marginal thought process.

One can view the development of knowledge in the fields of *management, management science*, and *financial theory* in this light. In the last twenty years, for example, our knowledge of the way in which managers attempt to deal with their environment has expanded considerably in response to the efforts of many businessmen and academic researchers to understand this process of management. The sheer number of scholars reviewing the subject clearly has been a major factor in this new knowledge. Similarly, if we define the process of management science broadly to include the use of computers or mathematical concepts as well as organization theory concepts to help solve management problems, then we may agree that the widespread use of computers in corporations for tasks of increasing complexity demonstrates the incremental growth of knowledge in this field. Finally, if we look at the sharply altered concepts of financial theory, which have changed in part because of new research techniques using mathematics, statistics, and computer facilities, then we can observe evolutionary growth in this field as well.

One cannot be a Dr. Pangloss, for one cannot know all concurrent developments in any field, nor can one be as unduly optimistic as Candide. Certainly,

1

there has been overemphasis and overpromise. The impact of much of the cost of capital research has been mixed, for example. We now think about the cost of capital for a corporation in a more rigorous manner than we did twenty years ago, but the empirical data and the research techniques are simply not adequate to support strong judgments on the optimum structure of debt and equity for any given firm at a particular point in time. Evidence can be brought to bear, but the problems of changes in variables which should be held constant, the definitions of risk for businesses in similar areas of operation, and so forth all render findings limited in their potential for generalization. Similarly, in the field of the management scientists' impact on management, massive overpromise (derived from honest overenthusiasm as well as self-interest in personal promotion) has resulted in disillusionment and abandonment of many expensive management science projects in corporations and elsewhere. Likewise, the popularly successful management science techniques (i.e., inventory control, account receivable management, credit policies) are all too often dismissed as "trivial" by their critics. The management scientist can argue, of course, that solving trivial choices gives management more time for important tasks and paves the way for the acceptance of quantitative techniques in the resolution of these more substantial issues.

These cross currents of opinion and the emotional intensity with which they are often voiced suggest the fiery and persistent medieval dragons. From these creatures who appear in the analysis of the impact of financial and management science theory on management, one might hear the following:

Dragon 1: "The theoretical framework of financial management is the critical variable. A computer model is only one means of implementing the theory. The timely availability of information at reasonable cost and the ability to manipulate it are relatively unimportant." (Financial Theorist)

Dragon 2: "The computer system and the model imbedded in the computer program are the central concern. The processing of masses of data and the rapid presentation of conclusions to the manager is the area of strongest impact on the decision. The nonquantifiable variables (if they exist at all!) are not usually critical to the successful operation of the model. After all, the exact and timely answer to the approximate problem is probably better than an approximate and delayed answer to the real problem." (Management Scientist)

Dragon 3: "Models and theory are irrelevant. The critical variable is judgment, and no model or theory can replace the executive's evaluation of a major problem." (Management Practitioner)

Dragon 4: "Regardless of their potential to revolutionize management, models and theory have not helped the managers to deal with any really important topic. They have failed in cost effectiveness. They exclude the relevant variables. Managers just are not comfortable with them." (Popular Empiricist)

Dragon 5: "Whatever the inputs of current managers, management scientists, computers, or financial theorists, what we really need is reorganization of the firm, and perhaps a reorientation of managers in their values and human relations skills. The problem is not how managers think or use computers, but the way in which large numbers of managers interact with each other. This area, not technology, is where we must work." (Organization Specialist)

These comments from the monsters, are, of course, exaggerated. However, the thrust of this monograph is the inevitable *interrelationship* of the management, the management science, and the financial theory judgments. No model of optimal financial behavior operationally can exist independent of awareness of computer devices and costs, independent of the limitations of data availability, or independent of the organizational and management elements which affect the potential for implementation. Similarly, the computer model which fails to filter the data, which ignores relevant theory, and which disregards the impact on the organization and the manager of sophisticated computers and programs is bound to be less effective than one which does not have these faults. Finally, the manager who steadfastly refuses to tolerate the combination of theory and management science to the firm, who refuses to train subordinates and him-herself for the benefits of these technological and intellectual contributions, is wasting resources for human beings within the firm and for those citizens who are dependent upon the corporation as the major economizing force in society.

This book is written for the corporate manager and for those scholars interested in a new model for management planning. The specialized scholar within management, financial theory, or management science may not find the latest "breakthrough" of the field discussed here. On the other hand, this book has the theme of the importance of *interrelationship*, of balance among these three fields. And its conclusion is that this relationship is symbiotic: that there is a magnificent potential for successful balance among these areas, in which each concedes some decisions to the other because of comparative advantage.

An Overview of the Book

This book is written for the researcher or corporate executive who is interested in a variety of approaches which are available for analyzing capital budgeting problems. Explanation of the various approaches is presented, and only a basic knowledge of algebra is assumed. The more detailed information which may be desired by some readers and the more basic knowledge required by others is presented in footnotes and appendixes. Thus, some academic readers probably will find technical material of interest to them contained in appendixes rather than in the basic text.

The rest of Chapter 1 discusses some theoretical and methodological findings of academic and management researchers as those results bear upon the capital budgeting decision. The discussion will center about what managers *do* (descriptive models) and what they *should* do (prescriptive or normative decision models). The "should do" models, of course, are based on specific assumptions. Usually an analysis of why the manager may avoid the normative models' prescribed behavior is presented.

Chapter 2 presents various systems for coping with risk in capital budgeting. After Chapter 1 has established the importance of a variety of criteria in any capital investment analysis, Chapter 2 carries this multiple goal analysis further to analyze the way in which risk can be considered. The chapter includes a brief discussion of probabilistic analysis for those unfamiliar with the concept. Appendix 2A discusses several analytical capital budgeting techniques, and indicates how risk evaluation has been incorporated in some of the models. Appendix 2B presents background analysis for the building of a computer simulation model.

Chapter 3 discusses the limitations of risk analysis. This chapter is based primarily on a survey of four major petroleum companies, and outlines the probable reasons for the success or failure of the attempt to implant risk analysis computer simulation in the capital budgeting process of a firm.

Chapter 4 broadens the analysis of earlier chapters by surveying published reports on what firms have actually done in the area of financial and strategic planning models. Although companies are often tempted to parade their successes, especially when the published reports are prepared by the model-builders, there is a contravening effect in that firms which have extremely sophisticated models may be reluctant to publicize them. However, this chapter does attempt to survey what is known generally about planning models in companies. The chapter also presents information about several particular companies, together with appropriate references for those who wish to study in more detail these companies' accounts of their own model-building efforts.

Chapter 5 introduces the concept of portfolio analysis. Since a company invests in a package of projects rather than a single project, the relevant context for the goals is the expected performance of the entire firm, together with whatever measure of risk for the entire firm is desired. Appendix 5A discusses the mathematics of portfolio variance calculations, comparing the calculations in a firm (whose portfolio is a package of individual projects) and the calculations in a security portfolio (where the portfolio consists of a number of securities). This appendix presents the changes necessary in the well-developed theory of security portfolios to accommodate the situation involving a portfolio of projects. Appendix 5B surveys the mathematical programming models for capital budgeting in portfolios which have appeared in recent years.

Chapter 6 outlines the characteristics of an interactive computer simulation program which allows executives to select a portfolio of projects at a remote computer terminal. This model, called SIFT, allows the executive to study the outcome of a portfolio of projects on a variety of goals, to review the risk characteristics of his portfolio on each of those goals using portfolio concepts of risk, and to revise the contents of the portfolio continually. Various screening and filtering devices are built into the model to aid the executive in his selection of the most desirable portfolio. Appendixes 6A and 6B present the framework of the model as it was related to a pair of cases which were used in experimental testing of the model with 102 executives. Appendix 6C shows the sample output from the model which was made available to these executives.

Chapter 7 analyzes the behavior of executives selecting projects for inclusion in a portfolio; the evidence is based on the use of the SIFT model described in Chapter 6. In addition to presenting the executives' reaction to this model, indicating that they were able to use the model successfully in their own minds to select portfolios with suitable risk and return characteristics, this chapter presents other information gathered from the testing of the SIFT model. Specifically, the chapter discusses their ability to fulfill their nominal goals, the manner in which they coped with risk, the variations in their project selection based on regional and professional background factors, and the manner in which they handled the complexities of certain financial subtleties. These subtleties included the ranking of projects by rate of return and present value (with alternative rankings), the problems of portfolio complexities, and the manner in which leases were evaluated.

Chapter 8 specifically outlines the possible installation of a model such as SIFT in a corporation. Nothing in the model is technologically or economically unfeasible. The experiment with the executives indicates that it seemed practically useful as well. The chapter, then, presents ideas regarding the implementation of the model.

Chapter 9 discusses the impact of information in a corporation and organizational change as they affect the potential use of SIFT. We also note that models not dissimilar to SIFT in some areas are being used. A summary of the book is at the end of the chapter.

The Choice Process in Project Investment Decisions

At the simplest level, the economic theory of the firm says that the firm invests in projects where the expected revenue net of operating expenses will cover the firm's cost of financing including a profit on the investment by owners of the business. Since cash is invested, cash is the criterion by which the firm measures its return on investment. Presumably, some adjustment is made for compounding: investors demand X percent per period, with either receipt of the cash each period, or reinvestment with compounded returns in a future period.

These are *studies of firm behavior* when investing in projects and pricing products. To understand why these results deviate from the simple economic theory, we will later survey the investment decision from the standpoint of *the single manager.* We can draw on material from academic and managerial sources which seek to understand the executive in terms of the psychological aspects of the position. Finally, we broaden our analysis to look at the *organization*, and review the evidence which examines the influence the organization has on the investment decision process.

Throughout this discussion, we will see contrasts and reference to "theories." This word should not be rejected by the practicing manager. Indeed, to paraphrase Lord Keynes, the man who roundly condemns "theoreticians" for their complex and/or irrelevant observations on the real problems of the world is himself biased by the views of some long-dead theoretician. There are good theories and bad theories, and the label attendant to each is dependent on the situation at hand. Some theories can be criticized as overly simple, yet simplification is the goal. If theory is as complicated as the world, what has one gained? The goal of a theory is to abstract the salient factors, to explain the major elements which seem to affect the process under study, and then to serve as a basis for prediction.

Some theories are normative (they describe the way a person, a firm, a country, or some other object ought to behave). Other theories are descriptive (they describe how the person, firm or country does, in fact, act). In terms of normative versus descriptive theory, what one seeks is an analysis similar to that suggested by MacCrimmon (1969). He distinguished *choice* theories versus *process* theories. In decision structures, choice theories are usually prescriptive (how an optimizing manager should behave) while process theories are usually descriptive (explaining how the decision is typically reached by the manager). "Thus, we would like to see a prescriptive theory that will help a non-idealized decision maker to improve the real choices he must make, and also a descriptive theory that will allow us to describe and predict how careful decision makers reach a decision."

Firm Behavior in the Market

Many writers seriously question the goal of profit maximization assumed in economic theory of the firm.[a] Thus there is evidence that:

1. In practice executives do not have profit maximization as the single goal;
2. Current management knowledge of cost and revenue functions is not sufficient to maximize profits even if that were the goal;
3. Organizational reality limits a manager's ability to pursue a single goal.

[a]For example, see Baldwin (1964), Baumol (1954), Chamberlain (1962), Cyert and MacCrimmon (1967), Cyert and March (1963), Katona (1951), Lanzillotti (1958), and Shubik (1961).

For example, Lanzillotti (1958) found that firms priced in order to realize a targeted *rate of return* on investment. In one sense, this conclusion leads to the chicken-egg situation, for the prices expected can determine the desirability of alternative investments, which in turn can prescribe pricing policies. However, given a plant and estimates of normal capacity utilization (e.g., 80 percent in the automobile industry), prices can then be established. If one assumes oligopolistic pricing and/or comparable firm costs, then the procedure can yield a stable outcome for the short run. Lanzillotti also found that a goal of nearly comparable importance to the targeted return on investment was a firm's desire for *market share*. Hence, to return to the example of the automobile industry, if the market develops and the firm wishes to maintain or to increase its share, then the investment decision pivots on location, size of plant, and so forth, with the tacit knowledge that some investment must be undertaken. In summary, Lanzillotti's questionnaire regarding the pricing behavior of twenty firms indicated that the criteria were:

1. pricing to achieve a target return on investment;
2. stabilization of price and margin;
3. pricing to realize a target market share; and
4. pricing to meet or prevent competition.

Gale (1972) presents a cross-sectional regression analysis based on 106 companies for which he evaluated the impact of market share, firm size, and concentration as explanatory variables for rate of return. Defining rate of return as net income on book equity over a five year period (1963-1967) and adjusting for leverage of different firms, he confirmed his hypotheses that positive relationships between market share and profitability were greater for: (1) high concentration industries versus low concentration industries; (2) moderate growth industries versus rapid growth industries; (3) relatively large firms versus smaller firms; and (4) large firms in high concentration industries with relatively moderate growth versus all other firms. He notes that, "the findings of this study would seem to confirm our belief that interaction effects, which tend to be overlooked in both theoretical and empirical studies of the firm and industry, play an important role in the determination of firm and industry performance." Hence, his conclusion is consistent with the strategy of a firm attempting to seek access to particular markets for the expectation of greater long run profitability by obtaining dominant market share.[b] Spitäller (1971) reviewed various quantitative studies of capital movements for both long term portfolio capital and foreign direct investment. He concluded that the decision to invest abroad was

[b]In decisions by American firms to invest abroad, the emphasis on market aspects as an operational goal is reinforced. From a National Industrial Conference Board (1966) study, the conclusion was that the main criterion dominating the decision process was a concern with *market position*.

primarily affected by the size of the foreign market, but noted the results were also consistent with differential rates of return. No other hypotheses for explaining the foreign investment level could be confirmed in these empirical studies. Because of the aggregate nature of the data on which the authors of the studies concluded the major impact was differential rates of return, Spitäller suggested that they did not consider the "unity of the investment decision of the international firm. This unity implies that the foreign investment decisions of a firm are interdependent."

Several elements in the Lanzillotti and other studies may be noted. First, the desire for liquidity, the hope for a quick payback of invested capital, and so forth all reveal management's concern over an uncertain future. Second, the return on investment criterion for a single investment was a consideration although the method of the evaluation varied among firms. Third, multiple factors were important in the firms studied. Whatever the relative merits of sales, profits, return on investment, and the like, the managers did seem to be concerned with more than one criterion. Fourth, broader aspects of the decision include not just sales or profits, but also concepts such as community relations, serving society, and the like. Although some of these points may be nominal goals not followed in fact or even may be surrogates for a long-run economic goal such as profit maximization, they nevertheless were stated by management as relevant. Finally, "political" and organizational factors were acknowledged as playing a part in the decision.

The Individual Manager

How does the single manager resolve conflicts over competing projects? There may be a multiplicity of goals which are fulfilled in a "scatter-gun" approach. A second conceptualization is one of sequential attention to goals; one goal is considered and then another is focused upon as the criterion. After the latter is met or exceeded, the manager seeks fulfillment of another lower priority goal, continuing in sequence. At the end of this trial, the executive may recycle to another solution with a higher value for all goals. A third approach involves achieving one goal subject to constraints on others. The manager may seek to maximize one criterion subject to minimum values on others, for example. A fourth approach is myopic concern with a single goal, allowing the other attributes to fall where they may in the outcome.

In practice, inclusion of *operational* goals (e.g., increase sales 10 percent next year) in place of *inoperable* ones (e.g., maximize the net terminal value of the firm as of 1990) is often seen. Furthermore, even in the area of near term performance, there is often a goal orientation related to growth in short-term sales or earnings per share rather than to discounted cash flow.

Concern for an attribute such as sales, long criticized by some observers as irrelevant to the basic problem of rate of return on investment, does have significance. Perhaps the executive is concerned with this criterion as indicating overall growth of the company. Perhaps it signals penetration of markets by the company which increases the potential for future profit-making situations.[c] Similarly, the individual manager, for reasons of self-interest or ignorance, may exaggerate the importance of a criterion (e.g., sales) because it is of immediate importance to him (e.g., he is a marketing executive).[d]

From the psychological work on cognition by George Miller and others, we know there are clearly restrictions on the cognitive processing capability of managers. While human beings consciously may hold certain topics in reserve, other ideas may rest beneath the surface. Somehow, these subconscious ideas are triggered by the system. That element notwithstanding, there is evidence that there are severe restrictions on the number of attributes which can be manipulated consciously at any given time. Miller (1956) concluded that the restriction was seven details on a single dimensional scale, approximately seven different dimensions, and perhaps seven objects over that span of attention. This conclusion is entirely consistent with the theory of bounded rationality from Simon (1957).

In summary, management lives of necessity in a world of imperfect and insufficient information. With positive costs of obtaining additional information, management uses rough standards for project selection. These standards are usually based on some set of operational goals (e.g., increase sales by 10 percent per year without decreasing earnings) which are applied to the firm's opportunity set of investment and acquisition possibilities. Then, limitations in quantity and quality of knowledge, restrictions on time and monetary resources, and constraints upon the evaluating capabilities of managers force executives to use the expedient standards which are available to them.

The use of rough standards for decision analysis is not inconsistent with one definition of *heuristics:*

... In problems that are very loosely structured, extremely complex, and otherwise sufficiently difficult, man requires intelligence to solve them. For such problems, "good" hypotheses for trial are chosen—using for criteria for "goodness" certain available information that may suggest which possible solution

---

[c]In one major study reviewing alternative rates of return from securities, Nerlove (1968) found a significant explanation of security returns derived from the *sales* level in one period. His approach was that returns adjusted for risk should be equal over time for various securities. If this outcome was not true, then presumably money should flow from the securities with returns below their risk-adjusted level to those with returns above their risk-adjusted level. Such arbitrage would tend to bring the risk-adjusted return securities into line over time. He found imperfections, perhaps because of tax features, inefficiencies in the markets, ignorance, or other variables. However, for the period of 1950-1964, he found that growth in sales was a significant explanatory variable for securities which had reached returns above the level which would have been predicted based on their potential risk.

[d]See "Selective Participation: A Note on the Departmental Identification of Executives" by DeWitt Dearborn and Herbert A. Simon (1958), pp. 140-144.

should be tried first, or that may rule all classes of solutions from being tried, or that may propose quick tests for distinguishing likely solutions from unlikely ones. Such criteria are called the heuristics of the problem.[e]

Organizational Interactions

Clearly, the organizational settings have an impact on the budgeting process. In the earlier stage, the basic impetus for a project, the firm's reward for risk taking, and the fact that managers have only short-term tenure in a given assignment, all affect the sort of project which will be submitted and approved [see, for example, Berg (1963), Bower (1970), and Carter (1971)]. From the control standpoint, the effectiveness in behavior and reaction also can be predicted. For example, Rotch (1958) found significantly different behavior depending on how the division was appraised. In his study, the condition under which the investment was measured, the return was measured, and the control of the division manager was executed all interacted. Simply increasing information is of no particular benefit. One must ask whether the information is more relevant or more useful. Perhaps the greatest guide is to structure information so as to improve the decision process. In a group setting, Shaw and Penrod (1962) found that moderate additional amounts of information for one particular group member would increase that group member's influence in the group. Beyond those moderate levels of information, the influence of the member was reversed, since the additional information was rejected.

There is also the question of whether a group will select riskier projects than the individual. For instance, Wallich et al. (1962) found in laboratory experimental situations that groups would take higher risks than individuals if the responsibility could be split. Woods (1965) argues the opposite. He believes there is likely to be more conservative analysis in groups than individuals, deriving from more complete analysis of the risks and pitfalls in a group setting. This (Woods') outcome applies only when the decision is required with no control aspects to be considered. The question is how one structures the data and the results so as to forge consistency in these two different sets of information in the real corporation.

Cyert and MacCrimmon (1967), March and Simon (1953), and others emphasize the influence of the organizational participants forming coalitions, bargaining units, and the like. Cyert and March (1963) stress the theory of organizational behavior based on variables such as the goals, the expectations, and the choice process within the firm. They suggest four major relational concepts which explain the interaction among organizational members (participants). The first of these is a process of conflict resolution, in which disagreements or inconsistencies are partially resolved in most cases and never fully

[e]See Ledley (1962), p. 349.

settled. The second concept is uncertainty avoidance: where possible, the firm's members avoid confronting the imprecision and risk inherent in their environment. The third concept is problemistic search: no issue comes before the firm unless stimulated by a "trigger": a lawsuit, too low earnings, declining market share, and so forth. Finally, Cyert and March suggest that organizations are adaptive, and learn from their experiences over time. Carter (1971) applied the Cyert and March framework to the decisions of a small growth company, and suggested a number of additional concepts or modifications which were useful when applying the Cyert and March framework to the context of project or acquisition decisions. These modifications included:

1. The need to consider the effects of multiple organizational levels on the decisions;
2. The elements of the bilateral bargaining process between a project sponsor and a manager who was to accept or reject the project;
3. The influence of technology and uncertainty in the environment upon the criteria used for evaluation;
4. The importance of active stimulus for search in contrast to the passive, problem-stimulated response of Cyert and March;
5. The concept of threshold levels, in which managers value projects as "very bad," "bad," "acceptable," "good," and "very good" on a variety of criteria, rather than cross-compare all projects on all criteria with unique values; and
6. The Pollyanna-Nietzsche effect, by which managers suppress the uncertainty in project forecasts which were present when they were evaluating the project, subsequently behaving as if there is to be the "most likely" outcome on the project after it has been accepted.

Finally, one may view the capital budgeting process in a typical organization as an inexact, changing, inconsistent, and unpredictable process. In the most cynical viewpoint, one may regard it as "organized anarchy," a situation referenced by Cohen et al. (1972) as having most relevance to a university. They suggest that an organized anarchy is an organization or decision characterized by three general properties. First, there is problemistic reference: no clear order of consistency exists, but references are only to the given situation. Second, there is unclear technology: the organization does not know what it is doing even subconsciously. Third, there is fluid participation: individuals fluctuate over time as participants and vary in the effort contributed to the solution of the problem.

In summary, at least three factors are important to corporate investment decision making:

Risk. The manager is concerned not only with *expected* return but also with the variability in that return.

Interdependencies. Individual project analysis is not adequate for handling an entire portfolio since interaction of returns among projects affects the portfolio profile.

Multiple goals. Firms consider a variety of goals (such as market dominance, growth in market share, earnings per share, rate of return) together with the "goal" of controlling the variability in many of the other goals.

Chapter 2 contains a discussion of the first of these topics, risk, together with a review of capital budgeting and simulation.

2

Risk Evaluation in Project Analysis

The quest for logic provides certainty and repose. But certainty is an illusion, and repose is not the destiny of Man.

Oliver Wendell Holmes

Introduction

In reaching long-term financial decisions for the firm, a corporate manager needs to consider (1) the selection and timing of projects in which to invest funds, (2) the total amount to be invested, and (3) the financial mixture for obtaining the funds to invest. Initially, we are concerned with a portion of the first problem: the selection of desirable projects in which to invest. As discussed previously, some of the criteria which a manager may consider are:

Cash flow. Ultimately, a project's financial return is measured in terms of cash invested and cash received. Moreover, a severe cash shortage in one period could bankrupt the firm.

Profits reported. Management is concerned with reported earnings for a variety of reasons. There may be an impact on the price of the stock (with possibilities of a corporate takeover), and there may be violation of loan covenants, for example.

Timing of profits and cash flow. The manager also considers how the value of cash and profits are altered with the passage of time.

Uncertainty. The predictability and range of probable outcomes are a focus of management concern. How does one wish to trade-off a relatively certain 10 percent return from one project against another project with either 50 percent return or a 5 percent loss?

Portfolio effects. The benefit of any single project is rarely independent of other projects the firm has previously undertaken or may accept in the future.

Business strategy. A manager must consider those areas of the economy in which he wishes the firm to operate, and how flexible its resources should be for future operations.

In dealing with the topic of capital budgeting, many managers have selected one or another technique for discounting future cash flows. Those readers who wish an introduction to the standards in capital budgeting are referred to Appendix 2A, which contains a discussion of payback analysis, internal and terminal rates of return, and net present value. As these models were moved in

13

application from a world of certainty to an uncertain environment, a variety of alterations were suggested. One means of coping with risk was simply to raise the discount rate which the project was required to meet. By having multiple discount rates (sometimes called "hurdle" rates), the firm applied a risk adjustment in any discounted cash flow evaluation of projects which had varying degrees of risk. We briefly will discuss this idea in the context of the corporation's cost of capital. Still other approaches have focused upon some explicit measure of the variability of future cash flows, and have then adjusted the ultimate value of the cash flows by some explicit function of the variability measure. One of the most popular adjustments has been based upon the variance in return or in net present value. Following an introductory discussion of probability and variance calculations, we will turn to the details of *risk analysis simulation*, a technique which has been used to incorporate the idea of dispersion of returns into an appraisal of projects. Risk analysis itself does not require a measure, such as the variance, for evaluating the uncertainty of an outcome. On the other hand, an understanding of the variance concept can stimulate some imaginative thoughts about the interpretation of results from a risk analysis evaluation.

The Cost of Capital and Risk

At the heart of most corporation finance courses is the idea of the cost of capital. The issue is central because the cost of capital has direct bearing on the required return for projects. Simply stated, unless the corporation can provide a return to those who provided funds for its operations, then it is not meeting its "cost" of capital. Accordingly, the firm must verify that the projects in which it invests meet that cost of funds.

Several comments are appropriate. First, *projects* refer to broadly defined entities. They are not just a new plant or a building, but can be thought of as topics as varied as the expansion of accounts receivable or inventories to stimulate sales, a new product which will be introduced, and so forth. Second, *return* can be defined in various ways. The return to debtholders and other lenders is the interest they receive together with any price appreciation or depreciation in the price they paid for the instrument of indebtedness compared to the price at which it is redeemed. The return to equity holders is more complex, but the return ultimately is also composed of dividend income plus price appreciation (or depreciation). Although many investment analysts focus upon earnings per share, the problem is that the equity holder does not receive earnings. This is a central issue.

For example, consider how much one would pay for an established business with excellent prospects and a good management, but a management which had specified that the firm would never pay dividends. Even with growing earnings which were assured, unless one can somehow receive cash from a business, the business has no value. Perhaps one can assume that the management may change its mind, or management itself may be changed. Alternatively, the firm may be taken over and liquidated, in which case the assets per share (which would have increased given the accumulated earnings that were never paid in dividends) would be distributed. This may be considered a liquidating dividend. Accordingly, with a little thought, one can conclude that it is dividends and the expectations of future dividends that give value to an investment. One does not hold a stock forever, but rather sells it to someone else. The price this rational buyer pays, however, may be based on the discounted present value of future dividends.

Earnings per share is a good guide to the company's probable growth and dividends. Thus, the analyst may quite properly focus on earnings per share even though not considering the process outlined above. For me to see a stop sign and halt my car, I can react in total ignorance of the neurological and physical laws involved. Thus, the image of the stop sign in my brain connects from optic nerves to sensory nerves, and a reaction is determined by my conditioning that I ease up on the gas, move my foot to the brake pedal, and press. This process, in turn, releases fluid from a reservoir under pressure which travels through a hose to ultimately press a plate or a drum against the wheels of my car. Friction reduces the ability of the wheel to turn easily, and since the wheel is attached to the tire, friction between the tire and the pavement stops my car. As noted, I do not need to know any of this process to *behave* in a manner consistent with this pattern. In similar fashion, the stock analyst does not need to understand or to believe any of the "cost of equity" analysis presented earlier to behave in a manner consistent with it.[a]

By historical record or judgment about the future, the financial officer of the firm can decide what costs apply to debt, preferred stock, equity, and other issues. Assuming this officer is concerned with financing future projects and raising new funds, the cost of these items is weighted by their proportion based on fair market value.[b]

If the business risk of the firm is taken as given (that is, the firm may be in a low risk business such as an established department store, or a high risk business such as a new computer company), then one can ask how the mixture of various

---

[a]Focusing on dividend yield and expected growth in dividends helps avoid the overly simple assumption of looking only at current earnings per share versus price as a "cost" of equity. If XYZ Corporation has a 50 price/earnings ratio, then the cost of equity in this model would be only 2 percent. That is, new stock sold at $100 would have to earn only $2.00 per share to have no dilution in earnings per share, given the 50 PE. Does that imply that IBM or any other high multiple stock company should sell millions of dollars in new equity and invest it in government bonds? The earnings per share would actually increase if the net yield after tax is above 2 percent. This point emphasizes the importance of growth; IBM's investors are not investing in IBM to have it behave as a bank or trust portfolio, but rather to achieve superior growth over time.

[b]Generally, market value weights rather than historical balance sheet weights are preferred.

sources of capital affects the cost of funds to the firm. Most financial observers today would agree that some debt is probably reasonable. Since equity holders take all the business risk of the firm plus the financial risk induced by the presence of senior financial securities (i.e., debt, preferred stock), they will demand a higher return. As a greater amount of debt is added to the capital structure, the equity holders will expect a higher return since the financial risk they face has increased because of the leverage.

Likewise, at some point the cost of debt will rise, for the debt-holders suffer increased probability of bankruptcy from the firm's inability to meet interest or principle obligations as they come due.

For the firm, this combination of factors creates a cost of capital curve which may appear as presented in Figure 2-1. The overall cost of capital of the firm is a function of the cost of debt and equity and their relative proportions. The cost of capital initially declines as the relatively cheaper debt is substituted for the more expensive equity. At some point, the steadily increasing equity cost combined with the increasing cost of debt will cause the cost of capital to flatten and then to rise. There is continuing controversy over whether there is a unique point or a range of points at which the cost of capital curve is low. Likewise, there is the continuing concern over how these curves differ for alternative industries (different business risks) and for more complicated financial structures than the simple debt-equity model suggested here.[c]

The job of the financial manager, then, is to schedule issues of debt, equity, and preferred stock so as to minimize the company's cost of capital over time. Thus, there are periods in the market when a debt or equity issue is relatively favorable. Hopefully, the financial officer can avoid the periods of highest cost for issuing these securities. Expectations may change, of course. In the last few years, many firms who refused to issue debt at an interest cost of 9 percent were rapidly seeking funds 18 months later at 9 1/2 percent. The difference was that the 9 percent rate was at a time of rising rates which eventually reached 10 percent for seasoned corporate debt issues. Then, when the market turned down to "only" 9 1/2 percent, many executives were happy to seize these relatively lower rates. This attitude reflected a crucial need for cash in some cases. However, it is also likely that 9 1/2 percent became more reasonable once the higher rates had been seen. Previously, even 9 percent seemed outrageously high.

By focusing upon the capital structure concept, one can avoid being caught in the bind of evaluating capital projects on the basis of the particular financing alternative being considered at a point in time. Thus, if the company is issuing debt with an after-tax cost of 4 percent, one might use a discount rate of 4 percent in evaluating projects. Some years later, an exceedingly high debt ratio induced by following this policy over time would force an equity issue. Assume

---

[c]For those readers more interested in the assumptions beyond this analysis and for additional references, see any introductory text, such as Weston and Brigham (1972) or VanHorne (1974).

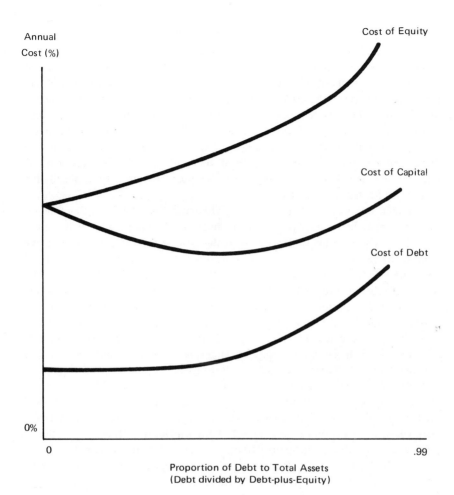

Annual
Cost (%)

Cost of Equity

Cost of Capital

Cost of Debt

0%

0

.99

Proportion of Debt to Total Assets
(Debt divided by Debt-plus-Equity)

Figure 2-1. The Cost of Capital.

the manager feels equity costs 15 percent; the implication is that the projects being evaluated that year should meet a 15 percent hurdle rate. Yet, such a mentality plays havoc with any sort of decentralized organization in which divisions must compete against each other for scarce funds. The motivation of a divisional manager would be to submit all the low return projects in debt-financing years and save the higher return projects for equity-financing years and/or to urge a competing division manager to meet the equity hurdle rate.

The conclusion is that the firm should decide on a cost of capital which represents the reasonable cost of the combined components of the capital structure over time. This cost is used as the hurdle rate each year regardless of the particular financing which is undertaken that year.

Obvious as this conclusion is to most practicing financial executives, its subtlety is often missed when evaluating major projects, or proposals which have particular mortgage debt attached to them. In most cases, a lender considers the overall capitability of a business, not just the security of a mortgage on a proposed new building. Likewise, the presence of a mortgage on a building may in turn affect the potential availability of debt from *other* lenders. Hence, to "give" the new building the benefit of all the debt (resulting in a lower hurdle rate for the new building as a project) ignores the effect of lessened debt availability for the rest of the corporation.

A similar confusion sometimes occurs when major projects are being financed by their manufacturers, as several competing shipyards who will arrange financing for their ships. Independent of the cost of the ships, many firms will look at the return to equity. That return, of course, is a function of the ship's cost, the revenues and operating expenses, and the timing of the particular financing scheme offered by a given shipyard. Holding the cost, revenue and operating cost assumptions constant, it is obvious that the shorter loan (faster payback) option will have a lower return to equity in normal settings. Essentially, the cheaper debt financing will be paid off sooner, meaning that the ship will be financed increasingly by larger portions of equity over its life. Lacking debt on which to leverage the return to equity, the return to equity will be lower than otherwise would be the case.

The analysis is valid, however, *only* if one assumes that no other financing is available in later years. One can argue that short term financing might be used in later years, or at the end of the period of the shorter debt financing option to replace some or all of that debt. Alternately, one needs to consider if the clean or low-debt balance sheet afforded by the rapid repayment of debt under the shorter-lived debt option would not permit more debt from other lenders for financing additional projects.

When the project's cash flows are discounted at the cost of capital, the presumption is that the capital structure of the firm remains *in balance* over the entire life of the project.[d] It is the failure to observe this condition that creates the confused analysis noted above.

In some situations the particular financing may be dominated uniquely and completely by the particular project at hand. Special joint ventures or subsidiaries in which the parent firm offers no guarantees may be looked at as unique projects, and the relevant cost of capital assigned. For example, Freeport Minerals traditionally operates in this manner. Nationalization of its huge Cuban nickel plant caused the parent to lose its equity, and several banks to lose huge amounts of loans to the project secured by that plant. However, the effect on the other lenders to Freeport and the rest of Freeport's operations was minimal.

---

[d]See Appendix 2A for a review of discounting.

This case is probably atypical. Often the corporation will feel a legal or moral obligation (perhaps induced by enlightened self-interest in assuring itself a welcome for future financing options) to pay off liabilities of legally separate entities, as American Express' behavior vis-à-vis its warehousing subsidiary in the wake of the salad oil scandal.

The cost of capital for the firm is one of the most unsettled issues in both theory and practice. When one turns to the evaluation of the appropriate cost of capital for a *project*, the confusion increases. Essentially, the cost of capital to the firm is related to the return and risk of the firm, which is derived from the underlying return and risk of the firm's investments, i.e., the projects. How does one determine the appropriate cost of capital for projects of varying risk classifications? The issue is important, for that cost of capital is reflected in the discount rate used in evaluating the project.

One can focus on the weighted cost of capital appropriate "for this investment." Where the corporation is a holding company, in effect one may view separate corporations as relatively passive investments. The weighted cost of capital may be computed for those subunits as separate entities either by looking at how the market evaluated competitors of those subunits which are publicly traded or by discussing with lenders and investors the appropriate capital structure of those entities.

Inductively, this same sort of logic can be applied to projects *within* a given firm. If the project carries more risk, one can argue that the relevant cost of capital is higher. This result is called the *risk adjusted discount rate*.

An alternative to these approaches which in practice should accomplish the same result is to focus on discounting the project's cash flows at a rate appropriate for an all-equity investment, and then adjusting for various loads of debt. If this adjustment is made, then (1) the amount and cost of the debt, and (2) the amount and cost of the equity will vary somewhat from project to project. The result is an analysis which is not dissimilar to the weighted cost of capital in practice. Whatever the intellectual justification, higher hurdle rates are used for riskier projects. In the Fremgen (1973) survey, 54 percent of the 170 respondents indicated their firms used higher discount rates when evaluating riskier projects.

The reasoning is straightforward. The project has a certain *business risk* which affects the amount and/or the cost of the debt. Yet this debt adds *financial risk* to the equity holders, and they demand a higher return to compensate for this risk. Accordingly, as one moves from project to project, the question is always how to consider the appropriate (business) risk of the project, then to evaluate the debt cost and amount, and finally to determine an appropriate cost of equity given these business and financial risks. Usually, particular debt or equity financing is considered part of the ongoing funds needed by the firm, and is not earmarked in the mind of the lender/investor for a particular project. Hence, the firm's executive has the job of determining the appropriate discount rates for projects *given* debt and equity available to the firm at certain rates and in certain proportions. Over time, of course, the firm's selection of projects will feed back to affect the costs of debt and equity.

In addition, there is the question of diversification. *If* one believes that the corporation has an advantage over individuals in diversification (because of management skills, the availability of large pools of capital, differential tax laws, limited liability of corporations, superior information, or some other concept), then the corporate-wide cost of capital may be *lower* than the appropriate cost of capital for all subsidiary unit or projects combined. This conclusion follows when one recognizes that diversification lowers total risk, hence allowing the overall return to diminish since the risk is no longer as great. This lower risk is available only to investors in the diversified corporation, given the assumptions, and not to investors who carve their investments among the company's projects.[e] Accordingly, the manager then has to consider how the surplus return from a portfolio of projects is to be divided. Some observers have suggested that the cost of monitoring and coordinating the broadly diversified firm may exceed any potential benefits from the spreading of risk. Alternately, some critics discount the existence of benefits from corporate diversification. They argue that the investor can adequately diversify. Of course, these two criticisms are not inconsistent with each other. If both are granted, the broadly diversified firm is economically inefficient, for there is a net cost of coordination which is not offset by any diversification benefits unrealizable by individual investors on their own.

A Measure of Risk

Central to the idea of an uncertain or risky world is the idea of *probabilities*.[f] The concept is straightforward: the chance of throwing any particular number on an honest die is one out of six, 1/6, or .166667 in decimal form. The chance of drawing an ace from a regular pack of playing cards is the probability of drawing the ace of hearts, the ace of clubs, the ace of spades, or the ace of diamonds. This probability is the number of aces (4) divided by the number of cards (52), or 1/13.

Probabilities of outcomes (often abbreviated "Prob" or simply "*P*") determine the expected value, or *mean*, of the outcome. To return to the die example, the expected value of many throws on the die is the sum of the probability of any outcome times the value of the outcome, or

[e]Related to this concept of the investor's ability to diversify is the "homemade leverage" argument of Modigliani and Miller. In a perfectly competitive market, the investors can lever themselves as wished; hence, they may act as arbitrageurs among differentially levered corporations. Corporate leverage, then, is irrelevant in the absence of corporate deductability of interest for tax purposes and bankruptcy risks. The relevance of this issue is discussed in Robichek and Myers (1965) and other corporate finance sources cited earlier.

[f]Statisticians and those familiar with the concept of risk can readily skip this section.

Outcome		P		P × Outcome = Value
1	×	1/6	=	1/6
2	×	1/6	=	2/6
3	×	1/6	=	3/6
4	×	1/6	=	4/6
5	×	1/6	=	5/6
6	×	1/6	=	6/6
		1		21/6 = 3 1/2.

Here, since the sum of all the probabilities is 1, we know that all possible outcomes are included. The "average" outcome is the sum of each outcome value times its probability of occurring, or 3 1/2. Similarly the average value for a card drawn at random from a deck, in which the cards are numerically valued from 1 to 13, is 7.

Suppose one applies this concept to the rate of return from a project which a firm is considering. After some study, it has been determined that the probabilities of various ranges of returns are as shown in Figure 2-2. In this Figure, the probability of a return is presented on the vertical axis, and the rate of return on the horizontal axis. One can interpret these graphs in several ways. For example, what is the probability of a return less than 10 percent? It is the sum of the probabilities of all intervals below that level, or

$$\text{Prob(loss to } 0\%) + \text{Prob}(0\% \text{ to } 10\%) = .05 + .25 = .30.$$

Alternatively one could plot the same results as a continuous curve (the middle graph of Figure 2-2), where the intervals for which the outcomes are shown in the first graph are made successively narrower to provide a curve of the probabilities.[g] Here, one can distinguish that the probability of a return of 1 percent is about .01 and a return of 9 percent has a probability of about .03. The top graph containing the large intervals allows no room to distinguish between these two outcomes; they both occur in the interval "0-10 percent" which has a probability of .25. One can look at either side of the range in an interval graph to have a better idea of probable returns at the ends of each interval, and the graph with the smaller intervals presents the results explicitly.

Another way of looking at the probable outcomes is shown at the bottom of Figure 2-2. The probability of a return of *more* than a certain level can be read directly since this graph sums the results from an interval graph. Similarly, one can determine the probability of a return *less* than a certain level. Since the sum of the probabilities must equal 1, and since all the probabilities are included, one can subtract the probability of returns *more* than (say) 5 percent from 1.00 to

[g]In fact, graphs such as shown in the middle of Figure 2-2 are usually "smoothed" data, interpolated from the midpoints of the bars on a graph such as at the top of the figure.

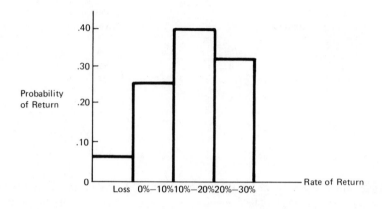

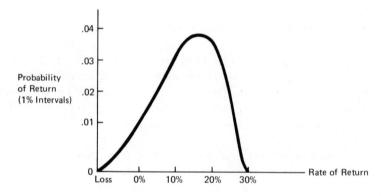

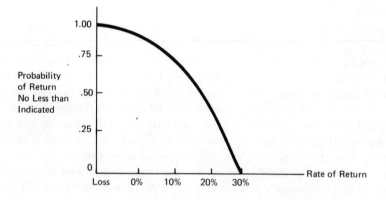

Figure 2-2. Probabilities of Rates of Return.

find the probability of returns *less* than 5 percent. In this present example, that return would be about

$$\text{Prob(less than 5\%)} = 1 - .85 = .15.$$

Suppose one project has a distribution of returns as in Project *A* in Figure 2-3, and another has a distribution of returns as in Project *B*. We may agree that there are many criteria to consider, but that we want at a minimum to decide whether Project *A* or *B* is likely to have the "better" rate of return. Yet, from the cost of capital discussion, we know that a riskier project requires a greater rate of return. *The dispersion of the returns is one way to consider risk.* Project *A* has a greater "spread" in probable outcomes, but we need a summary statistic to measure that dispersion.

One measure of the dispersion of the returns is the *variance*, or its square root, the *standard deviation*. If the distribution is a statistically *Normal* one as shown in Figure 2-3, then the standard deviation has the convenient quality that

1. The interval from the average *minus one* standard deviation to the average *plus one* standard deviation includes .65 of the probable returns;
2. The interval from the average *minus two* standard deviations to the average *plus two* standard deviations includes .95 of the probable returns;
3. The interval from the average *minus three* standard deviations to the average *plus three* standard deviations includes .99 of the probable returns.

The calculation of the variance is a straightforward process. When the returns and the probabilities associated with each return are determined, then the average is computed in a manner similar to that explained in connection with the "average" roll of a die. This average is then subtracted from each return and the differences are squared, which eliminates the minus sign. The squared differences are then multiplied by the respective probabilities and the products added together. The answer is the variance.[h] Variance is usually written as σ^2 (sigma, squared).

Variance is a measure of the *variability* in outcome of a project on some particular dimension. But how does one compute the variance of a *portfolio* of projects? Suppose three projects are considered. Each is a cement plant, with one in each of two Brazilian states and one in Vermont. Each will have some expected return and variance. Suppose a manager wants to invest in two plants, but is unsure of which two are preferred. The variance of an investment in the two Brazilian plants may be very close to the sum of each plant's variance; each of them shares most of the same risks with respect to the world cement market, imports to Brazil, the value of the Cruzeiro, inflation, and so forth. On the other

---

[h]Variance in algebraic terms is computed as follows. Let "trial" denote an observation or a sample outcome, and (footnote continues on p. 24)

hand, the variance in return on the same money invested in the Vermont plant and either one of the Brazilian plants may be substantially less than the simple sum of the two projects' variances. Here, there is obvious *diversification*. The executive has reason to hope that a labor strike, or severe inflation or devaluation in one country, for example, would not necessarily follow in the other. It is true that both pairs of investments are subject to the same technological and world market conditions of cement. But there is a benefit from geographically spreading the risk.

Finally, our hypothetical manager might elect more diversification by investing in one Brazilian cement plant and a department store in Atlanta. There is then geographic diversification and business diversification.

These examples should present intuitive reasons for rejecting variance sums as a measure of *portfolio* variance. The variance pays no heed to any other project. Accordingly, another statistical measure is used, the *covariance*. Between each project and every other project, the covariance can be computed. Further, the variance of a portfolio of two or more projects can be found by combining the respective variances and covariances.[i] Hence, the portfolio variance can be found readily, and it reflects the effects of diversification!

Y_i be the value of variable Y on trial i

P_i be the probability of trial i occurring, and $\sum_{i=1}^{N} P_i = 1$, where

$$\sum_{i=1}^{N} P_i \text{ means } P_1 + P_2 + \ldots + P_N$$

$\overline{Y}$ be the average of all Y_i values, weighted by the probability of occurring

$$(= \sum_{i=1}^{N} P_i Y_i),$$

Then the variance is equal to

$$\sum_{i=1}^{N} P_i (Y_i - \overline{Y})^2.$$

[i]Following the earlier terminology, let

Y_i and X_i be the value of variables Y and X on trial i, respectively,

P_i be the probability of trial i occurring,

$\overline{Y}$ and $\overline{X}$ be the average of all values of Y and X, respectively.

Then the covariance is equal to

$$\sum_{i=1}^{N} P_i (Y_i - \overline{Y})(X_i - \overline{X}).$$

(footnote continues on p. 25)

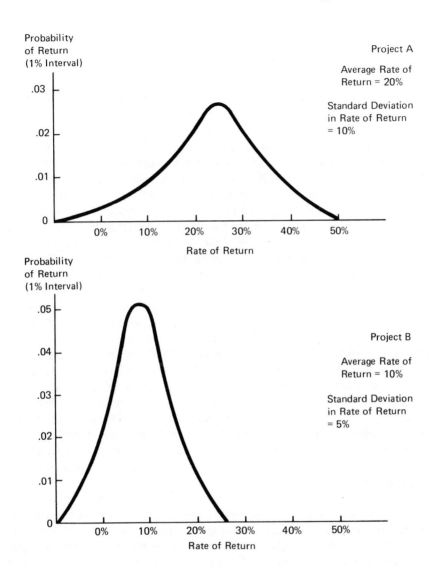

Figure 2-3. Probabilities of Rates of Return, Projects *A* and *B*.

The calculation of portfolio variances for projects will be discussed in detail in Appendix 5A. For more detailed discussions of probabilities and related concepts, see Kemeny et al. (1959). For a discussion of these concepts in addition to an expanded discussion of evaluating investments, see Quirin (1967), pp. 199-247. Variance is not an unambiguous measure of risk, as should be apparent. Different measures of risk may result in a different ranking of projects. For an example of this divergence in the area of stock portfolios, see the paper by Schlarbaum and Racette (1972).

Risk Analysis Simulation

The technique of risk analysis simulation has been available for many years. Basically, the technique requires estimates of the *distribution* of possible outcomes of a project's major factors (e.g., sales, market share, advertising costs, wage rates, etc.). The crucial variables are linked together in a model (e.g., if market share increases by 6 percent in year 3, sales will increase by an expected value of $1,000,000 with a standard deviation of $20,000). Then the model is converted to a computer program, and the manager employs simulation to determine the range of possible outcomes on any number of criteria for the project. Simulation involves repeated chance trials using outcomes from a random number generator adjusted to provide various probability distributions.[j]

Thus, from probability information about the variables which determine the rate of return of a project, we may create a computer simulation model which will provide output concerning the distribution of probable rates of return. Using a chart in conjunction with a statistic such as the standard deviation, we may then make a judgment about whether the expected return and risk of a project are consistent with the cost of capital for that project. Computer simulation allows us to aggregate many different distributions to find the resulting distribution of the rate of return, for example. Combining these different distributions, some of which may not "fit" any standard distribution, can be a tedious analytic job even for an experienced mathematician. Risk analysis simulation permits a relatively easier means of combining those distributions, and in some cases represents the only practical way to combine them. Furthermore, it allows rapid changes in the form of the distributions and the completion of a new risk analysis simulation. Steadily decreasing computer costs per calculation and judicious model building make risk analysis simulation a practical tool of management. Additional details of simulation are presented in Appendix 2B.

If the criterion is rate of return and the company is considering Project *C* and Project *D* as two mutually exclusive alternatives, there might be a distribution of returns as shown in Figure 2-4. Notice the greater risk in Project *D*. Note also that Project *D* has a higher median rate of return than Project *C*. One management might prefer Project *D*, arguing that a higher risk is fully justified by the return. Another management might prefer the safe (and lower) return of Project *C*.

In addition to showing explicitly the possible risk/return conflict, risk analysis reveals to the manager that some projects are not what they seem at first. Thus, in comparing the net present value of Projects *E* and *F* on the basis of the most likely single value (mode) for each of the many underlying variables, a manager might find Project *E* has the higher value with certainty. However, on

[j]An early published article is by Paine (1963). Other discussions may be found in Hillier (1963) and McMillan and Gonzalez (1965). A popular article is the one by Hertz (1964).

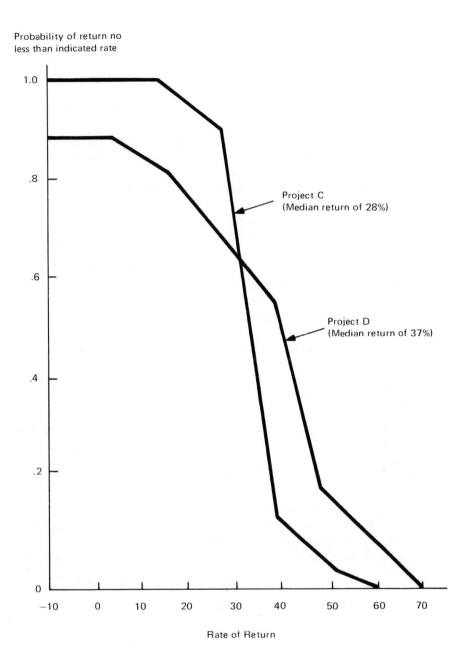

Probability of return no
less than indicated rate

Project C
(Median return of 28%)

Project D
(Median return of 37%)

Rate of Return

Figure 2-4. Cumulative Rate of Return Distribution.

the basis of simulation, the executive may learn that Project *F* has a higher mode for net present value because of the form of the underlying distributions which must be combined. Finally, risk analysis simulation may be useful for sensitivity analyses which enable one to explore the effect of shifts in any or all of the underlying variables.

In addition to the problem of obtaining estimates of the variables, a basic drawback of risk analysis is the indeterminacy of the technique. In some cases, a project will be eliminated if it is completely dominated (i.e., there are other alternatives which have a higher return for any level of risk). However, in most cases there will be no clear domination. The manager now sees risk added to the analysis, and the choice will be based on the attitude toward risk of the executive.

In dealing with the portfolio effects of capital budgeting, one is confronted with an even more involved problem. Because of the complexities of this issue, the technique of *mathematical programming* was increasingly recommended by some writers to managers as an aid in solving the capital budgeting problem.[k] Some of the earlier formulations ignored considerations of risk in exchange for a consideration of the portfolio effects. However, a later formulation of the capital budgeting problem sought to solve the risk-return tradeoff in a portfolio context by using the Markowitz "efficient frontier" concept. This concept was originally related to selecting a portfolio of securities from the universe of all investments, and the selection was made from those optimum portfolios which had minimum risk for any given return [see Markowitz (1959)]. Hence, the manager could gain a higher expected return only at the "cost" of accepting a higher risk.

The Markowitz approach was suggested for capital budgeting projects by Van Horne (1966) and by Cohen and Elton (1967). Essentially, each of these writers used computer simulation of the expected returns where the simulation was done jointly with all projects at once. From this array of possible returns, a table of the variances and covariances was computed. This table (or matrix) could be used to generate the "efficient frontier."[l]

Thus, using a body of knowledge about Normal distributions and mathematical programming techniques, these approaches have attempted to provide techniques for dealing with capital budgeting problems under conditions of risk,

---

[k]Some of the mathematical programming approaches to capital budgeting are discussed later in Appendix 5B.

[l]Among the conceptual difficulties are the existence of fractional projects (which can be eliminated by the development of an integer quadratic programming code), the single period optimization, the equating of *variance* with *risk*, and the question of multiple goals of firms. In addition, there is the practical problem that many firms do *not* face capital budgeting questions in a portfolio context [see Chamberlain (1962)]. Thus, a project is suggested, investigated, and approved or rejected individually. Then another project may appear several weeks or months later. To some extent managers could consider project proposals on a portfolio basis. On the other hand, often they must accept or reject some projects in a short time span independently of other possibilities.

with allowance for some of the interrelationships of projects. In Chapters 5 and 6, we will return to the discussion of risk in a portfolio context, and explain the risk aspects of the SIFT model.

Before discussing what corporate managers in several firms are attempting in conjunction with computerized models (Chapter 4), we will appraise some of the limitations of risk analysis. These limitations are considered from the standpoint of experience with the technique in several petroleum companies.

Appendix 2A:
An Introduction to
Capital Budgeting
Standards

This Appendix will review the concept of discounted cash flow, and three popular standards for evaluating projects: the payback period, the internal rate of return, and the net present value. In addition, the Appendix will discuss the newer concepts of the net terminal value and terminal rate of return, and indicate some features of these standards of evaluation.

Payback Period

One form of analysis of projects is the payback period. Basically, this method ranks projects on the speed with which cash is returned from the investment. Consider yearly cash flows of Y_0, Y_1, Y_2, $Y_3 \ldots Y_n$. Y_0 is negative representing the cash invested at time $t = 0$, and other Y's may be negative. The payback period is $t + \in$, where

$$\sum_{i=1}^{t} Y_i \leqslant - Y_0 \leqslant \sum_{i=1}^{t+1} Y_i \text{ and } \sum_{i=1}^{t} Y_i = Y_1 + Y_2 + Y_3 + \ldots Y_t$$

and $\in$ is the interpolation between t and $t + 1$ based on

$$\frac{- \left[\sum_{i=1}^{t} Y_i + Y_0 \right]}{Y_{t+1}}$$

If cash is received only at the end of the period, the $\in$ does not apply and the payback (or pay*out*) period is simply the period which finally permits the cash flows to equal or exceed the cash invested.

Several criticisms can be offered. The payback criterion places a premium on a quick payout of the investment; thus Project G in Table 2A-1 has a payout of 2.5 years. It would be favored over Project H with a payout of 3.2 years, even though cash inflows from Project H in years 4 through M are higher. Thus the payback period is a crude measure of *liquidity* and not one of *profitability*. It ranks two hypothetical projects equally if the payback period of one equals that of the other, regardless of the pattern of cash flows within the early years and

31

Table 2A-1
Alternative Investment Cash Flows

Year i	Project G Y_i	Project H Y_i
0	($100,000)	($100,000)
1	40,000	20,000
2	40,000	30,000
3	40,000	40,000
4	40,000	50,000
5	40,000	60,000
.	.	.
.	.	.
.	.	.
M	40,000	60,000
Payout	2.5	3.2

Project G, $t = 2$, since

$$\sum_{t=1}^{2} Y_i \leqslant -Y_0 \leqslant \sum_{t=1}^{3} Y_i \quad = 40 + 40 \leqslant -(-100) \leqslant 40 + 40 + 40$$

$$= 80 \leqslant 100 \leqslant 120$$

and $\epsilon = \dfrac{-\left[\sum\limits_{i=1}^{t} Y_i + Y_0\right]}{Y_{t+1}} = \dfrac{-[40 + 40 - 100]}{40} = \dfrac{20}{40} = .5$

so payout $= t + \epsilon = 2 + .5 = 2.5$ years.

Project H, $t = 3$,

and $\epsilon = \dfrac{-[20 + 30 + 40 - 100]}{50} = \dfrac{10}{50} = .2$

so payout $= 3.2$ years.

regardless of the pattern (or existence) of cash flows in later years. As commonly used, cash flows are not even discounted to calculate the payback period. The criterion also ignores risk; no thought is given to the likelihood of Project G's having a cash flow of $-\$10,000$ or $+\$60,000$ in year 2.

Nevertheless, managers continue to use payback as an indicator of profitability and/or risk. Executives argue that a fast payback is relatively more likely to be realized; a slow payback inherently has much more risk. Unfortunately, this view confuses the rapidity of cash flows with certainty. There is no reason to believe that Project G is more likely to realize its projected cash inflows than Project H.

Discounting: Net Present Value and Internal Rate of Return

These two concepts are designed to rank alternative projects taking into account the total expected cash throwoffs of the projects and the time value of money. Both rely on an estimate of cash flows and a projection of the firm's cost of capital.

Suppose one has X dollars (e.g., $10) and the discount rate is r (e.g., 10 percent). At the end of one year, the value of Y_1 of the holding is:

$$Y_1 = X(1+r) \qquad\qquad Y = \$10\,(1+.10) = \$11.00$$

At the end of two years:

$$Y_2 = Y_1(1+r) = X(1+r)^2 \qquad\qquad Y_2 = \$10(1+.10)^2 = \$12.10.$$

Y_2 represents the *terminal value* of investment X at the end of the second year, compounded annually at the rate, r. One can reverse the procedure. Given Y_2 dollars at the end of two years, and the rate of discount, r, then X, the amount of money now which is the same as Y_2 dollars two years hence can be found:

$$X = \frac{Y_2}{(1+r)^2} \qquad\qquad X = \frac{\$12.10}{(1+.10)^2} = \$10$$

and X is the *present value* of Y_2.

In capital budgeting, it is assumed that one knows the Y values (yearly net cash flows) for the investment. One selects a discount rate which is the opportunity cost of funds to the firm (the cost of capital), r. Then it is possible to compute X, the *net present value* of the stream of cash flows including the initial investment, Y_0, which is negative, and the other Y_i's which may be negative or positive.

$$X = Y_0 + \frac{Y_1}{(1+r)} + \frac{Y_2}{(1+r)^2} + \ldots + \frac{Y_n}{(1+r)^n}\,.$$

If the present value is positive ($X > 0$), then the investment is considered desirable, as it covers the cost of funds to the firm.

The *rate of return* is also called the discounted rate of return, internal rate of return, or return on investment. It is obtained using the same equation but slightly different analysis. Rather than using a given discount rate, r, the equation is solved for that rate for which the present value of the stream of cash outflows and inflows of an investment equals 0. That is,

$$0 = Y_0 + \frac{Y_1}{(1+r)} + \frac{Y_2}{(1+r)^2} + \ldots + \frac{Y_n}{(1+r)^n}$$

Y_0 is negative, representing the cash investment by the firm in the project.

One of the more troublesome problems that may arise is that the rate of return may not be unique. Under some conditions, it may not even be possible to compute the rate of return. Lorie and Savage (1955) point out that this situation may arise with investments which have initial cash outflows, subsequent cash returns, and later cash outflows. They give the example of an oil pump that extracts a given amount of oil from the ground more rapidly than the current model. There is an initial outlay (for the new pump), later gains in cash inflow (from the sale of the extracted oil), and final net incremental cash outlay (caused by the earlier exhaustion of the oil reserve through use of the new pump). Figure 2A-1 indicates the present value of the investment, AA', at the firm's cost of capital, A. Two internal rates of return, B and C, both equate the present value of the income stream to 0.

Multiple returns can be understood by noting that the present value of the project approaches the sum of the net cash flows for low rates of interest. If this sum is negative, the present value is negative. With a higher cost of capital, the present value of the final net cash outflow diminishes relative to the earlier flows, and the present value of the project becomes positive. Finally, as the cost of capital increases further, all flows after the first few years tend to diminish in importance and the total of the discounted cash flow stream is swamped by the initial negative investment.[a]

---

[a]Mathematically, this can be understood by Descartes' rule of signs. First, the rate of return formula can be presented as a polynomial expansion in powers of K, where K equals $(1 + r)$. Thus,

$$0 = Y_0 + \frac{Y_1}{(1+r)} + \frac{Y_2}{(1+r)^2} + \ldots + \frac{Y_n}{(1+r)^n}$$

Multiplying both sides of the above by K^n [$= (1+r)^n$], one obtains,

$$0 = Y_0 K^n + Y_1 K^{n-1} + Y_2 K^{n-2} + \ldots + Y_n.$$

(footnote continued on p. 35)

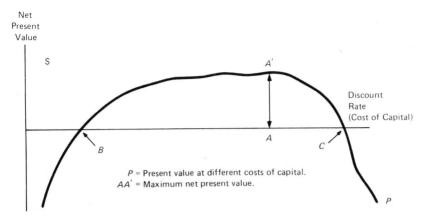

Net
Present
Value

S

A'

Discount
Rate
(Cost of Capital)

A

B

C

P = Present value at different costs of capital.
AA' = Maximum net present value.

P

Assume an oil company can add a new pump which will extract oil faster than an old pump. With the old pump, cash flows are $10,000 in one year and $10,000 in two years. At a cost of $1,600, a new pump can provide cash flows of $20,000 in one year and nothing thereafter. The relevant cash flows for the project are thus:

Time Period	Incremental Cash Flow from Investment
0	($ 1,600)
1	10,000
2	(10,000)

The "internal rate of return" of the pump is either 25 percent or 400 percent, since both equate the stream of cash flows to 0. Even if one accepts the lower rate as the standard, note that in this situation a *higher* cost of the pump would result in a *higher* return (e.g., $2,500 for the pump would result in an internal rate of return of 100 percent).

Figure 2A-1. Present Value of an Investment with Two Rates of Return. Source: Example based on Solomon, Ezra, *The Management of Corporate Capital,* The Free Press, New York, 1959.

Another problem is that the rate of return and present value criteria do not always lead to the same ranking of proposed investments. Terborgh (1956) gives the following extreme situation which has been adapted slightly for this example. The four investments provide cash flows of $1,000 per year for 5, 10, 15, and 20 years, respectively. The cost of capital is 10 percent. In this example,

---

Descartes' rule states that *at most* there will be "R" positive roots to a polynomial equation with real coefficients which has "R" changes of sign. Given negative Y's initially turning to positive ones in later years, there will be one change of sign, and at most one positive root. (In fact, there also may be imaginary roots, although the rate of return focuses only upon real roots.) The extraction example presented by Lorie and Savage has two changes of sign, since the early Y's are negative, later Y's are positive, and the final Y's are again negative. See Jean (1968) for a recent discussion of this issue.

the possible inconsistency of the rate of return and the net present value rankings is clearly apparent.

Investment Outflow	Present Value of Income Stream at 10%	Net Present Value	Rate of Return	Ranking According to N.P.V.	R.O.R.
1. ($2,991)	$3,791	$ 800	20%	4	1
2. (4,494)	6,145	1,651	18	3	2
3. (5,324)	7,606	2,282	17	2	3
4. (5,929)	8,514	2,582	16	1	4

A partial explanation for this inconsistency as well as for some of the other unusual situations which may arise lies in the way the two methods treat the cash inflows from the investments. The rate of return method assumes implicitly that yearly cash inflows can be *reinvested* by the firm at the same rate of return which applies to the project. For example, if a project had a 20 percent internal rate of return, then a $1 received in the sixth year could be replaced with an additional $1/(1 + .20) = $.83 in the fifth year, leaving the rate of return unchanged. This example indicates that the rate of return calculation implicitly assumes the reinvestment rate of cash flows is equal to the rate of return. The present value method, in contrast, assumes that the cash inflows are invested at the "cost of capital" rate. Clearly, both methods make rather strong assumptions about what the cash throwoffs are worth. Forced to pick between the two, however, one can say that the present value assumption is more realistic.

Much of the disparity in rankings in the above table is caused by imprecision about the reinvestment rate, the rate the $1,000 returned each year will earn in future years. To compare these projects with very unequal lives, one can assign a reinvestment opportunity rate to cash flows received in various years, compound the inflows, and compute a *Net Terminal Value*. One can then compute the *Terminal Rate of Return*, which is the rate of return which will compound an initial investment of X dollars to a Net Terminal Value of Y dollars. For these four investments, the Net Terminal Values and Terminal Rates of Return are shown below for a 10 percent reinvestment rate. Note the rankings here are consistent with each other and with the original NPV rankings above.

Investment	Terminal Values of Investment	of Income Stream	Net Terminal Value at 10%	Terminal Rate of Return	Ranking
1	($20,122)	$25,503	$ 5,381	13%	4
2	(30,233)	41,337	11,104	14	3
3	(35,817)	51,170	15,353	15	2
4	(39,887)	57,275	17,388	16	1

Current business practice is such that only a small minority of firms probably explicitly consider the reinvestment rate, based on the Fremgen (1973) survey. However, the same study found 15 percent of the 170 respondents reporting their firms encountered multiple rates of return "fairly frequently" or "very frequently."

A Historical Footnote

As the above remarks have indicated, the intellectual progression of discounting techniques has been rapid in recent years. Typically, no one solves the indicated equations. First, one can use a Table of Present Value Factors. In essence, these tables show the worth of $1 received at some future point, discounted at a particular rate to give the present value. These tables may be for $1 received annually for so many years, or for $1 received at the end of a single year. The discount rates typically range from 1 to 30 percent or more. In addition, some tables give the value of the funds when they are received monthly rather than annually. In fact, these tables are simply the reversal of Compound Interest tables; instead of $1 compounded forward 10 periods at 8 percent, for example, the Present Value tables show the value of $1 received in ten years discounted at 8 percent. Hence, when the manager uses these tables, he or she computes the present value of a project's cash flows by multiplying the respective cash flows times the factors taken from the table. After subtracting the initial outflow, the manager has the net present value. For the rate of return analysis, the manager tries different present value calculations until locating the discount rate which provides a present value of 0. That discount rate, then, is the rate of return.

Alternatively, and practically, many managers use a computer time sharing system. A variety of packaged programs allow one to enter various cash flows and to have the present value at several discount rates as well as the rate of return calculated and printed at the executive's console.

Today, most finance texts have come to acknowledge the importance of discounted cash flow. Quite simply, it is recognition that a future receipt has less value than cash now, simply because the holder of current funds could invest them at some interest rate. Alternatively, some accounting textbooks continue to emphasize return on net worth concepts in which the return is (say) an average of five years' earnings over an average of the five-year net worth summation. In evaluating the impact of a particular project, the profit contribution of the project (not even the cash flow) is averaged over the life of the project and divided by one-half the investment (the "average" investment, assuming the salvage value of the investment is 0) to compute the "return" of the project.

One might have excused this analysis on the simplest grounds if the present value tables are recent. With computer-induced precision, the accuracy of such tables today is dependent on the high speed of computer systems which can prepare the tables.

The tables for the present value of money are not new, however. Mining engineers have utilized such tables for many years in their evaluations of properties. One of the earlier works in the mining fields is Hoskold (1877). He presented exact tables for the pricing of annuities where there was a sinking fund compounding at a safe, risk-free rate. This sinking fund was determined so as to permit the funds to compound at a rate sufficient to retire the principal amount of the investment at the end of the period. The excess funds above the sinking fund requirements were the amount on which the "speculative rate of interest" was calculated (i.e., the rate of return, thus defined).

Prior to this mining analysis, the ideas of both simple and compounded interest were related to the present value concept. Among the basic tables for this purpose are Ward (1710) and Smart (1726). In addition to extensive compounding tables, the latter work contained detailed tables for the present value of one £ as a single payment or as an annuity for up to 100 years. The discount rates were from 2 to 10 percent, and the results were to eight decimal places of accuracy. These tables are probably among the earliest ones.

At a prior period, tables for simple interest and sums were presented with addenda containing a limited number of compounded items. Instructions were offered for finding the "just price or value" of a future interest. For example, note the *third* edition of Webster (1634).

With regrettable delay, the impact of the present value concepts which moved into the field of mining came to economics in a formalized sense most notably with Fisher (1907). Subsequently, the idea of discounting emerged into finance and accounting literature, returning to the field from which it began at least 300 years earlier. Of course, if the concept is not limited to present value, but is based on "interest," the idea of the time value of money is many thousands of years distant. The point of this historical note, however, is to indicate that both the concept and the tables for the present worth of a future receipt are a minimum of three centuries old.

Appendix 2B:
Building a Simulation
Model

There are a number of relevant books and articles dealing with the creation and use of simulation models or systems [for example, Gershefski (1969), Naylor (1970), Hare (1967), or Meier et al. (1969)]. Risk analysis adds the element of probabilistic outcomes to the major input variables. This Appendix will indicate the general pattern for building a model. We will also dwell upon the practical means by which the probability distributions may be obtained.

After an outline of how a computer model is created, we will discuss the technique of flow-charting (by which the analyst organizes the project). There also will be a survey of approaches from which the analyst may develop the relationships among variables by quantitative techniques or by inquiry of line managers. Finally, the task of interpreting the risk analysis output will be discussed. These introductory comments should give the reader unfamiliar with model-building an awareness of the process involved.

The Process

All the steps involved in preparing a simulation model are crucial even though the emphasis in much of the literature concerns the techniques used in encoding the simulation for the computer (step 3 below). The steps may be sequenced as follows:

1. Decide upon the particular aspects of a problem which are to be simulated. The net present value of several alternative investments, the estimated daily sales of a product under various advertising campaigns, and the probable voting patterns in an election are all possibilities for a simulation study. In the usual management situation, an executive will become aware of the simulation tool and will ask a subordinate to construct a model to aid in the decision process for a problem.

2. Analyze historical data and interview personnel to obtain (a) an idea of the most important factors which need to be considered and (b) a first premise or operating basis for the interrelationship of the important factors.

3. Flow chart, code, and debug a computer program for the particular model. At this stage, one also will reanalyze the input data gathered from individuals in order to assess an executive's reaction to the final output when the various assumptions and hypotheses are combined.

4. Simulate the problem to be studied and present the results to the relevant personnel. The computer simulation combines the various probabilistic relationships and calculates the project's distribution of outcomes.

39

5. Interpret the results to individuals who are not familiar with the technique of simulation. Further analysis may be useful as a result of the study. For example, the simulation results may indicate that variables which a priori the executive believed were very important in fact had a minimal effect on the outcome. The model builder may then suggest that staff time and effort could be better spent forecasting some elements instead of others.

Flow Diagrams

Flow charts are widely used in computer programming, project analysis, production process studies, industrial engineering applications, and other areas. These diagrams are particularly useful in computer simulation modeling. First, a flow chart is a logical predecessor to the encoding of the simulation model. It makes the transition from the system which is under study to the computer program used in the analysis much easier. Second, a flow chart helps create the logical design of the basic system. Thus, the flow chart would be useful even if it were not required for creating the computer program.

The symbols and terminology used in flow charts vary widely. Three types of "blocks" found in the flow chart will be shown as examples. First, a transformation or *conversion* block alters the variable in a particular way. The flow chart shown at the top of Figure 2B-1 is the conversion required to change pre-tax profit to after-tax profit.

A second type of block is the fork or *logical* block. Here, the path of the simulation changes depending on the value of a particular variable. In the lower part of Figure 2B-1, the diagram forks to make allowance for whether sales were for cash or on account, since the decision affects the cash balance.

Finally, a *loop* exists to either correct an error condition or (in the example shown here) to repeat an operation a given number of times. The simple loop shown in Figure 2B-2 indicates how the yearly total of monthly sales is computed.

Each of the basic building blocks can be merged in turn to create extremely complex flow diagrams. Since the complexity expands very rapidly, experienced analysts often attempt to make the flow charts *modular*. That is, particular components of the simulation which will be required more than once (e.g., depreciation calculations, taxation figures) are made into separate "modules" which are coded and referenced. Figure 2B-3 shows one module system which might be used. When the simulation is converted to a computer program, these modules are often made into subroutines or functions.

Developing Functional Quantitative Relationships

Certain data within a model can be estimated with certainty once the underlying figures are known. For example, "cash flow from operations" is equal to "net

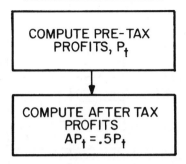

CONVERSION BLOCK

COMPUTE PRE-TAX
PROFITS, P_t

COMPUTE AFTER TAX
PROFITS
$AP_t = .5P_t$

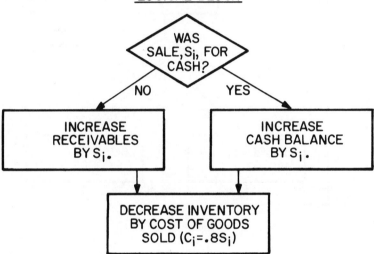

LOGICAL BLOCK

WAS
SALE, S_i, FOR
CASH?

NO   YES

INCREASE
RECEIVABLES
BY S_i.

INCREASE
CASH BALANCE
BY S_i.

DECREASE INVENTORY
BY COST OF GOODS
SOLD ($C_i = .8S_i$)

Figure 2B-1. Blocks

profit after tax plus the net of noncash expenses minus noncash income." Thus, simple accounting regulations or basic economics specify some figures. On the other hand, the real difficulty in model-building usually comes when one attempts (1) to estimate the functional relationships among various unknowns and unknowables, and (2) to forecast the unknown variables on which the accounting or economic relationships are based. For example, one could hypothesize that the market for a product can be explained by the income distribution of the surrounding population, the size of the immediate buying public, the number of teen-age children in the home, the percentage of home owners among the public, and any number of other variables. Since one is trying

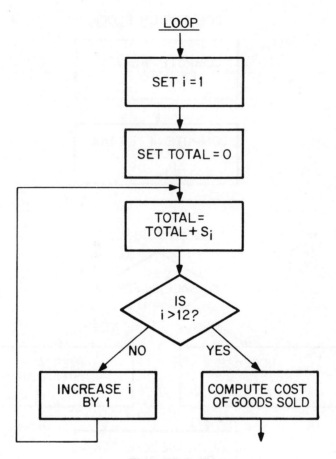

Figure 2B-2. Loop.

to predict (not necessarily explain) sales, detailed analysis might show that the past evidence indicates the two most important variables in predicting Sales in period t (S_t) are (1) the number of people within a five-mile radius of a store who are in the \$12,000-\$15,000 income bracket, and (2) the level of Gross National Product. Specifically, one might form the equation

$$S_t = .02 \times I_t + .06\,\mathrm{GNP}_{t-1}.$$

Where I_t is measured in hundreds and GNP_{t-1} is measured in billions, S_t is the expected, or mean, estimate of sales. Nothing is said about the variance or range likely in the figure since another equation (or set of equations) would handle that issue. Further, note that the income group is measured as the current period

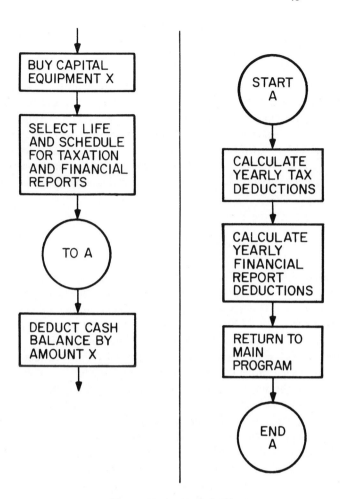

Figure 2B-3. Modular Design.

(I_t) but that the GNP predictor is lagged one period. That is, GNP in the *previous* period (GNP_{t-1}) is the variable which is required.

The above relationship gives the functional dependency of the change in sales upon some other variables. The next question to be faced is how one estimates the variables such as I_t and GNP_{t-1} in this case. The initial problem of the model builder is to find the relationship between the dependent variables he seeks to estimate and the other variables. He then must develop a reasonable system for forecasting those other variables. One technique available in resolving this problem of forecasting is regression analysis. A major problem in using regression analysis is the selection of the appropriate data with which to test the relationships. The underlying assymption of any regression study is that the data are all from the same (homogeneous) population. *Time-series regression* means using observations of the variables over different years, quarters, weeks, or some other period. Even if one agrees that two variables are logically related, unless one believes that the relationship itself remained stable over the time period, then one should not expect valid results from time-series data. An alternative is the use of *cross-sectional data*. Thus, instead of investigating how one firm's sales related to profits of that firm over time, we study, for instance, the relationship between sales and profits for many different sized firms in a single year. Again, however, the crucial question is whether the underlying relationship is the same from firm to firm.

Obtaining Estimates of Distributions

Although regression can be useful in attempting to estimate many variables, the model often must depend, partially or exclusively, on the data provided by executives and other officials who are knowledgeable regarding the situation for which the model is being constructed. Ideally, perhaps, the executive could say, "I forecast sales in five years as a log Normal distribution with mean value of M and variance of V." In practice, however, one usually must extract forecasts accompanied by vague probability relationships. Subsequently, one attempts to fit a statistical distribution to the projections. The question is how one obtains the forecasts from the executive.

. The type of approach used depends on the statistical awareness of the manager; a knowledge of basic statistics would permit him to draw a distribution of sales, earnings, production costs, or whatever. With that task accomplished, one could move to a discussion of the link between sales and earnings, for example. However, if one is dealing with the manager who is not particularly familiar with distribution patterns, then the evoked response could be chaotic. Consider a situation in which the interviewer is attempting to ascertain the form of the underlying distribution of some factor the executive considers important in determining the project's outcome. As a suggestion, the following question-answer sequence could occur:

Q1: What is the most likely value for X? (X may be sales in Year 1, for instance.)
A1: A (This will be considered to be the modal value.)
Q2: What value of X' is there which, of all the possible values you see as reasonable, will be halfway between all of them? That is, you believe there is a 50 percent chance of the actual value of X being larger than X' and a 50 percent chance of it being smaller?
A2: B_1 (This value, which could coincide with A, will be accepted as the median.)

Q3: Given B_1, what is the minimum value you see as possibly occurring under the worst circumstances?

A3: B_2.

Q4: Now, from B_1 and B_2, what outcome for X is likely to occur such that of all the possibilities you see between B_1 and B_2 that value of X would have half the probable outcomes above and half below?

A4: B_3.

One can continue this line of interrogation and obtain as many discrete frequency observations as desired and the executive is prepared to give. From these observations it may be possible to create or to estimate a frequency distribution which can be employed in the model.

Such a process helps determine the probabilities for variables. But how are the variables related to each other beyond the accounting relationships? An important joint product of this interviewing of managers for potential outcomes in given years is the allowance for open-ended comments by the manager. Thus, the manager could well preface a remark with, "Well, that depends on the preceding year, since I suspect sales should be about 15 percent higher that year, give or take 10 percent, if we sold at least $100,000 the year before. If not, sales will be roughly unchanged, and if we sold less than $50,000, I suspect they would drop more." From such a response to a basic question, one can progress to a discussion of the likelihood of various deviations around the figures mentioned. This discussion helps build the model by establishing the link between the yearly forecasts of sales, for example, and the determining factors for the final outcome. This linkage can be gleaned both from commentary of the managers and by reference to historical company and industry data. Similar comments help establish a manager's impression of the relationship between sales and operating expenses, and so forth.

Analogous to the techniques followed in the PERT (Program Evaluation and Review Technique) approach, one can ask an executive to specify an optimistic estimate, a pessimistic estimate, and a most likely estimate. Using these projections, one can input these into a Beta distribution which presumes that the standard deviation is 1/6 of the distance between the lower bound and the upper bound.[a] Although the Beta distribution has bounded tails instead of going to plus and minus infinity as the Normal, and also need not be symmetrical, it can be a useful distribution with which to approximate a frequency schedule given these three points provided by the user. With these estimates, the estimated mean value is 1/3 of the sum of twice the most likely estimate, plus 1/2 of the pessimistic estimate and 1/2 of the optimistic estimate. The variance is, as implied, the square of 1/6 the distance between the optimistic minus the pessimistic estimates.

There is the question of accuracy and consistency among the various forecasts

[a]For a discussion of PERT, see Meier et al. (1969), pp. 37-43. One discussion of the Beta distribution is found in Mood and Graybill (1963), pp. 129-131.

elicited from several managers who are involved in a given project. Each manager may be operating from different assumptions. This problem may be solved by requiring the managers to give the open-ended answers noted before and by stating assumptions made by one manager to another manager. This restatement may not involve "office politics" per se; the quarrel could be over the reasonableness of the assumptions. Such a discussion, of course, is just what a manager needs to formulate accurate estimates. The responsibility for insuring that disagreements over assumptions do not lead to organizational chaos rests with the top executive since there is clearly a possibility of the manager constructing the model being caught in the middle of executive disputes over assumptions.

A second problem derives from conscious or subconscious bias. That is, managers may "overshoot" in estimates (to gain a project's acceptance) or "undershoot" (to appear talented when the project performs better than expected). This problem is partly reduced by a careful note that the forecasts made by managers when seeking project acceptance should be the same forecasts which will later be used for *control* and *evaluation* of the project (and the manager). Furthermore, decentralized operations can require the division manager to forge a common forecast from his subordinates since he knows he will be evaluated by the accuracy of his subordinates' forecasts.

3 The Limitations of Risk Analysis Simulation

The problems are more difficult, the responsibilities are greater, and the limitations are more sizable than I had imagined . . . It's always easy to make the speeches . . . The advisors may conflict, but in the end the President must make the decisions. If it is wrong, as I have been on occasion, he must bear the responsibility. The advisors go on to new advice.

John Fitzgerald Kennedy

There are relatively few corporations which explicitly consider risk in all variables. (See Chapter 4 for a discussion of the models employed by some firms.) One can suggest a number of reasons for this state of practice, and one might learn more from an analysis of the general problems of risk analysis simulation encountered by those firms which do use the technique. One then can consider the effect of these weaknesses on the model proposed here.

Some observers criticize simulation for being imprecise and cumbersome, among other things.[a] Sensitivity analyses ("what if" one variable is 10 percent higher, for example) often require completely new computer runs. Another criticism is that the manager needs guidance on how to use the mass of data generated. One of the argued benefits of the SIFT model presented in Chapter 6 is that it will help the manager cope with the volume of data by the use of time-sharing which greatly simplifies interaction with the computer. Furthermore, it is suggested that the SIFT model enables the manager to be more comfortable with his results. Usually, the manager is either (1) presented with the answer, derived in a manner he may not understand or in which he may have little faith, or (2) given a wide variety of choices which he resents being forced to confront. With the SIFT model, the manager can examine all outcomes which might be considered relevant.

The "Hows" and "Whys" of risk analysis simulation's success are debatable. This chapter is designed to highlight some general observations on the application of this old technique. While the results can be generalized, perhaps to other industries and other techniques, this commentary specifically is related to a survey of risk analysis simulation in four major international oil companies. Two of the companies are using the technique with apparent success (where "success" means some use in analyzing exceptionally risky projects); the others, after an

---

Portions of this chapter are based on Carter (1972), ©The President and Fellows of Harvard College.

[a]For example, see Hillier (1969), p. 84ff.

expensive initiation, have seen the technique dissolve into partial disuse if not total discard. The observations here are based on discussions with management at various levels in each of the companies.[b]

For purposes of this exposition, consider two hypothetical firms, called Aztec and Cherokee. In Aztec, the results were consistently "unfavorable," in the sense that risk analysis failed to be implemented after considerable expenditures of man-hours and money. In Cherokee, the composite result of the various aspects detailed below was a successful implementation. No single company interviewed had all the characteristics of either of these hypothetical firms. Rather, these firm characteristics are based on impressions of plausibility, not just possibility. In a topic as uncertain as the causation of success or failure of the implementation of techniques one can only deal with evidence, not certainty. However, if a firm had an environment that resembled Aztec, then the probabilities of successful implementation seemingly would be drastically lower than the probabilities in a firm which paralleled Cherokee. That is not to say that a firm which had many of the aspects of Aztec could not have successfully implemented the technique, nor that the meeting of all the criteria in Cherokee would have assured successful implementation. All that is done here is to make an intelligent assessment of the probabilities.

There are two major discussions of difficulties encountered in the application of risk analysis in the twin composite firms. In the area of *implementation*, there is an analysis of (1) when in the history of risk analysis simulation each firm attempted to use it, and (2) where in the organization the pressure for trial originated. There are comparative accounts of (3) the organizational location of the management scientists and the computers, (4) the introduction of managers to the technique, (5) the specification of data, (6) the utilization of the technique by senior management, and (7) the transition in personnel and computer systems. In the second section of the chapter, the *inherent problems with risk analysis* per se as perceived by managers are noted. These problems relate to (1) the obtaining of data, (2) the relevance of the technique to a large corporation, (3) the interpretation of the results, (4) the rate of return of risk analysis itself, and (5) the limitations imposed upon ex post appraisal. The chapter concludes with some general comments on why the "implementation problem" developed, and how it might have been lessened somewhat.

Problems of Implementation

Time of Introduction

Aztec introduced the technique almost prior to appearance of several popular articles in 1963-64. This timing was early in the life of the development of the technique, and many problems of both staff support and executive support

[b]For an earlier discussion of this study, see Carter (1972).

perhaps could have been avoided had the technique been used later. Indeed, many executives would argue that a company implementing management science techniques should avoid being the first using that technique. By waiting for others to proceed, the company not only uses a filter to screen techniques which are unlikely to be successfully implemented, but may also have a tool to prod its own executives ("XYZ Corporation has been using this for two years and they find it helpful"). Finally, later users usually can profit from the experiences of pioneers given the professional discussions between various management scientists. This argument rests on the premise that the loss from attempting to implement techniques which become unusable is substantial compared to the small gain from early successful utilization of a new technique.

In this situation, Cherokee successfully implemented the technique five years after the initial effort by Aztec. Cherokee found broad support within the company was as a result of external threats (i.e., other industry users). In addition, five years of additional familiarization with computer manufacturers and software vendors allowed Cherokee management scientists to draw upon a wide range of external resources, reviewing a variety of approaches prior to creating their own general models. Given the evidence of successful implementation of the technique in some firms today (see Chapter 4), this limitation ("avoid being the guinea pig") should not be a restriction on future installations of the technique. This caveat is a relevant restriction on the potential impact of the SIFT model proposed in Chapter 6.

Impetus for Creation

At Aztec, popular articles and the curiosity of top management induced the top planning committee of Aztec to require every operating subsidiary to attach risk analysis proposals to its capital budgeting analysis. In Cherokee, the stimulus was not a popular article which showed the technique was feasible, but a major operating crisis stimulated by the 1967 closing of the Suez Canal. The top management of Cherokee realized they needed more detailed projections of what would happen under a variety of conditions, and asked their management science group to assist in creating systems to provide that information. Both of these situations parallel what is often found in the implementation of management science techniques. That is, the imposition of the new approach is mandated by top management. Cherokee's management clearly was much more committed to risk analysis than the Aztec group. However, Aztec and Cherokee differ from the normal example in that top management was stimulated by external events in both cases. The typical example is probably that both ideas and impetus for innovative techniques are from the management science staff.[c]

---

[c]See Seligman (1967). In the impact of this element on the implementation of the portfolio simulation model, SIFT, one can see conflicting aspects. If it is a "crisis-induced" psychology, then a time of crisis is just the time major expenditures for staff activities are truncated. To the extent that there is risk analysis in place, however, the incremental costs for the portfolio model suggested here would not be great.

*External Versus Internal Staff
and Facilities*

One of the critical aspects of success seemed to be the location of the management science department vis-à-vis the division. In Aztec, the management science staff was an excellent professional group which operated independently of any particular division. When requested by top management to complete risk analysis results on all projects, the operating subsidiary managers turned to the staff group, working with management science officials who were not directly responsible to the subsidiary managers. Not only did this arrangement force the subsidiary managers to work with a person who was often unknown to them, but they also perceived a divided loyalty from the management science people. On the one hand, the management science staff member was to aid the subsidiary or division in obtaining a successful resolution of the problem. On the other hand, some subsidiary managers believed the management science officials were disposed to reveal unfavorable data regarding the projects to senior management.

In Cherokee, by contrast, a management science trainee initially was employed in a central staff where he remained for several years. In this period, he was rotated throughout the firm and saw many of the operating divisions. The novice management scientist then was transferred permanently to a particular division where he was a "management science staff officer." This approach had two benefits. First, the burgeoning management scientist became familiar with the resources available in the company during his previous two-year tour of duty with the central staff area. Second, as a management science staff officer he was seen as having primary identification and responsibility to the division or subsidiary manager. He was perceived as much less a threat to this operating manager than was the case in Aztec.

A centralized computer system in Aztec required the subsidiary manager not only to turn to the management scientist who was external to his operating subsidiary, but to execute the computer programs on a machine which was beyond his control. There was resentment by the management science staff in Aztec that they had to "waste" time running computer programs for divisions since the divisions were directly responsible neither for their budgets nor for promotion of the individuals in the management science group. In comparison, the division manager did not have to depend upon an "external" person in Cherokee. Also, each subsidiary had its own computer facility. In Cherokee, the internal divisional capability of both staff consultant and computer facilities coupled with a requirement that results must satisfy the division manager for salary increases and promotion imbued the management scientist with an altered ranking of priorities. Here, the orientation was to produce results which would help the division.

Education of Users

Although both companies imposed the technique from above, the approach followed to achieve an understanding of risk analysis was drastically different. In Aztec, some subsidiary and division managers noted they never exactly understood why (or if!) the technique worked. One manager resented risk analysis because it was impossible for him to replicate the results by hand. Others felt that risk analysis was imposed by top management and they had to employ a technique developed by someone outside their division. They regarded the management science group as distinctly separate. Further, they perceived the management scientists as knowing more about their division activities than they (the division managers) knew about management science activities. Cherokee, on the other hand, used a massive training program for executives at all levels of management. These "schools" were conducted by management science staff officials as well as by management science staff members within the divisions. Furthermore, the educational program was completed prior to initial use of the technique by the division.

Data Input and Model Building

A feature which probably had devastating impact at Aztec was the fact that the division managers perceived risk analysis as a threat to them. It implied that they were being placed in the middle; whatever confidential results were derived from the risk analysis would be relayed to top management. Second, they disliked being forced to specify ranges of outcomes. Third, they encountered obstacles in the computer program itself since the problems they wished to analyze often required substantial modifications of the program. Modifications not only were difficult for them to understand ("Why doesn't the program fit my problem instead of my problem always having to fit the program?"), but also the cost of the modification was charged to their own division budget. As a result, they preferred to avoid modifying programs and allowed their assistants to "shoe-horn" their problems to fit the program. The results were discounted even more by the division managers since they were cognizant of the limited parallel between the real project under analysis and the risk analysis output.

At Cherokee, by contrast, the extensive schooling and the in-house staff capability helped mitigate the natural resentment of division managers at being forced to specify copious amounts of data. In addition, a flexible program and a willingness on the part of the management science staff to meet the needs of their immediate superiors (the division managers) seemed to induce greater willingness to adjust the program to accommodate the needs of that manager. Most important, it seemed, was the education. This element allowed Cherokee to overcome somewhat the nascent fear of a foreign person and tool. Such fear, after all, was the basic attitude of a division manager to a management scientist and to risk analysis. Once the fear was overcome, trial results received a more tolerant viewing by the division manager.

Top Management Review and Analysis

At the budgetary hearing in which division managers competed against each other for funding, Aztec managers continually found individual division managers, competing division managers, and top managers disagreeing about the merits of various inputs. Not only were the probabilities a source of conflict, but even the "most likely" estimates often were controversial. Since groups rarely could agree at the annual review sessions on relevant probability data, the outcome was a diminution of impact on the decision from the distribution of possible results. Yet such a distribution is the prime output of risk analysis. Cherokee, noting the possible impact of computers on the organizational structure, recognized a need for a two-stage cycle. In contrast to the previous policy under which the competing division managers would meet annually for a one-week discussion with top management resulting in the establishment of the final budget, Cherokee realigned its proposal review meetings into two, four-day sessions. At the initial session, the basic projects were proposed and agreement was reached on what were reasonable ranges and probabilities for critical variables. When division managers disagreed with each other, a consensus was forged or the results were computed under alternative conditions. After the computer results based on agreed upon specifications were prepared, a final four-day session was held in which the risk analysis results were reviewed. Here, the risk analysis output was utilized since the data input had been agreed upon by consensus.

The impact of computers on management in the organizational structure is a popular topic for managers, computer experts, and management scientists alike. The above situation is an example of how technology, in order to be employed usefully, required a small change in the organizational process. One should note that the use of time-shared computer systems can mitigate even the organizational change cited here. In the case of time-sharing, the console might well be in the same room with the top management committee as these executives review projects. At any point when various division managers disagree about probabilities, the results quickly can be found there in the board room and presented via teletype or a completely silent television screen. Not only is the output returned immediately after agreement on input data is reached, but one readily can find which criteria are most important and can concentrate on those. Often disagreement over the probable ranges of certain attributes disappears when participants perceive the miniscule impact of that attribute on the final results.

Such useful byproducts of the simulation can also be employed in the project review process. The usage of time-sharing, preferably in the form of a television-like Cathode Ray Tube (CRT) with an option to produce a hard copy of any output desired is technically and economically feasible today and is used in corporations. It is well suited to the application of the SIFT model, as discussed in Chapter 8.

Changes in Personnel and Computer Systems

Aztec found itself dependent upon sparse documentation prepared by a single official in its management science group. When he later left his assignment for another job, the limited documentation was coupled to the identification of project with the official. This combination of factors meant that any new person merely would be continuing a predecessor's work, not developing imaginative ideas of his own. Further, the new person faced substantial difficulties in modifying and updating the program. In addition, confronted with heavy turnover in equipment because of new computer models introduced by the various manufacturers, the firm inevitably faced serious problems modifying the computer system or the program to allow execution of the old program on the new machines.

Cherokee assigned a team to develop the project, and the interdependency of the team members forced detailed documentation from the inception of the project. As new computers were received, prime emphasis was placed on convertibility. Indeed, if a new computer system required massive conversion costs or created transitional difficulties, it simply was not accepted. Finally, the identification of the management scientist with his division induced greater interest on convertibility and implementation than in Aztec.

**Problems with the Technique
of Risk Analysis**

Whatever the causes of eventual nonuse of the risk analysis technique in various companies, throughout the course of the conversations with executives in these petroleum firms one could note concerns which limited the usefulness of the risk analysis technique. First, executives in all the companies stressed the difficulty of obtaining good input data. It was not clear to them how they could assess reasonable ranges of probabilities for many of the key factors. What was the probability of expropriation in any particular country? What were the likely ranges of crude tanker rates in the late 1960s? Thus, the inability to develop probabilities or even likely ranges of variables seriously inhibited the use of the technique in many of the companies. One executive stated that he felt the most useful research academicians and management scientists could present would be usable guidelines for probability assessments. While he was familiar with some techniques for accomplishing this end (see Chapter 2), he felt that the probable dispersions in most input data were so large as to make the results meaningless.

As a rule, efforts to obtain the data were limited at best. The real problem was not "bad" data, it seems, but more often was a function of (1) managers who did not wish to be forced into a precise statement of the probabilities, and (2) managers who were uncomfortable with the concept of probabilities. Those executives who did not wish to be precise can receive some sympathy. They perceived precision about project uncertainty as linked to a forced admission that the world is uncertain. Hence their performance in it is even more uncertain. When a manager says, "This project is too risky," he is implicitly making an assessment (1) about the uncertainty, and (2) about the tradeoff in uncertainty and return. Yet, risk analysis forces more explicit consideration of what "risky" and "too risky" mean. Perhaps the greatest benefit from risk analysis comes from making the disagreements among project managers more explicit during the preparation of the model, not from the output. Of course, many managers were unfamiliar with the idea of probability and this obstacle may be overcome by education within the organization and by an influx of other managers familiar with the concept.

The difficulty of deriving good input data can be substantial in terms of the cost. One of the benefits of risk analysis is that the relative impact of the uncertainties of different factors can be seen. With only crude distributions of uncertainty in various components, the rate of return or other results quickly can reveal where it is worth the firm's spending more time refining the data, and where the final outcome would be changed minimally even with a large magnitude of error in the input data.

Second, several companies questioned the relevance of risk analysis to a large corporation. In most of the oil industry cases, even the largest of projects would be no more than 2 to 3 percent of the total corporate assets of the firm. There was some doubt as to whether the firm should be concerned with the risk or volatility of a particular project. Indeed, the law of large numbers should imply that by investing in a portfolio of projects, the corporation average would be close to the expected values of the projects. Some managers expressed interest in the problem of the correlations among the various projects they were considering. Clearly, they saw the relationship to the idea of diversifying outside the petrochemical business in order to reduce the total corporate risk. However, they stressed that this diversification benefit was a function of reducing the correlation of the projects with each other, and not just the riskiness of a given project. They noted that it was only the variance of the project that entered into the risk analysis in their firm.

The evolution of thinking from return, to return plus variability in return, to portfolio return plus portfolio variability may make risk analysis more relevant in the future. To the extent that the covariances among proposed projects can be derived with minimal effort and can be handled explicitly in a portfolio simulation, then the relevance of risk analysis may be increased. This increased interest stems from the facility of portfolio risk analysis to deal with a larger part of the real problem (the performance of the corporation when viewed as a collection of projects) than simple project risk analysis.[d]

Third, several officials indicated their disappointment that the academic and professional communities had failed to indicate what the tradeoff in risk and return should be. Although risk analysis might be beneficial for eliminating projects with greater risk for the same return or lower returns for the same risk, essentially there seemed to be very little guidance on what sort of tradeoff the company should demand. How much higher return should it receive for a proportionately greater increase in volatility? They felt the financial theorists specializing in the field of capital structure had failed badly in giving supportable guidance in this area.[e] Thus, one of the alleged benefits of risk analysis (that it leaves this decision on the risk-return tradeoff in the manager's hands) seemed to be a major liability when many managers indicated they were incapable of dealing with the problem.

It is true that a financial scholar or a financial vice president of a major corporation would have difficulty in saying what the tradeoff in risk and return is. However, most parties would agree that higher risk requires a higher return. What concerned the managers who complained about the "imprecision" of risk analysis in this context is simply that they were being forced to make a decision about the tradeoff they would make. Here, they seemed very happy to surrender the decision making to a model, rather than to employ "management judgment!" In short, the difficulty of knowing the tradeoff in risk and return is a fact of life which is not the fault of risk analysis. It is true that greater detail in any area where one does not know how to employ the detail is worth little. However, one would still hope that most managers would have some feeling for trading off risk-return combinations even if they are not comfortable about the correctness of their own tradeoff. Should they wish to have the model make the risk-return tradeoff decision, then it is a simple matter of programming risk analysis outputs to flag acceptable and unacceptable projects. All that is required is for someone (manager, management scientist, or finance professor) to say what tradeoff function he wishes to use. Given that function, the technique is perfectly capable of discriminating among acceptable and unacceptable projects.

Fourth, many managers indicated that if capital budgeting standards were applied to risk analysis, *it would never pay its way*. In conjunction with (1) the

---

[d]For additional comments on portfolio approaches in strategic planning, see Carter and Cohen (1972).

[e]A reader unfamiliar with the controversy surrounding the cost of capital/risky investment discount rate may wish to consult a basic finance text or book of readings. Examples are Van Horne (1974), Chapters 5-8; Weston and Brigham (1972), Chapters 8 and 9; and Archer and D'Ambrosio (1967), Part II. See also Chapter 2 of this book.

organizational and computer costs, (2) the low impact of a single project on a multibillion dollar corporation, and (3) the limited knowledge about how to use the results, several executives noted that there was no problem *funding* good projects on an expected value basis. Rather, the difficulty was in finding enough good (equals high expected value) projects. Hence, these officials argued the company resources spent on risk analysis could be employed more profitably on seeking additional proposals. Furthermore, these executives argued senior management time was more usefully employed on broad questions of policy and budgeting; junior management, on the other hand, did not have the expertise to prepare good risk analysis input data.

The problem with discounted cash flow applied to risk analysis is the same as discounted cash flow (or risk analysis!) applied to any project: how does one quantify the relevant variables? When one takes into account the benefits and costs of forcing executives to be more explicit about their forecasts, to select numbers which they will put on paper, to discuss their differences in arguments with their colleagues and superiors, and to work with techniques with which they are unlikely ever to be fully comfortable, then it is difficult to make an assessment. But what are the relevant comparisons? Would time released from this analysis be used to search for more profitable projects, or simply to massage the qualitative or subjective arguments for existing proposals which the division manager prefers? Even if the free time is spent on searching for more profitable projects, how is their greater desirability to be ascertained other than by more subjective generalizations? Results of expected returns shown in risk analysis can be strikingly different from the expected returns under single-point estimates. What is the value of this improved knowledge? The point is not that this criticism of risk analysis is invalid. Rather, the relevant opportunity costs of management time and money have to be judged explicitly, and what those opportunity costs are is rarely stated.

Finally, managers emphasized that the use of probabilities and ranges of outcome made the control function and the ex post evaluation of project outcomes extremely difficult. Many of them felt that the lack of precision or the lack of determination in the final output meant no one could evaluate a project's performance since the final outcome was almost certain to be somewhere in the ex ante probable range of outcomes. Some executives in companies which were successfully using risk analysis argued that the existence of the range of outcomes made ex post evaluation more difficult but still left it a reasonable possibility. Indeed, if the various key input factors could be assessed after the event, one manager argued he could see how closely the results paralleled what should have happened given the outcome of the external, uncontrolled variables.

Genesis of "Implementation Problem"

The observations presented here specifically were in the context of risk analysis as used by four major international oil companies. However, as anyone who has worked with the implementation of management science techniques will observe, the "elements of difficulty" detailed here indeed are not unique to either the petroleum industry nor to risk analysis. In addition to the generalization of the above concepts, one naturally wonders about the key factors which seem to create difficulties in implementation. Perhaps a major irritant is that of identification. Management scientists, whether academic researchers or staff consultants in the corporation, often receive greater role fulfillment from the scholarly pursuit of their field than from the success of the corporation. In addition, the financial and psychological rewards are often greater for creating new techniques and publishing results than for implementing established techniques. As a palliative noted earlier, increased corporate identification can be achieved by placing the management scientists within divisions after a suitable initiation period in a management science staff department. While many management scientists would be unhappy in this environment, they can be left in the staff area or sent to other academic or corporate settings. From the standpoint of the firm, such an approach does increase the probabilities of the management scientist who remains in the division having greater identification with the firm than colleagues would have.

Second, there is the inevitable problem of a consultant. Even in the implementation strategy suggested here for Cherokee, in which staff operations research people are later transferred to division responsibility and locus, these people remain essentially in-house consultants. Their job is to advise and to propose, not to act upon the result of those actions. As President Kennedy observed, "The President must live with the decision. If it turns out badly, he must still live with it, while the advisers go on to new advice." Many management scientists feel that once they have presented the basic components of a technique to the managers, their job is done. If the manager wishes to use the techniques, so be it. In any case, they proceed to other projects.

Third, the human relations and organizational problems which have been noted briefly are extremely critical. The physical location of the management scientist, the position in the hierarchy, the vis-à-vis that of the division manager to whom he must report, and the very basics of personality all tend to interact. Management scientists tend to have a technical background. As a result, many of them are neither particularly gifted with nor enamored of the smoothing qualities which allow many organizations to function. There is resentment of the "game playing" that occurs in the corporate world.[f] Again, there is greater role identification on the part of the management scientist with the purity of ideas and intellectualism. The organizational disadvantage of this factor can be cushioned with greater identification of the management scientist with the division, from which concern for the corporation as a whole may evolve.

Fourth, time, in terms of not just the technique "state of the art," but of

---

[f]Some observers who have viewed corporations, universities, and government institutions argue that the "games" of government and academia can be much more intense because of the more limited institutional rewards in these two organizations. Salary differentials and offices (for example) do not have as wide a diversity as in industry. Hence, this argument goes, the "games" in nonprofit institutions are all the more aggressive.

education, hardware, and software is critical. As engineers and business school graduates become more widely available to firms, the utilization of any particular technique is facilitated. Furthermore, (1) steadily decreasing costs of computers per calculation, (2) larger memory capacity models at reasonable prices, and (3) the wider use of terminals, CRT's, and minicomputers will allow the analytically trained MBA or MS executive to use quantitative skills economically. *These complementary aspects of the impact of newer computers are probably the most underrated element of the so-called "computer revolution." The reinforcing effect of these three factors is critical, and one major basis for the potential of a model such as SIFT.*

Fifth, sabotage of techniques by those who feel it will lessen their budgets/ staff/influence is always a problem. This "implementation" problem may be confronted by sensitive and/or determined senior executives who can handle the threatened individuals. However, given the realities of organizational life, perhaps this "problem" is a recurring one which is both critical and resistant to the management scientist's efforts. Resentment of techniques often will come from those who dislike having their (unspecified) judgment questioned, who do not like being forced to be specific about their statements on the merits of a project, or who are simply very effective at "beating" the current system and see no reason to take a chance on a diminution in their effectiveness in "getting their piece of the pie" by tolerating a new appraisal system.[g]

Finally, although many management scientists are reluctant to acknowledge the fact, it often is true that their exact solution to the approximate problem is not as good as an approximate solution to the exact problem. Technical problems with the proposed models for dealing with situations often cause the models to be inapplicable. The technical problems are not restricted to problems of computers and processing. They also include the basic assumptions which are made in the model that may do gross injustice to reality, the optimization or analysis presented by the model which may not relate to the real problem, and so forth. Indeed, one of the larger causes of implementation problems may be simply the basic inadequacy of the model which is to be implemented.

Following this detailed discussion of one technique in one industry, let us now turn to a summary of what particular firms are attempting with computerized financial and strategic planning models.

---

[g]See Argyris (1969a). In his study of research and development activities, he concluded that top-notch men rarely needed formal budget arrangements to pursue the activities they wished in research and development. Rather variant research interests and the central interests of the system "were highly congruent." On the other hand, there was still a major problem of ambivalent feelings between the executives. Many of them had doubts about their own interests vis-à-vis the interests of the corporation. The broader impart of this issue is discussed later in Chapter 9.

4

Financial and Strategic Planning Models in Corporations

The age of chivalry is gone; that of sophisters, economists, and calculators has succeeded.

Edmund Burke

Many companies are today involved in computer-assisted approaches to long-range financial and strategic planning. Often, these systems involve relatively simple pro forma five-year income statement and balance sheet projections. In other cases, highly sophisticated techniques of management science such as mathematical programming and advanced statistical models are used as part of the planning process.

In the previous chapter, some of the specific problems were discussed which firms in one industry have encountered with the technique of risk analysis simulation. Beyond that issue, what are the general requirements for model building? Are there factors common to many situations?

Lippermann (1968) cites a number of conclusions drawn from his observation of IBM's planning system.

First, there must be a recognition of the need for operating plans and long-range forecasting. Furthermore, that activity should be acknowledged as an ongoing function of the firm.

Second, the planning personnel themselves should be interested in improving the capacity of planning. This improvement may take the form of considering a greater number of alternatives and considering more sophisticated alternatives. These planning personnel should be involved in the design and development of any planning system.

Third, the system should be designed to allow the planning personnel to specify and to evaluate various plans, and to relieve them of the tedious calculating tasks which are a part of any planning project.

Fourth, the formalized plan can be a supplement to an accounting system. The objectives which brought forth the particular plan and the forecasted results can be retained as a record which may be used to evaluate the consistency and accuracy of projections over time.

Fifth, the planner can focus on better analysis of those inputs which are shown to be most critical in the ultimate outcome of the plan.

59

General Surveys of Corporate Models

The Gershefski (1970) survey of corporate managers and corporate models confirms many of Lippermann's comments. Most of the models were built after 1966 and involved straightforward pro forma simulations, with no explicit risk appraisal. Only 12 percent of the 323 respondents had models which included probability distributions for each of the underlying factors. If there was any study of the dispersion of returns, it was a "what-if" analysis. One or more variables would be changed ("what if sales increased 10 percent") and the entire projection model rerun. Only 5 percent of these models incorporated mathematical programming elements. Typically, models were regarded as "most useful" in those firms which had formal planning procedures; 91 percent of Gershefski's respondents felt the value of the model justified the cost.

In another survey of twenty firms' models for planning, Dickson et al. (1970) found that all were deterministic models, although one model featured a PERT-type analysis. Typically the models allowed the managers great flexibility in the specification of account labels, relationships among variables, and so forth. Dickson et al. concluded that the advent of time-sharing facilities will substantially change the economics and the effectiveness of many computer models.

Miller (1971) surveyed simulation models, and found a multiplicity of uses in particular companies. Most of the firms used "simulation" in the sense of a pro forma generator, with the balance sheet, income statement, and cash flow results under a variety of assumptions regarding growth in sales. Other uses included airline fleet planning, R & D project selection, possible joint ventures and acquisitions, and also external financing strategy. Miller reports similar uses for "risk analysis simulation." It is not clear that the companies involved understand what "risk analysis" really implies, however, since the tasks (evaluation of investments, mergers, and alternative marketing strategies, for example) and the output (standard financial statements) are similar to the tasks and output noted by Miller when reporting the use of simulation. Miller indicates that risk analysis is gaining a foothold: 55 percent of the 40 respondents to his survey indicated they were using the technique in some form.

Miller (1971) also found a number of company managers applying regression analysis. Most uses concerned projection of growth rates in industries from historical data, or general relationships such as sales to Gross National Product. Some emphasis was based on market penetration and seasonal factors, with the typical orientation of the forecasting being aggregate sales data.

In a study emphasizing the capital budgeting part of planning, Klammer (1972) evaluated the nearly 200 replies to a questionnaire from respondents who are biased toward high technology, rapid change and capital intensive industries, and are therefore more likely to be using more sophisticated techniques than United States industry in general. He found little difference among the industries from which he had responses. Among his results, 45 percent of the respondents attempted explicitly to deal with risk (an increase from Gershefski's 12 percent two years earlier). Fifty-one percent of the respondents used some management science techniques broadly defined. Among these techniques previously discussed are computer simulation (used by 28 percent of the Klammer sample), probability theory (32 percent) and linear programming (17 percent).[a]

One of the most significant findings of Klammer was the rapidly increasing use of some variant of discounted cash flow in evaluating projects as discussed in Appendix 2A. When asked to indicate their "most sophisticated primary evaluation standard" in 1970 compared to 1964 and 1959, Klammer respondents indicated the following:

	1970	1964	1959
Discounting (rate of return or present value)	57%	38%	19%
Accounting rate of return	26	30	34
Payback	12	24	34
Urgency (sic)	5	8	13
	100%	100%	100%

A variety of models are commercially available for use by any firm willing to contract for them. A survey of many pro forma models is found in Eiolart and Searle (1972). Carter and Harris (1971) and Carter (1973) survey the attributes of several financial pro forma models. An excellent survey of the commercial risk analysis packages for both time-sharing and batch processing is Berger (1972).

Company Models

From this broad survey of the uses of models in firms, one can turn to a brief discussion of particular models employed for specific tasks in major corporations. Sources of these descriptions will be indicated, so that the reader may pursue the discussion for any model in more detail.

The discussion of individual companies is drawn exclusively from published sources. Several notes of caution must be made prior to presenting this material. First, the public speeches and articles are usually offered by those officials of the company who are responsible for developing the model. There is a natural tendency found in mankind to overemphasize one's importance and impact in an organization. Hence, the models discussed here may not have the pervasive impact which the tone of the primary source material would indicate. This is not

---

[a]Readers unfamiliar with linear programming are referred to Appendix 5B for a brief introduction.

to say there is conscious distortion or exaggeration. It is merely to emphasize the fact that the impact of the model within the company may not be that extensive. Second, and conversely, most of these speeches are given only after they have been released by higher officials of the company. There are a number of very sophisticated planning techniques implemented in various corporations of which the author is personally aware, which are not released for public discussion. The companies see no reason to advertise their success when they consider the techniques or application relatively sophisticated. This effect, in conjunction with restricted internal rewards to systems officials for publicizing their activities, acts to limit the published material drastically.

American Can

One major model for long-range planning involves sensitivity analysis [referred to as "simulation" by Miller (1971)], with the initial application being a joint venture. In that case, the question focused upon the returns to participants under various divisions of equity. After running a market model which projected required funding and revenue for various sales strategies and resulting competitor reaction, the manager used the output from that basic market model as input for the financial model. The financial model was of a standard form: profit and loss statements, balance sheets, cash flows, and present value calculations for alternative investments. Although American Can had not attached risk analysis to the financial model, they indicated they anticipated risk evaluation. The officials observed there was continued interest in risk analysis, and suggested that the firm would be moving in that direction in the future.

Boston Edison

This company developed a long-range planning model which had sufficient accuracy to be used for short-term financial forecasting as well. The company started with an extremely gross model, and then refined it to include smaller sections in much greater detail. The major outputs of the model were income statement, balance sheet, and cash reports. The various subroutines prepared special calculations for fuel costs, load demands, expected revenues, property taxes, alternative book and tax depreciation figures, labor rates and earnings per share and dividends. The model was designed for sensitivity analyses for alternative regulation rates, demand, expected costs, and so forth, and a maximum time horizon of 25 years. The model is discussed in Miller (1971).

Combustion Engineering

In conjunction with Arthur D. Little, Combustion Engineering began in 1967 to do detailed work on an input/output analysis. This model was employed exclusively to predict sales in the particular industries in which Combustion Engineering was operating, such as products for the electric power, steel, and coal industries. In conjunction with this model, regression analysis was used extensively to forecast reasonable input data. In addition, Combustion Engineering officials emphasized their enthusiasm for input/output analyses because of the internal checks and forced consistency required. Another major asset of the input/output analysis, according to Combustion Engineering executives, was the way they themselves developed a sense of the interdependencies among the sectors. A brief account of the model may be found in Miller (1971).

Corning Glass Works

Although there is no complete planning model, Chambers et al. (1970) described components of the total corporate model which was envisioned. In the area of financial planning, the Corning model aided in the evaluation of alternate strategies for meeting loan commitments. The results involved pro forma income statements, balance sheet and cash flow figures for various periods. The study indicated there were detailed models dealing with multinational investments analysis. At the time of the article, Chambers indicated that the company was moving to more integrated models and to risk analysis simulation models.

Dow Chemical

Beginning in 1956, a pro forma model was designed which was placed on their computer. After a second generation model in 1963, the company turned to the latest version created in 1968 [Morgan et al. (1970)]. The model is described as "basically a deterministic accounting model which calculates income and expense statements, consolidated balance sheets, cash flow balances, and performance measurements for future years." The company had no single overall corporate planning model because of the basically decentralized organizational structure and the amount of effort required to develop a unifying model. The model language was Dow's own, Planning Simulator One (PS1), primarily written in ALGOL. The typical projection was for ten years. There were no disaggregations by product line, region, or general business. The model was used for "what if" analysis. Although there had been effort at probabilistic simulations, Morgan et al. indicated that the simulations were overly demanding of computer time, providing results which, in the opinion of Dow managers, did not warrant the effort. The model primarily served to estimate cash needs and target capital structure strategies.

Exxon (Standard Oil Company of New Jersey)

Based on a paper by Abe (1970) and personal interviews, this author has the impression of a modular system of corporate pro forma models in Exxon. In addition to a variety of linear programming and computer simulation models used to prepare input data for various subcomponents, the master corporate models aggregate results from 15 regional and operating organizations and over 300 affiliates. This is a deterministic simulation model used for long-range corporate planning. It provides pro forma results for many years into the future, giving various operating and financial ratios. Various modules provide volumes, prices and cost, and capital coefficients for the analysis. A financial module presents financial information and the analysis of financing policy impacts upon working capital, dividends, and debt. Output could be presented for twelve areas, eighty different products and functions, and a total of 24 time periods. From a base case on operating results, the financing module also could simulate various financing strategies. Among these were the option to permit any of the variables (working capital, debt, or dividend) to float; to use upper and lower limits for debt figures; and to interact the dividend rate with the constraints on debt. The end result was a cascading one as the inputs for various business lines in particular areas were fed into regional allocations which in turn became part of the particular Exxon affiliate.

This company has had many advanced uses of corporate planning models for a number of years. It was an early user of mathematical programming for production and refining operations, and has since derived mathematical programming models for a number of other areas of business such as transportation of crude oil and exploration programs. The output from these models are inputs for the company's general financial planning model (discussed above) which is processed twice a year for the corporate office itself. Output is a balance sheet and income statement for future periods. Relatively great detail is presented for five-year forecasts, with lesser detail from six to twenty years or more in typical use.

General Electric

As many computer manufacturers, General Electric was one of the early users of corporate models. For long-run strategic planning, General Electric employed models primarily on the basis of sensitivity studies and evaluation of alternative policies. G.E. also made extensive use of econometric analysis. The manager of their long-run planning operation noted that executives were heavily divided between quantitative and more qualitative approaches. The former group utilized the model for long-term economic forecasting as well as short-term forecasting. Some emphasis was given to the particular subcomponents of the economy in which General Electric tends to operate. The latter, nonquantitative group was more concerned with an entrepreneurial approach to the businesses likely to be profitable for the future. The group employed the model for projected outcomes based on contingent results from product/market strategies. These efforts are discussed in Raymond (1966) and Miller (1971).

International Business Machines

In the writings of Lippermann (1968) and Lande (1968), one has an image of the system developed for the IBM Corporation. Dr. Lande, the IBM office products division's first manager of divisional planning, began his efforts in 1959. He first needed the once-a-year compendium of departmental projections for the preparation of financial statements for five years into the future. Part of the effort involved assuming both accurate forecasting and consistent assumptions among departments within the division. From 1962 through 1967, throughout various planning cycles, the system was altered to accommodate the experience of the organization. The general process at IBM for planning involved two cycles. An operating plan was created in the fall of the year, focusing on near-term projections and the following year's budget. The long-range plan, comprised of much less detail, was the projection for five years of future operations. Following the planning cycle of 1960-1963, IBM determined that the operating and long-range planning projections should be converted to a compatible system. This task was subsequently accomplished. However, by the end of 1963, there were over 6,000 parameters involved which naturally limited the flexibility of the program. As Dr. Lande observed "With a 6,000 parameter system . . . you are constrained by an input problem. You have to review too many inputs. In addition you have to maintain consistency between them."

Pro forma projections for the five-year plan include "what-if" projections with the resulting cash flow income statement and balance sheet output. Dr. Lande, by 1968 the manager of corporate planning systems at IBM, noted that the firm planned to provide computerized planning tools for other divisions of the corporation as well as for the corporate and group staffs. By the use of remote terminals, he expected to have a common facility available to various divisions.

International Utilities Corporation

McSweeney (1972; 1973) describes an optimization model used by this billion-dollar diversified corporation for strategic planning. This is a mixed integer programming model which involves aspects of capital budgeting, acquisitions, divestments, debt creation and repayment, stock issue and repurchase, and dividend payout. It is an on-line model which allows a variety of sensitivity runs following the multiperiod optimization output. The objective function is to maximize reported average earnings per share for the period in the planning horizon. Minimum growth rates per year are forced by appropriate constraints. There is a linear approximation to the fractional objective function which would be required from the consideration of expansions and contractions of the number of shares outstanding.

This "model" initially evaluates projects on a risk analysis basis, suggesting "optimum" portfolios for any given risk level. These portfolios are then inserted into the integer programming submodel to handle the issues raised in the earlier paragraph. Output is presented in numeric and graphic terms to executives by means of Cathode Ray Tubes, which are in turn linked to a copier. Thus, the manager can "freeze" for later reference any results he views which are especially interesting.

X_1 Company

One of the earliest and more imaginative uses of optimization techniques such as linear programming in the program of pro forma analysis is from Carlton (1970). This model was in part supported by First National City Bank, and customers of the bank have used it for their financial projections. The model permits optimizing an objective which is the maximum discounted stream of dividends plus the terminal stock price as of some period in the future. The model, designed for time-sharing terminals, begins with the initial balance sheet and income from the firm's current operations. Preestablished loan take-down or repayments are supplemented by an allowance for new loans. The program permits accelerated depreciation for tax purposes with the resulting changes in the deferred account for shareholders. Preferred stock and convertible issues are permitted, although the latter can only be established initially. Conversions to equity are handled on the basis of a management-specified time and rate. New equity issues are permitted, adjusted for transactions costs.

In handling investments, Carlton observed that a major problem in models is allowance for investments which will arise beyond the current period, but whose exact form and yield is not known in the initial period. He makes an assumption consistent with much of the finance literature, namely that future investments will contribute earnings at a constant percentage of the invested amount (which amount, in turn, is determined in the solution of the program). This earnings increment from a new investment may occur coincident with investment, or may be lagged one or more periods. Furthermore, the rate at which investments earn is steadily decreasing, based on the dollar value of new investment that period relative to the total assets of the firm in the previous period.

The model allows a variety of management policy constraints, such as a target capital structure for the terminal period, maximum limits on debt within the periods covered by the model, minimum interest coverage rates, limitations on additional current debt not to exceed current new investments, and cumulative and annual limitations on the dividend payout rates. Also, the model allows the manager to specify minimum growth rates in dividends and earnings per share if no new shares are issued. Under the formulation published, however, when new shares are issued the constraints can be reformulated only to assure the dividends and earnings per share will not decline. The manager indicates specified data for the periods under study, and establishes a terminal value for the payout and growth rate of the firm beyond that terminal period. The optimization model then proceeds, creating a balance sheet, income statement and sources-uses statement for each period studied, together with per-share data. Given the sample study, the formulation shown does not explicitly incorporate uncertainty constraints because of the excessive complexity.

An imaginative extension of the Carleton (1970) and other models is the recent planning model suggested by Myers and Pogue (1974). Their objective function includes the net worth of the investments based on all equity financing and a risk-adjusted discounted rate, increased by the tax savings derived from debt issues associated with projects and the investment in various liquid assets which are required, less equity issue transaction costs and any penalties inserted. Their constraints permit liquidity and debt buffers for the cash flows in coming periods, based on Normality assumptions. Although the formulation permits the inclusion of contingent projects, interdependencies in the sense of probabilisitic interrelationships among the cash flows are not included. Naturally, where there are major interdependencies involved, the user has the option of creating a dummy project, mutually exclusive of its components, which includes the features of the composite investment in several of the projects which are interdependent. Additional constraints permit optional mandatory growth rates for aggregate reported earnings as well as minimum dividend payments, and the authors indicated a forthcoming version of the model will accommodate earnings per share constraints.

Xerox

According to Brown (1968; 1970), the Xerox efforts to build a computerized financial planning model began in late 1964. This early model was SCRAM (Strategic Corporate Resource Allocation Model), although, as Brown indicates, it was neither strategic nor did it allocate. The model was a basic five-year forecast written in FORTRAN II for an IBM 7010. With the creation of a corporate planning staff, Xerox moved into formalized planning models which were based upon clearly stated quantitative and qualitative objectives (earnings growth, return on investment, etc.). The goal was a consistent forecast for various items, with formalized procedures to achieve a unified objective. The result was XPM, by which managers could use the corporate model to study how demands upon their divisions would alter if corporate plans were changed. Faced with the reorganization of Xerox in 1965, the planning group created a new version of XPM. In this version, it was realized that data handling, storage and retrieval were the critical problems, rather than computations or logic. Hence, separate modules which fed key variables into the system were employed. Random access storage and remote terminals were utilized. With the retirement of the director of planning in 1967, the model builders recognized that the rest of the planning staff had not been sold on the model nor was the model institutionalized into the corporation. As a result, the model was used at much lower levels in the organization than had originally been planned. As Brown (1970) indicated, XPM was used as a planning tool only within the business products group of the corporation. Hence, Xerox no longer has a computer model of its entire corporation although there are computer aids to assist planning in most divisions.

A variety of brief descriptive commentaries of other company models are available. However, the above survey of firms indicates the range of approaches, some of the implementation problems, and possible future evolutions. Linear programming is ideally suited for certain problems, and a brief description of Boise Cascade's timber harvesting L.P. model is found in Dickens (1970). The most frequent "model" is a financial statement generator, and other models of a "pro forma/what-if" variety are used by Pennzoil [Meyer and Jennings (1972)] and Johnson and Johnson [Anderson (1972)].

Problems with Models

Some general management literature is concerned with the problems of using models in corporations; an even greater proportion of the management science literature is concerned with the "problem" of implementation. Chapter 3 discussed specific problems with risk analysis. Are there general "catalogues of complaints" about corporate models?

One of the most incisive general critiques comes from Boeing Aircraft's director of corporate planning, Harry J. Goldie, who argued (1970) that managers found three major sources of irritation in the models:

1. models always take three to four times longer to build than promised (and cost more than budgeted),
2. the models take very long lead times to incorporate any changes, and
3. the data are not readily available for most models.

Mr. Goldie also cites several sources which induce a severe lack of confidence in the model on the part of the manager. These sources of worry include:

1. "the model is never quite correct—but it soon will be,"
2. the problem is translated from the manager's terms to the model,
3. the model can be explained, but requires highly technical language,
4. the processes that are being simulated change faster than the model can change, and
5. no one can find the probable range of error in output.

In addition, Boeing faced the typical problem of most corporations which build models. There is usually a rapid turnover of model builders, limited documentation of the work done by previous builders, and steady alteration in computer facilities.

Simulation models may be more flexible than other models, and may be changed relatively quickly. General models, such as that developed by Exxon and others described earlier, usually allow fairly rapid alterations and specifications of risk details with a reconstruction of the various cash flows.

The problem of unavailable data noted earlier is most critical; many managers are simply not confident enough in their ability to specify the data. However, one can hope that an increasing awareness of the ways in which risk evaluations might be incorporated together with better training of future business managers in these concepts will mitigate this problem in the future. The tests of SIFT reported in Chapter 7, as well as some other evidence, indicate that some practicing executives can use "risk data."

Are Models Successful?–The
Issue of Causation

In analyzing the particular success (or failure) of risk analysis in a corporation, one is involved in an appraisal crucial to the SIFT model proposed here. One wishes to use knowledge of the qualities which induce success or failure in order to improve the probabilities of future success. Yet, the issue of causation of success is very hard to appraise.

Suppose, 10 years after introduction of the technique, one simply focuses upon the number of managers using a technique versus those not using it. Does a low percentage of users indicate any limitations of success? It certainly suggests limits, yet can one say what a relevant time period is? How can one verify if responsible officials of the firm were ever aware of the technique no matter how well it may be known among professionals in the area?

Gershefski (1970) found many companies using risk analysis (12 percent of his survey of 323 respondents). In his overall appraisal of those who were using models of any kind versus those who were not, he tried another analysis. He evaluated performance on some simple goals (five-year earnings per-share growth and sales growth). Using small samples in the chemical and manufacturing industries and a larger sample in the petroleum field, he computed an *effectiveness ratio*. This measure was the compounded growth rate in the period after planning became formalized divided by the growth rate before planning. All formal planners had strikingly high ratios, indicating substantially greater growth after the introduction of the models in both sales and net income. However, to eliminate the effects of a general economic upsurge causing bias, he contrasted their ratios with those firms not having formal planning programs at any time. In all cases, the formal planners' effectiveness ratios exceeded those of the informal planners.

But what faith can one have in these results? Would the opposite outcome dissuade the previously convinced observer of either the merits or demerits of models? It is doubtful, since the issue of association is not the same as causation. There is evidence which might indicate a relationship, but one cannot be certain of the cause. A company with an aggressive, enlightened and talented management may be the one which responds to proposals for models, and may use those models. Is subsequent success (and how difficult that element is to measure!) the result of those models, or is it the results of an unknown element which may have also stimulated the use of the models? One cannot answer this question, and different readers will have different conclusions based on their own personal experience.

But this question continually recurs. The question may be one of the success of a mutual fund which uses technical analysis, or computers, or fundamentals of the stocks renewed. Or the question may involve whether firms with MBA graduates are more profitable (better managed, faster growing, etc.) than those without MBAs. Even if there is a positive association between the quality being evaluated and the desirable results, one can never know what was the cause of the desirable results. The answer is unknown and unknowable. One can say that many managers like to use models once they are familiar with them and think they can handle the limitations. Other managers have been disenchanted because models were oversold to them in the past. Some people's hostility to models is induced by fear or ignorance. In any case, models are growing in usage; Klammer's (1972) and Gershefski's (1970) studies and the typical articles in many management journals so indicate. As to their usefulness and impact, one can only guess. And the long-run results again will be indecisive.

Conclusion

This brief survey of particular models employed in particular firms should indicate several attributes of planning models as currently operating.

First, the formalized models are relatively recent in origin. This nascent quality is a function of many factors. One can suggest the factors include the assembling of a critical mass of technical and managerial talent interested in formal models, the increasing awareness of a need to plan for the future on more than a back-of-the-envelope basis, and the decreasing cost of computer time.

Second, the models are used for a variety of purposes in the firms. That is, there is no consistent use of pro forma models for cash management, or capital budgeting analysis, or merger-acquisition studies. Generally, the ad hoc nature of model-building is a function of the same "interested-parties" phenomenon noted above.

Third, the typical model does not attempt to cope with risk explicitly; rather, the approach tends to be use of "what-if" models in the form of sensitivity runs on key variables, or the raising of the discount rate for riskier projects.

Fourth, throughout the accounts there is a very brief discussion of the ex post results; usually the impact of the model is difficult to assess, or at least not discussed publicly. Klammer's respondents indicated 85 percent of them conducted post performance audits of projects. The question is what such a post audit of the models themselves would reveal as to the models' cost effectiveness. The "implementation problem" so often referenced in management science courses is quietly present in most accounts of models in firms. Yet, there seems to be limited publicity of its presence, let alone a discussion of its character.

Generally, it seems probable that the future impact of computers in the corporation will be concentrated in presenting preprocessed information in usable form. This requirement means that there likely will be increased use of time-sharing systems and cathode ray tubes. The computers will employ simulation and optimization models for the evaluation of various projects, where the projects may range from a regional marketing program for a product up to the firm itself. Top managers of major corporations have made such public statements, as Cole (1973) for General Motors. Likewise, some relatively recent surveys have suggested optimization techniques are gaining a foothold. For example, 15 percent of 170 respondents to a questionnaire indicated their use of linear programming in their capital budgeting decisions [Fremgen (1973)].

We now turn to the issues upon which the SIFT model is built. Since a manager may use models, may be concerned with risk, and must invest in portfolios of projects where interrelationships are present, how can he evaluate potential projects? The next chapter discusses a number of potential issues which affect the ability of anyone to cope with this problem.

5

The Measurement of Risk in Portfolio

. . . real-life problems are open ended in the sense of not having correct answers, but only answers that may be shown by subsequent experience to have been better or worse.

Elliott Jacques

As the previous discussion of various approaches to capital budgeting and risk has indicated, there is the possibility of using the standard deviation as a measure of risk. The model described here, SIFT, uses this approach. It also assumes a Normal distribution of possible outcomes for all attributes under review. This allows a simplification of the portfolio calculation. However, there are limitations to the use of this assumption. Some of these limitations stem from the fact that some outcomes are non-Normal and cannot be fitted by the Normal distribution. Other limitations to this assumption are derived from the basic limitation of the "standard deviation" as a measure of risk. Finally, one may question how the variance of a proposed investment project can be derived at all, let alone the covariance between projects. These drawbacks will be discussed briefly in this chapter building on the analysis of project risk measures contained in Chapter 2. Presentation of the SIFT model will be found in Chapter 6.

Normality of Outcomes

In order to compute the portfolio results generated in the SIFT program, it is necessary to combine the project variances and covariances using standard statistical techniques. Since the confidence limits on both sides of the mean can be computed with the help of the standard deviation if the distribution is Normal (see Chapter 2), this is a convenient distribution. On the other hand, one can object to the assumption of Normality, arguing that typical forecasts of sales for a project are not Normally distributed at all. There may be a highly skewed forecast for sales, with a minimum level assured at some level (e.g., $10,000,000), a probable outcome in the first year at a higher level (perhaps $14,000,000), and various chances of much higher outcomes (e.g., $25,000,000). Similarly, one could contend that the operating cost and investment estimates are known to be non-Normal. Such analysis would seem to challenge the Normality assumption employed in SIFT and in many other models.

However, it is likely that the assumption of Normality for the distributions of expected values of the various criteria need not be invalidated. First, there is a sampling process involved in which sampled attributes are combined to find cash flow and profit figures. Even if particular distributions for certain variables within a project are non-Normal, the project's profits and cash flow often will tend toward a Normal distribution. For example, operating expenses and administrative expenses may both have non-Normal distributions. However, regardless of the form of each underlying distribution, to the extent that administrative expenses are not related to the level of operating expenses, the combination of these expenses will result in a Normal distribution over many simulation trials.

The relative magnitude of the variables and their independence are the critical elements. If one variable (e.g., sales) is so large as to swamp all others (e.g. operating expenses, depreciation of the investment), then the summed variable (cash flow or profits) will have a distribution patterned after the sales distribution. Likewise, even if there is no dominant variable, major dependencies (i.e., nonindependence) of variables can limit the Normality for the summed variables. (An example is the estimate of operating expenses heavily dependent on the level of sales.) The limitation stressed here is one of degree. The issue is *not* whether the summed variables are perfectly Normal, but whether they are close enough to a Normal distribution to make the approach useful. This outcome, of course, is dependent on the particular projects involved.

Second, to the extent that cash flows or profits of projects flow into portfolio results, the process of sampling from any non-Normal distribution would result in portfolio expected values which tend toward the Normal distribution. Indeed, the estimation of the variance of the portfolio results of a Normal distribution stems directly from the calculations of covariances among projects. Furthermore, the portfolios of such projects move toward the Normal as the number of projects composing the portfolio are increased, presuming no major projects overwhelm the results of all others. Again, this result derives from the summing process involved. Hence, as one moves to portfolio considerations, the assumption of Normality is not as invalid as it might at first seem to be.[a] If the assumption of the Normal distribution does not seem warranted, one can rely on the use of some other estimator, such as Chebyshev's inequality. Thus, given a standard deviation, σ, the probability of an outcome for a portfolio (or a

---

[a]One can review Jean (1970) and Hillier (1969), pp. 24-29 for the severe limits on the Normality assumptions. Hillier (1969) assumes independence (although not Normality) among many project cash flows in his own models (pp. 96-98) whereas SIFT accepts the dependence among projects and proceeds on the assumption of Normality. SIFT and Hillier follow the same pattern in partitioning the potential project *portfolio* to create new "projects" where combinations of other projects could have complementary or competitive effects resulting in outcomes not equal to the sum of the basic projects. In this framework, the partitioned results must be constrained so that the "combined project" is mutually exclusive to the underlying projects upon which it is built, which in turn may be mutually exclusive of each other.

project) outside an interval from $-t\sigma$ to $+t\sigma$ either side of the mean will be less than $1/t^2$, where t may be an arbitrary number. In the case of a manager wondering what the probabilities are of being within ±2 standard deviations of the mean, the Normal assumption would presume that only $(1 - .95F_n) = .05$ of returns would fall outside the ±2 standard deviation interval. Chebyshev's inequality, being less restrictive on the form of the distribution, would say there is $1/2^2$, or .25 chance of the outcome occurring beyond the two-standard deviation interval.[b]

Does the Variance Measure Risk?

Before reviewing some studies which have attempted to verify whether variance and risk have a direct relationship, it is helpful to discuss the concepts of utility and risk aversion. Utility is the value of something to the individual (or the firm). It is distinct from the dollar value. For example, one might be twice as happy with $10 as with $5. Alternatively, if one were very rich, for example, the difference between $5 and $10 might appear to be very small. Hence, one cannot say that the basic *dollar* difference between two figures measures the *utility* of the difference in outcomes. A utility *function* is simply a functional relationship which transforms the dollar (or other value) into the utility value. There are a number of utility functions which have been hypothesized to "fit" an individual, and there are a variety of techniques for deriving individual or group utility functions. Many of the techniques have been used successfully with management groups.

Risk aversion is a measure of one's disinclination to take risks. Its opposite is risk proneness. Quite simply, risk aversion is expressed by index numbers which measure the willingness of an individual to gamble in given situations. If one assumes that most individuals prefer less risk to more risk for a given level of expected return, then one can see how the level of risk an individual is willing to accept in exchange for a potentially higher return changes with income or with wealth.

Consider the investor who has a choice between a risky asset and a fixed income asset. He can transform his expected income into some combination of the risky investment and the fixed income investment. Then, if he increases the absolute *dollar* amount invested in the risky asset as his wealth increases, the investor has decreasing *absolute* risk aversion. If the *fraction* of total wealth invested in the risky asset increases with wealth, then the investor has decreasing *relative* risk aversion. Pratt (1964) and others have indicated that it is plausible that individuals would show decreasing absolute risk aversion.[c] Intuitively, one

---

[b]See Kemeny et al. (1959).

[c]The commonly used quadratic utility function shows increasing absolute risk aversion, however.

can find plausible explanations for either increasing or decreasing relative risk aversions as wealth rises.

Actual results in experimental settings of the reaction of executives or MBA students to risky situations are mixed. In a study by Gordon et al. (1972), the results with advanced MBAs indicated that standard utility functions did not fit the data well. The results were consistent with decreasing absolute and increasing relative risk aversion as wealth increased, however.

Alderfer and Bierman (1970) found that subjects in a gambling situation consistently had a strong aversion to loss and preferred an alternative with a lower mean and higher variance but with a lower probability of loss to another alternative with a higher mean, lower variance, and higher probability of loss. (Such an outcome is possible if the skewness of the investment outcomes is such as to cause the distribution to have a long tail on one side.)[d] Furthermore, the choices and utility values were a function not just of mean and variance, but of the average distance from the breakeven point. The Alderfer and Bierman study also found that executives were far more willing to tolerate low returns or losses than student MBAs were, at least at Cornell! Similar findings in general among individual decision makers is found in Slovic (1972).

From a field study of eight firms, Mao (1970) concluded that the negative semivariance (the variance of outcomes below the mean) is a far better measure of risk. This conclusion coincides with the above analysis of the importance of avoiding a loss since the negative semivariance refers to returns below the expected level. Other conclusions in the Mao study were the preoccupation of executives with earnings per share analysis, a concern with stable growth as opposed to stable earnings, and a preference for payback versus present value or rate of return analysis.[e]

Below are some common implicit or explicit rules of thumb which reflect these concerns with loss.

1. No project shall have more than X percent probability of (a) loss, (b) a return below 5 percent, or (c) a return below our cost of capital.

---

[d]This result indicated a utility function inconsistent with the "quadratic" function upon which the mean-variance results are usually predicted.

[e]Such preoccupation with the zero limit or loss limit is not inconsistent with the use of payback. Payback has long been criticized in the academic literature, for ignoring the time value of money, cash flows beyond the payback period, and the general pattern of cash flows prior to the period. Weingartner (1969) attempted a slight resurrection on these same grounds. He argued that it can be used as a breakeven figure for telling the manager "when the firm will be made whole again." This number can be used to reduce concern for uncertainty. The knowledge of break-even or profitable outcomes in repeated situations has direct benefits to the manager who receives rewards for a wise decision. Given high uncertainty in the environment, the result is that both the *time* of the payoff and the *amount* of the payoff are unknown, all of which increase the computational difficulty and lack of comfort of the manager. Payback is an information reduction process; it limits the amount of search by focusing on the point in time at which the firm will be "made whole again."

2. No project shall have more than X percent probability of leaving our firm's reported earnings per share (a) less than the prior year's earnings, or (b) less than earnings would have been in the nth year.
3. Any project must pay back its investment in Y years. Any project whose investment is above $\$Z$ must pay back the investment in Y' years.

Conrath (1973) has also observed results consistent with these findings in an industrial setting in Canada. He found that the executives he observed could cope with probabilities. Risk of loss was a major factor of concern, independent of variance. In addition, there was sequential attention to various issues, a management style commented upon in Chapter 1. Finally, the form of the data presentation was critical; essentially identical projects could be accepted or rejected depending on the form in which the risk was presented. Conrath hypothesized an accept/reject decision process based on the forecasted return and the probability of a loss. In this model, if the forecasted return exceeded 30 percent plus three times the probability of a loss, the project would be accepted. However, the absolute probability level of a loss could not exceed 10 percent, or the project would be eliminated regardless of expected return.

For the reasons discussed above, the variance which follows from the use of a Normal distribution assumption in the portfolio models may be useful. The manner in which that variance is used is an empirical question to be answered by experience. To the extent that the underlying portfolio results tend toward the Normal distribution, the use of the variance in place of the negative semivariance is warranted. First, do the managers using the model complete a deliberate risk/reward calculation? Second, alternatively, do they follow the pattern implied in some of the above studies? If so, there should be evidence of preoccupation with the zero-confidence level of returns on whatever criteria are found to be important. Third, is there concern with selecting project(s) with a particular probability distribution of returns?

Fortunately, the SIFT program allows a specific option in which the managers can focus on the probability of a project outcome which is either negative or below what would occur without the project. Although the particular calculations are simplified, the frequency with which they are chosen may help to confirm the preoccupation of these managers in a laboratory setting with the "no-loss" or "no-worse-than-we-are" dictum for selection of projects.

The Derivation of Portfolio Variances

It is important to note that this SIFT model assumes that the variances and covariances of the project present values and other criteria found by simulation prior to the use of SIFT. The assumption of Normality is then offered as a way to permit the manager to select portfolios of projects, observing the resulting risk characteristics along many dimensions. In the event such variances and covariances are not found by prior simulation, there are restricted ways for handling the results. First, one could ask managers to specify correlations between projects. This task is difficult to accomplish even if the manager is thoroughly familiar with the concept. If it is possible in a given situation, such correlations can generate the covariance matrix. On the other hand, if the existing firm is huge in relation to any proposed project, the loss in accuracy in the variance of firm and project portfolio is minimal when the correlations between new projects are ignored. Rather, all that has to be estimated is the correlation of outcomes between each new project with the existing firm's asset base or some "market" standard.

A second approach is to find equivalent formulas which allow one to estimate the maximum variance in portfolio net present value from some compendium of project present value variances, ignoring the covariances between projects or between projects and the firm "market."

Under either alternative, as Jean (1970), pp. 102-106, has indicated, the problem created by the possible combinations that can occur for a portfolio of projects is not trivial. Thus, if one calculates all possible combinations of projects, and analyzes the outcomes, the task is enormous. Jen (1969) calculated that a portfolio of one to twenty potential projects would involve computing over one million combinations unless some simplifying rule is used, probably under a Normality assumption.

A third approach is to ignore the variance approach altogether and to ask managers to accept gambles or judgments which reveal their certainty equivalent preferences for future cash flows of projects or portfolios. *Certainty equivalents* have been discussed in business decisions by Raiffa (1968) and others. Briefly, one can demonstrate that a rational consistent decision maker will be indifferent between some certain value and a distribution of uncertain returns. For example, one may choose to accept 50¢ rather than a gamble with equal probabilities of nothing and $1. Depending on whether one is *risk averse* or *risk prone*, one might accept (for example) 45¢ or 55¢ respectively, rather than accept the gamble. Similarly, one can generalize this concept of (1) uncertain payments at some future time period and (2) a distribution of outcomes other than the two possibilities (0 or $1) shown here. Hence, in analyzing a capital budgeting project or a portfolio, one must obtain a distribution of cash flows which may be expected in each year, ask the manager what payment (s)he would accept with certainty in place of that uncertain cash flow in that year, and discount the certainty equivalent value at the appropriate rate.[f]

Apart from management specification problems, the disadvantage of this approach is (again) selecting the combinations of cash flows and finding the

---

[f]The rate would be a "risk-free" rate (U.S. Government bonds, for example) since the risk of the project has already been considered. In making this decision operationally, several simplifications can be employed which somewhat distort the results from the theoretical values. Thus, one may assume α_i, a coefficient for transforming the expected value of the

probability of their outcome. The certainty equivalent of a portfolio distribution in the nth year is not the sum of the certainty equivalents of the projects within that portfolio unless the projects, individually and in total, are so small as to warrant the assumption of a linear utility function for the manager over that interval. Hence, portfolios of projects must be completed. Then, (1) how does one decide which projects are to be combined to give a portfolio result of probable returns with maximum utility and (2) how does one find the distribution of probable returns?

Thus, one is back to the problem of finding "combinations."

This problem is not insurmountable. A manager can take a first guess at probable portfolios (as done in the SIFT model), the results can be simulated with the full distribution of outcomes, and then returned to the manager. Such an approach is not inconsistent with the SIFT model although the version shown will use the given variance in place of the full distribution of outcomes in order to derive the benefits of interaction with a time-sharing system. Complete resimulation of entire portfolios in time-sharing mode is not feasible on any but the largest and fastest machines fully dedicated to one interacting manager.

The Capital Asset Model

In recent years, corporate financial theory increasingly has responded to the contributions from capital market theory and the ideas surrounding the capital asset pricing model. Many of these concepts were initially applied to the area of investments, perhaps most notably in the evaluation of mutual fund performance. Briefly, the capital asset analysis focuses upon (1) the return of a risk-free asset, (2) the return of a broadly-measured market portfolio and its risk, and (3) the return of a particular security or fund, and its risk. "Risk" is measured solely in terms of standard deviation. The analysis has highlighted the need for a risky asset to have a higher than average return to compensate for that risk. Stated another way, one may conclude that "outstanding" performance of a particular mutual fund may have occurred because it contained a portfolio of

---

cash flows in year i (Y_i) to the certainty equivalent ($\alpha_i Y_i$). Hence, under this simplification, the net present value of the certainty equivalents of an n-year project is:

$$\sum_{i=1}^{n} \frac{\alpha_i Y_i}{(1 + r)^i} \qquad [0 \leqslant \alpha_i \leqslant 1].$$

Essentially, the selection of α_i is designed to compensate for the parameters of the cash flow distribution other than the expected value. For other comments on the "forms" of popular mathematical models of utility and why they may not "fit" the manager well, see Applewhite (1965).

securities which were riskier than the average security. Accordingly, when "performance" is measured simply as rate of return compared to the average, the fund appeared superior. On the other hand, when one adjusts that return by charging it for the higher risk (recalling that one demands a higher return for accepting risk), then the performance has often declined to average or below.

This same sort of analysis has been applied to the concepts of corporate financial theory. Corporate financial theory probably will move in this direction. In terms of the SIFT model, the most immediate application would be in the determination of the projects with "excess" return.

The previous chapters have demonstrated the importance of considering the project's variance and its covariance with both the firm and other projects under consideration. As an alternative formulation in the capital asset framework, one can focus on the variance and covariance of projects in relation to some market return. Likewise, one could make some judgment about the future return which can be earned by a risk-free asset. Then, given a measure of the proposed project's variance and covariance with the market return, the required return of the project can be calculated. In the case of net present value, one computes the NPV at the risk-adjusted discount rate, where the particular rate reflects the value required given the risk of the project and its covariance with the market. If there is an excess net present value associated with the project, then it is a desirable investment.

In one sense, this capital asset model is a simpler one than proposed by SIFT. In the event there is not simply educated guessing of the covariances of projects with the market, the simulation trials are done in relation to projects and the market, rather than in relation to each other. Furthermore, the model directly incorporates a charge for risk, based solely on the standard deviation. Such an analysis can be determined within the confines of the SIFT model: each project can be evaluated in terms of whether the return is satisfactory when adjusted for risk.

The application of capital asset pricing model to corporate financial theory is progressing. Currently, the theory equates standard deviation with risk, ignores the risk of bankruptcy, does not handle debt of the corporation when evaluating risk, and assumes investors are perfectly diversified (which implies that the typical corporate investment is unwarranted if based largely on diversification grounds, unless there are substantial economies of scale or other joint effects present). There is a reasonable expectation that these assumptions can be relaxed in future research, providing a richer analysis of the decision process.

Those readers particularly interested in this emerging field of financial theory are referred to Bierman and Hass (1973), Rubenstein (1973), or the text by Mossin (1973). A readable example of the application of the capital asset model assumptions to a corporation's investment decisions may be found in Weston (1973).

Risk in the SIFT Model

In summary, the SIFT model uses the variance-covariance matrix for analysis of project interrelationships created by a joint-simulation of projects in a risk analysis context. Alternatively, that matrix could be derived by asking managers to specify the correlation between projects on each criterion, or at least between each proposed project and the existing firm or a "market" return if no single proposal is that large relative to the firm. From this correlation estimate, the variance in any portfolio could be roughly estimated. Otherwise, the variance could be ignored and the complete distribution of probable portfolio outcomes printed at a terminal.

In any case, the major problem of the selection of projects for inclusion in portfolios is left unsettled. Using the variance-covariance matrix in the SIFT model allows one to fall back upon the variety of mathematical models which deal with capital budgeting in the mean-variance approach, although these models are not used in the results presented here. After those trials, the SIFT model usage would imply resimulation in the full model of those portfolios deemed to have the most potential. This full portfolio resimulation would return to the basic project models, combining results as they occur in the model rather than using the variance-covariance matrix to estimate the portfolio variance.

For readers interested in the process of computing capital project portfolio variances of various criteria, and in seeing the calculations differ from the typical security example, Appendix 5A discusses these topics. A brief summary of several of the mathematical programming approaches to capital budgeting is contained in Appendix 5B.

Appendix 5A:
The Calculation of
Portfolio Variance

In measuring the risk in individual project returns, we have stressed that the cash flow from portfolios of projects may tend toward the Normal distribution. This Appendix will show how to compute the variance of portfolios of projects, and why a series of Normal cash flows will result in a Normal distribution of net present values but a non-Normal distribution of rates of return.

In the case of portfolios of securities, there is evidence that the rate of return from securities may be Normal or log Normal, and there is a copious amount of academic research regarding portfolios of *securities*, but not portfolios of *projects*. The examples will contrast the process for computing project variances with that for computing security variances. Finally, the Appendix will present a discussion of another measure of risk, the coefficient of variation.

The Normality of Rates of Return
and Net Present Values

As an example, consider an average yearly cash flow from a project of $50, $60, and $70 following an investment of $100 in the first period. Assume the resulting yearly cash inflows have a standard deviation of $20, and are Normally distributed. Even if one were to assume that these yearly cash inflows were independent of each other, the distribution of the rate of return would not be Normal. With cash inflows plus and minus one standard deviation away from the average (either equally probable, given the assumption), the rates of return and net present value are as follows:

Yearly Cash Flows

0	1	2	3			ROR	NPV @ 10%			
($100)	$70	$80	$90			57%	$97.37			
				difference	23%				$49.74	difference
($100)	50	60	70			34%	47.63			
				difference	25%				$49.73	difference
($100)	30	40	50			9%	(2.10)			

The nonsymmetrical outcome of the rate of return is expected. In the case of the net present values, the variables are divided by different factors for each year in the discounting process, although those factors are constant in a given year regardless of the particular cash inflow that year. For the rate of return, however, the factors for division vary depending upon the particular outcome of the cash flows in combination, which means the variations in the rate of return on either side of the "expected" outcome are not symmetrical. Furthermore, for the case in which the yearly cash flows are Normal but not independent, the rate of return will continue to be assymetrical and the net present value again will be symmetrical.

Jean (1970), page 105, shows that the variance in the net present value of a series of cash flows can be determined directly from the variance of the cash flows if the cash flows are independent over time. Thus, if F_i is the cash flow in year i, then the variance in the present value is

$$\text{Var}(PV) = \text{Var}(F_1)\left(\frac{1}{1+r}\right)^2 + \text{Var}(F_2)\left(\frac{1}{1+r}\right)^4 + \ldots + \text{Var}(F_n)\left(\frac{1}{1+r}\right)^{2n}$$

Clearly, this approach is inapplicable in the case of most projects, for the value of the cash flow in period j is likely to influence the expected value of cash flow in period $j+1$. Failing this independence, Jean notes that one must specify all combinations of cash flows and probabilities, deriving the variance in the present value from the result. For portfolios of projects, an assumption of independence in intertemporal project cash flows is even less warranted. The SIFT approach substitutes a variance calculation based upon simultaneous risk analysis simulation. The variance in present value cash flows is found from the simulation variance-covariance results of projects. This simulation option in place of Jean's complete specification of all probabilities is available to any manager attempting a risk analysis of a project.

Portfolio Variance Calculations—
the Security Example

One should consider the difference between the calculation of portfolio variance used in the SIFT model and the usual approach followed in calculation of portfolio variance for securities. In this project portfolio case, the portfolio variance on a typical criterion is,

$$\sigma_p^2 = \sum_i \sigma_i^2 + \sum_i \sum_j \sigma_{ij} \ (i \neq j) \tag{5A.1}$$

where σ_p^2 is the variance of the portfolio, σ_i^2 is the variance of project i, and σ_{ij} is the covariance between project i and project j.

In the typical security portfolio case, the total amount invested is considered fixed, and the fraction of the total investment in security i, a_i, is used in the calculation, such that $\Sigma a_i = 1$. Here the variance of the security portfolio's rate of return, for example, is

$$\sigma_p^{\,2} = \sum_i a_i^{\,2}\,\sigma_i^{\,2} + \sum_i \sum_j a_i a_j \sigma_{ij}\,(i \neq j). \qquad (5A.2)$$

The distinction between (5A.1) and (5A.2) is most important. In the case of $1000 dollars to be invested in up to 100 securities, the mean expected rate of return is the sum of the dollars invested in each security times the expected rate of return from that security. The a_i weights can be used in the estimate of the mean, for if .2 of the portfolio is invested in Security A with an expected return of 6 percent, .4 in Security B with an expected return of 8 percent, and .4 in Security C with an expected return of 9 percent, the expected return of the portfolio is then,

$$E\,(\text{Return}) = .2(6\%) + .4(8\%) + .4(9\%) = 7.8\% \qquad (5A.3)$$

and the variance is

$$\sigma_p^{\,2} = .04\sigma_A^{\,2} + .16\sigma_B^{\,2} + .16\sigma_C^{\,2} + 2[.08\sigma_{AB} + .08\sigma_{AC} + .16\sigma_{BC}]. \qquad (5A.4)$$

In the case of the portfolio SIFT example in which all of the standards are *absolutes* which are additive, the situation changes. The mean earnings per share from investing in Project X and Project Y is the simple sum of the earnings from each of them separately. Furthermore, adding Project Z to the portfolios does not change the mean earnings generated from Projects X and Y, for the investment budget is increased. *Thus, there are no* a_i*'s which are redefined with each addition or deletion from the portfolio.* This outcome is in contrast to the security portfolio example where only a fixed amount of dollars are committed and adding another security necessarily diminishes one or more other securities' absolute returns.

Another form of stating the same consideration is to note that *the "optimum" mixture (* a_i *'s) in the security portfolio can be selected independent of the size of the budget. In the project portfolio, this selection is not possible.*

The distinction, then, is that the criterion is an *absolute*, not a *rate*, in case (5A.1). Where standards are absolutes, as net present value or earnings per share, then the summation in (5A.1) is correct. Where standards are a *rate*, as rate of return, then (5A.2) is the proper calculation of variance. Equation (5A.2) will give the same answer as (5A.1) if the restriction that all a_i's must sum to 1 is replaced with the constraint that each a_i equal 1; the equations are then identical.

Many capital budgeting writers have applied this security portfolio model (5A.2) to the capital budgeting situation with nominal adjustment for this situation. Thus, Vaughn et al. (1972) use the standard security model, recalculating a_i for each additional capital project added. They focus upon rate of return, as is proper. However, when Vaughn et al. consider the cash flow outcomes, they incorrectly assume that a rate of return corresponds to a yearly cash flow. This assumption is rarely valid. A $10 million project with a 15 percent internal rate of return is very unlikely to yield $1.5 million in a single year, let alone in every year. Clearly, a cash flow portfolio analysis needs (a) to be calculated specifically on the standard of cash flow, not rate of return, and (b) to be found using Equation (5A.1).

The Coefficient of Variation

Alternatively, if one wishes to study the *coefficient of variation* instead of the variance as a standard according to which a project is being evaluated, then the summation shown in Equation (5A.1) will be rejected. The coefficient of variation (CV) is the standard deviation per expected unit on a given criterion. It is a rate, as is the rate of return, and the appropriate formula is (5A.2). For example,[a] consider two projects, J and K. Let them have the following attributes:

	J	K
Expected Net Present Value ($E(X)$)	$1000	$100
Standard Deviation (σ_X)	100	20
Coefficient of Variation (CV) $\left\{ = \dfrac{\sigma_X}{E(X)} \right\}$	.10	.20
Correlation (ρ_{JK})	.6	

Since the covariance (σ_{JK}) between the two projects is equal to the coefficient of correlation times the respective standard deviations,

$$\sigma_{JK} = .6 \times 100 \times 20 \qquad (5A.5)$$

$$= 1200.$$

Then the standard deviation of the portfolio is, from (5A.1),

$$\sigma_P = \sqrt{(100)^2 + (20)^2 + 2 \times 1200} \qquad (5A.6)$$

$$= \sqrt{12800}$$

$$= \sim 113.$$

---

[a]For similar examples showing the effects of diversification as the correlation between projects changes, see Quirin (1967), pp. 223-228.

In calculating the portfolio coefficient of variation (CV_p), the result is, from (5A.2), and (5A.5)

$$CV_p = \sqrt{\left(\frac{1000}{1100}\right)^2 (.10)^2 + \left(\frac{100}{1100}\right)^2 (.20)^2 + 2\left\{\left(\frac{1000}{1100}\right)\left(\frac{100}{1100}\right)(.6)(.10)(.20)\right\}}$$

$$= \sqrt{.00826 + .00033 + .00198}$$

$$= \sqrt{.01057}$$

$$= \sim .103. \tag{5A.7}$$

Here, the relative net present values of the projects to the total, 1000/1100 and 100/1100, become the a_i's which sum to 1, and the CV's of the projects (.10 and .20) replace the σ_i's in Equation (5A.2). The covariance calculation between coefficients of variation is patterned upon Equation (5A.5).

Again, the distinction here is between the variance (5A.6) which is a measure of absolute variation, and the coefficient of variation (5A.7) which is a measure of the rate of variation.

Appendix 5B:
Mathematical Programming
and Capital Budgeting

Rapid development of mathematical programming approaches to the capital budgeting question have occurred in the last two decades. A few of the various proposals will be discussed briefly here.

A variety of techniques now exist for solving portions of the portfolio problem. Indeed, such techniques can be used in the corporation as a means for providing "first approximation" or target portfolios for a manager. Perhaps the most standard model is a mixed integer mathematical programming algorithm which would maximize the net present value subject to various restrictions. These restrictions, called *constraints*, relate to the inclusion or exclusion of a project in conjunction with possible limitations on a minimum earnings contribution, sales growth, cash flow or the like. Alternatively, one can maximize the sum of discounted or undiscounted earnings subject to various other constraints, as in the International Utilities example discussed in Chapter 4. Finally, one may sequentially maximize each of many criteria using any of the other criteria as restrictions.

Perhaps the most widely known approach is that of Weingartner (1963; 1966a). In one formulation, the following values are defined:

c_{ij} = cash investment in year i in project j,   (5B.1)

C_i = total cash budget constraint in year i,   (5B.2)

b_j = present value of project j, and   (5B.3)

x_j = fraction of project j accepted.   (5B.4)

Then the *linear* programming problem is

Maximize $\sum_{j=1}^{n} b_j x_j$ (*Objective function*)   (5B.5)

Subject to

$\sum_{j=1}^{n} c_{ij} x_j \leqslant C_i$ for all i periods   (5B.6)

$0 \leqslant x_j \leqslant 1$ for all j projects   (*Constraints*)   (5B.7)

$C_i , c_{ij} \geqslant 0.$ (5B.8)

89

Such a formulation would allow fractional projects (x_2 = 3/4, for example) to occur. With a mixed integer programming approach, these fractional projects are prevented by the constraint,

$$x_j = 0,1 \qquad \text{(i.e., } x_j \text{ must be either 0 or 1.)} \qquad (5B.9)$$

instead of (5B.7).[a]

The model can be expanded to include yearly cash throwoffs from each project which is accepted (the flows on which b_j is based). These flows can be added each year to the budget constraint, C_j. In such a case, the cash throwoffs of accepted projects are used to finance other projects.

Another variation in the constraints concerns contingent projects. Suppose Project 6 is a fleet of trucks and Project 7 is equipping the trucks with extra large flat beds for hauling. Clearly, Project 7 is to be considered *only* if Project 6 is accepted. The appropriate constraint is then

$$x_7 \leqslant x_6. \qquad (5B.10)$$

With x_j constrained to 0 or 1, (5B.10) means that x_7, the extra large flat beds, can be included only if x_6 also is part of the optimum solution.[b]

Another constraint concerns mutually exclusive projects. Suppose Projects 20, 21, 22, and 23 are to build a new plant in four New York suburban areas, but only one plant is to be built. Then the appropriate constraint is

$$\sum_{j \in J} x_j \leqslant 1 \text{ where } J = 20, 21, 22, 23 \text{ and "} j \epsilon J \text{" means "} j \text{ an element of } J.\text{"}$$
$$(5B.11)$$

(5B.11) insures that at most one of the new plants will be accepted in the final solution if all x_j are also constrained to be integers.

We may add to the Weingartner formulation additional constraints that allow a richer analysis of the problem. As an example, consider how one would describe a problem with a minimum level of earnings per share, a minimum growth in earnings per share, and a minimum growth in absolute sales each year.

To the above formulation of maximizing net present value, we add the following constraints. First, define new variables

$$e_{ij} = \text{earnings per share contribution in year } i \text{ from project } j, \text{ or} \qquad (5B.12)$$

$$s_{ij} = \text{sales contribution in year } i \text{ from project } j. \qquad (5B.13)$$

---

[a]The constraints presented here are the form in which they are usually written. The actual form of the constraint when inserted into the computer program is quite different.

[b]Generalizing, assume Project 8 is also available, and that Project 7 must be included *if and only if* Projects 6 and 8 are both accepted. Three constraints (in addition to the integer 0-1 constraints) assure this outcome: (1) $x_7 \leqslant x_6$, (2) $x_7 \leqslant x_8$, and (3) $x_6 + x_8 - x_7 \leqslant 1$.

Then the growth in earnings per share or sales in absolute terms can be found. For example, the growth in earnings per share contributed by Project 10 from the first to the second period is

$$\Delta e_{2,10} = e_{2,10} x_{10} - e_{1,10} x_{10} \qquad (5B.14)$$

where Δ means "the difference." $\Delta e_{2,10}$ is a new variable, where "2" means the growth for period two (the difference between the absolute earnings per share contribution from period one to period two) and "10" refers to the project. By similar analysis, one can compute the growth in sales for any two periods from a given project.

To insure either a minimum level or a growth in earnings per share, sales, or any other variable where the contribution of a given project to those goals is assumed with certainty, one adds sufficient constraints to insure that the portfolio as a whole will meet the standard. For example, to insure that earnings per share will be at least \$4.50 per share in year 2, the constraint is

$$\sum_{j=1}^{n} e_{2,j} x_j \geqslant 4.50 \qquad (5B.15)$$

To insure that earnings per share will increase in *dollar* terms, the above constraint is modified and included for year 3 at \$5.00, for year 4 at \$5.70, and so forth if desired.

To verify that the earnings per share will show a certain minimum percentage increase, then the formulation can be understood if one considers

$$E_i = \text{total earnings per share contribution from all project in year } i \qquad (5B.16)$$

$$= \sum_{j=1}^{n} e_{ij} x_j$$

and then the constraint is, for year two versus year one,

$$E_2 - 1.1 E_1 \geqslant 0 \qquad (5B.17)$$

to insure at least a 10 percent earnings per share growth.

More complex formulations with mathematical approximations where the exact formulation cannot be handled are possible [e.g., Carleton (1970), Hamilton and Moses (1971)]. In the basic programming formulation presented here, the constraints bear the burden of achieving various satisfactory (or minimum) levels for criteria deemed to be important. Should a management be concerned about earnings per share rather than net present value, then EPS could be placed in the objective function instead of net present value. However, for reasons noted in the introduction such a judgment is inconsistent with generally accepted financial theory. In addition the formulation to account for periodic issues of common stock is complex. In the linear programming framework, no unknown (the x_{ij} here) can be involved in a multiplicative product with another unknown. The restriction is eased in the quadratic programming framework discussed below.

Other alterations allow an increasing cost of funds, differentials in borrowing and lending rates, and restrictions on other scarce resources (such as management). In addition, one may believe that cash throwoffs for short-term investment have differential reinvestment rates depending on the year in which the flows are received and the fact that short-term funds often can be invested only at the marketable securities rate which is lower than the return from a long-term investment in capital goods. In situations such as this, one seeks to maximize the terminal value of the firm as of some horizon date with appropriate reinvestment rates specified in the constraints. This formulation typically will result in selection of a different subset of projects than a net present value objective function produces because of the valuation of the intervening cash throwoffs.

Note that the linear programming solution solves one problem in contrast to a popular alternative standard. *Profitability indices* of projects, the ratio of the net present value of cash returns from a project to the initial investment, are often proposed as a means of ranking projects. With a budget constraint, the decision maker selects projects in decreasing index ranking until the budget is expended. One problem with the index is the ambiguity regarding treatment of cash investments in a project in more than one year. Are investments after year 0 to be netted against cash inflows in later years (i.e., included in the numerator) or added to the initial outflow (i.e., included in the denominator)?

The above problem can be solved by a definition followed consistently. The second, more serious, problem is that the approach is fundamentally wrong in confusing the maximization of the average ratio with maximization of the net present value of the projects, the presumed goal. Table 5B-1 shows a sample conflict. Although most writers in the finance area have seen the conflict and avoided the ratio method, most of the research in cost-benefit analysis still seems to be concerned with selecting projects on the basis of the highest ratio of benefits to cost.[c]

cSome additional weaknesses of the profitability index are inability to handle multiperiod budget constraints and the lack of consideration of interdependency among projects. *Given* a standard of accepting or rejecting projects on a net present value basis, *then* both the profitability index and the rate of return methods separate acceptable (greater than 1 and a return greater than the cost of capital, respectively) from unacceptable (less than 1 and a return less than the cost of capital) projects. The problems arise when one tries to *rank* projects on the basis of either the profitability index or the internal rate of return. Such ranking may be required in selecting one project from several mutually exclusive projects, or for selecting a portfolio of projects under a capital constraint on outlays in one or more periods. See Weingartner (1963) for an extension of these criticisms.

Table 5B-1
Portfolio Selection with the Profitability Index

(1)	(2)	(3)	(4)	(5)
Project	Investment $t=0$	Net Present Value of Cash Throwoffs $t=1,\ldots,n$	Net Present Value of Project (3)–(2)	Profitability Index (3)/(2)
1	($1000)	$4000	$3000	4
2	(2000)	4000	2000	2
3	(2000)	4200	2200	2.1
4	(3000)	6600	3600	2.2

Budget constraint: $5000

Projects selected by index: 1, 4
    NPV = $6600

Optimum project selection: 1, 2, 3
    NPV = $7200

This mathematical programming approach clearly permitted a consideration of interdependency in the sense of contingent or mutually exclusive projects. However, it did not deal with risk or uncertainty explicitly in the projects and likewise did not handle the probabilistic interdependency of projects. Further, the approach seeks a single goal (e.g., net present value as of time $t = 0$ or terminal value as of time $t = T$). However, this original conceptualization of the problem has served as a foundation for further work in the area of mathematical programming approaches to capital budgeting. General surveys by Weingartner (1966) and Bernhard (1969) of the mathematical programming approaches to capital budgeting in a portfolio context also are available.

Goal programming allows variables in the objective function to be included directly in the constraints. Thus, Ijiri (1965) presents a goal programming approach to multiple goal situations using a basic linear programming technique coupled with multiple goals under certainty. In this approach, a requirement level for each goal (such as cash flow, earnings, or the like) can be specified. Only after all goals had met one level of performance would the solution proceed to a higher level, thus assuring a given lower bound for all goals at each outcome. The difficulty with the approach is the requirement that all goals be specified in detail by an executive, and the certainty required in all the projections. Another drawback in the approach is the problem of valuing all the goals on a common criterion. Either one assumes linearity of marginal valuations (one apple is equal to two oranges regardless of the number of apples and oranges currently in the package) or else one must specify massive tradeoffs of goals for different levels of achievement.

A variety of approaches have been proposed for dealing with risk, as noted. One approach in linear programming is to use the coefficient of variation. The coefficient of variation, as explained in Appendix 5A, is the ratio of the standard deviation of a variable to the mean value of that variable. Either the objective function can be set to minimize the sum of these coefficients over all projects for some variable (earnings per share, net present value), or a constraint can be formulated in which the coefficient cannot exceed some base amount.

Another approach was presented by Naslund (1966) using chance-constrained programming. Briefly, Naslund sought to maximize net present value (or some other criterion) where the constraints must meet or exceed a certain value with a given probability. Hence, the technique allowed for explicit consideration of risk in the constraints themselves. There is the problem that the algorithm may work well only where the distribution of the constraints approximates a Normal distribution. In addition, there is the problem of specification. Management must explicitly state the forecasts, risk preferences, risk distribution of factors, and the like. However, the problem is encountered in most programming approaches.

Alternately, one can truncate the variables to a mean-variance analysis and use the Markowitz quadratic programming formulation. Here, one can seek a minimum variance portfolio outcome for a given criterion subject to a fixed return on that criterion. Again the results could be computed for multiple portfolios and the first approximations studied. Unfortunately, this method still leaves the manager with the requirement of prespecifying restrictions on all minimum levels for other criteria in any given program. This can be solved using another variant of mathematical programming, chance-constrained programming (see above). Here, the results again are assumed to be Normal. However, the portfolio effects (e.g., diversification arising from portfolio considerations) cannot be taken into account directly. Hence, while the manager then could require a return subject to a certain probability of not falling below that return, interdependence among the projects which generate the return is not permitted, where interdependence is related in such terms as correlation or covariance as used here. Furthermore, under this chance-constrained programming option, the ability to induce constraints on the other variables is restricted.

The above comments should not be seen as eliminating the chance constrained, mixed integer, or quadratic programming algorithms as viable tools in selecting portfolios. Indeed, some practicing operations research departments within firms might wish to use these techniques as scanning devices for selecting potential projects. These comments are merely to indicate that the SIFT interactive program at its full potential conceivably deals with a greater variety of interdependency and risk considerations than the current proposed mathematical programming solutions, and may be more useful operationally to the manager as he works with the results. The latter point is critical, given the emphasis on organizational and managerial decision models mentioned earlier.

6

The Interactive Model—SIFT

The open mind never acts: when we have done our utmost to arrive at a reasonable conclusion we still, when we can reason and investigate no more, must close our minds for the moment with a snap and act dogmatically on our conclusions. The man who waits to make an entirely reasonable will dies intestate.

George Bernard Shaw
"Androcles and the Lion"

Explanation of some of the background factors in the SIFT program will be presented in this chapter. The specific manual prepared for executives operating this model program will be shown together with an example of how the program processes data. A description of the executives who used the model and the results of their experience are given in the following chapter.

Individual Project Simulations

For reasons of economy, the actual project and portfolio simulations required for this model were not made in these sample runs. Rather, estimated values for the relevant figures were computed, and the resulting mean values, variances and covariances were calculated.[a]

Actual simulation of these data is not unreasonable for most computer systems. Risk analyses on the basis of individual projects can be completed as described earlier. However, the simulation of projects must be done jointly in order to derive covariances among projects. The requirements of the joint simulation are simply that the outcome of each project be computed on a given trial and stored in relation to the outcome of all the other projects on that trial. Then the sampling process is restarted and the simulation repeated. Hence, where projects are dependent on some common variable (such as GNP, growth in a particular area of the economy, and so forth) a common value for those underlying factors is assured.

From this joint simulation, the results may be stored as shown in Table 6-1. Table 6-1 shows a joint simulation for a single criterion, net present value. For each simulation trial (column), the outcome for each project (row) is stored.

---

[a]The merits of using variance as a measure of risk has been discussed previously in Chapters 2 and 5, together with the means of calculating the covariance between any two projects.

Table 6-1

Computation and Storage Procedure for Joint Project Simulation on Criterion "X" (Net Present Value)

	Simulation Trial 1	Simulation Trial 2		Simulation Trial N
Project 1	X_{01}	X_{02}	$\cdots$	X_{0N}
Project 2	X_{11}	X_{12}	$\cdots$	X_{1N}
Project 3	X_{21}	X_{22}	$\cdots$	X_{2N}
.	.	.	$\cdots$	.
.	.	.		.
.	.	.		.
Project M	X_{M1}	X_{M2}		X_{MN}

Note: Each simulation trial is completed for all proposed projects before computation of the next simulation trial.

When all simulations have been run and stored, it is possible to compute means and variances for each project, as well as covariances for each pair of projects.

The calculations contained in the SIFT program can be understood in the context of the flexibility given to the user of that SIFT program. Before presenting the SIFT program commands and the sample runs with that program, it is helpful to review the business environment which was simulated for executives using SIFT in the experiments which will follow. All the participants in this experiment were given descriptive material in the form of "cases" which described a hypothetical business situation and presented various quantities of data about the company and the 20 projects under consideration.

The Decision Environment

In evaluating the project selection decisions of a group of executives, the essential information about the situation was given to these managers in two separate packages. The first package [or (A) case] consisted of a brief description of the company and its history, brief outlines of the characteristics of 20 projects, and tables showing the expected outcome and standard deviation of the outcome on ten criteria for each of the projects. The criteria were net present value, and the impact on cash flow, on earnings per share, and on sales for each of the next three years. As additional information, each project's rate of return and profitability index were produced together with the expected cost of the project. Participants were given a general budget ceiling, but it was emphasized that this was a flexible limit. The company was described as a family-owned, diversified manufacturer of specialty machine equipment for various industries. In the most recent year, sales were $10,500,000 and earnings were $950,000. Earnings per share had grown from $2.50 three years ago to $4.75 in the most recent year. The firm was considering an additional issue of stock, and becoming a public company. This stock issue was expected to dilute current earnings per share to $3.41. In addition participants also were given information relating to previous years' cash flow, depreciation and capital outlays, as well as income statements and balance sheets for the preceding three years. For those participants unfamiliar with simulation, a brief description of the technique also was presented.

The second package [or (B) case] included a brief description of portfolio theory and presented the correlation coefficient matrix for all of the projects on each of the ten criteria previously noted.[b] These materials are included here as Appendixes 6A and 6B.

In conjunction with the (B) case, the computer program SIFT was made available. This program allowed a participant to observe the effects of his/her decision on the portfolio. For any portfolio, the calculations presented the expected outcome and the variability of that outcome on any criterion the participant wished to examine. These results were derived by combining the means and variances/covariances for the projects the executive selected. Furthermore, expected debt financing accruing to the company as a result of capital outlays in the first year was included in the cash flow figure. The interest charges on this debt were considered in the firm's income statement and earnings per share results. As the participant signed on to the system, (s)he was asked to state the goals and select an initial portfolio from among the projects. Certain illegal project combinations (e.g., one of two new products might be accepted, but not both) as well as the forced inclusion of the current operation (Project 1) were imbedded. Should these constraints be violated, error messages would be returned. These same requirements were also stated in the text of the (A) and (B) cases.

When an executive first connected to the SIFT system, (s)he would receive a welcoming message and an explanation of the common codes which were available:

WELCOME TO THE COULTER CORPORATION CAPITAL BUDGETING SIMULATION

WHAT IS YOUR NAME(S)?G. WELLS,A. MILES

PLEASE EXPLAIN YOUR OBJECTIVES ON THE NEXT THREE LINES
?TO MAXIMIZE
?EPS IN
?YEAR 3

[b]Early preliminary testing indicated that correlation coefficients (see Appendix 5A) were more readily used by executives than the covariances. Accordingly, this measure was presented to them for these studies.

MAXIMUM BUDGET LIMIT = $ 8000

WHEN THE COMPUTER TYPES—OPTION?—PLEASE ANSWER WITH ONE OF THE RESPONSES SHOWN BELOW

OPTION	DESCRIPTION
NP	STARTS A NEW PORTFOLIO
PC	PORTFOLIO CONTENTS
EC	LIST PROJECT ENTRY COSTS
IP	LIST ILLEGAL PROJECT COMBINATIONS
A	ADD A NEW PROJECT TO YOUR PORTFOLIO
D	DELETE A PROJECT FROM YOUR PORTFOLIO
P	PORTFOLIO STATISTICS
SP	SHORT PORTFOLIO OUTPUT
C	COMBINE PROJECTS
MR	RANK PROJECTS BY MEAN VALUES
VR	RANK PROJECTS BY VARIABILITY(STD. DEV.)
END	STOPS PROGRAM

WHEN THE COMPUTER TYPES—CRITERION?—PLEASE ANSWER WITH ONE RE-SPONSE SHOWN BELOW

CRITERION	DESCRIPTION
S1	SALES IN YEAR 1
S2	SALES IN YEAR 2
S3	SALES IN YEAR 3
CF1	CASH FLOW IN YEAR 1
CF2	CASH FLOW IN YEAR 2
CF3	CASH FLOW IN YEAR 3
EPS1	EARNINGS PER SHARE IN YEAR 1
EPS2	EARNINGS PER SHARE IN YEAR 2
EPS3	EARNINGS PER SHARE IN YEAR 3
NPV	NET PRESENT VALUE

In using this SIFT program, the executive had a number of filtering options available as shown in Appendix 6C:

1. The program could be used to determine *portfolio* data. SIFT would present the capital outlay and the results for any of the criteria for any combination of projects legally allowed. As noted, the program would include costs for debt.

2. *Confidence levels* using Normality assumptions were printed for the portfolios chosen by the executive for whatever criteria he wished. These confidence intervals used the standard deviations of the portfolio to compute 25/75 percent, 10/90 percent, 5/95 percent, and 1/99 percent intervals for the criteria as the executive requested.

3. *Compare* options permitted the participant to study the effectiveness of

the proposed portfolio vis-à-vis the current operation in meeting various goals for future years. For example, the executive could view the probability that earnings per share in the second year would be no less under his proposed portfolio than expected second-year earnings per share of the existing firm alone. These probabilities were explicitly presented for each of the ten criteria.

4. *Portfolio-project comparisons* permitted the executive to view how his proposed portfolio would be altered for each of the ten criteria by adding or deleting a particular project. These results were similar to those obtained for the existing firm/portfolio comparison indicated above. The comparison indicated the amount by which the expected values and standard deviations of the portfolio would be changed by addition or deletion of a project.

5. *Mean search* routines permitted the executive to seek altered values from the expected outcome of his portfolio for any criterion. When using this option, the participant indicated his criterion and the number of proposals he would like (N). He was asked whether he wished to increase or decrease the mean value. The program then returned in ascending or descending order (as the executive had specified) the N projects which would have the greatest effect in increasing or decreasing the expected value under consideration. Depending on what the participant specified, the program would review all projects, those currently in the proposed portfolio, or those currently out of the proposed portfolio. The participant's specification, of course, depended upon whether (s)he was attempting to eliminate projects from her/his portfolio which had an unfavorable impact on a criterion (e.g., a binding budget constraint and low earnings per share in the first year) or to add projects which would improve an outcome (e.g., find projects to boost sales in the second year).[c]

6. *Variance search* routines required the participant to input the same information as under the mean search routine. The program then would search for those projects in and/or out of the current portfolio which would do the most to increase or decrease the variance on a given criterion. The routine operated by means of comparing the impact of each new project on the existing portfolio's variance, computing a new portfolio figure which was then compared with the existing portfolio. After all projects under possible consideration were evaluated, the ranking procedure permitted the participant to learn the N most desirable projects for the criterion (s)he had selected.

Examples of these commands in operation are presented in Appendix 6C, which shows actual output from a pass through the SIFT program. The particular projects and their descriptions are contained in Table 6A-2 of the Coulter (A) case presented in Appendix 6A. When interpretation of the results are made in Chapter 7, reference and description of the projects will be made as appropriate.

---

[c]Since the portfolio model operated on the basis of a Normality assumption, the mean is an acceptable average. In typical risk analysis models for a non-Normal outcome, the median is the relevant figure.

Discounting: Selection of the Rate

In terms of the mean/variance approach used for the project portfolio evaluation in SIFT, one can argue that the correct discount rate is the risk-free rate, which would be less than the 10 percent rate employed in the raw data. Thus, the manager discounts the cash flows for time, but should not discount them for risk. The risk-adjustment is made when the portfolio is selected using the appropriate mean-variance tradeoff the manager wishes to apply. Hence, a more appropriate rate would be lower, perhaps 6 percent.[d]

An opposite approach would be to *vary* the discount rate, raising it for the riskier projects. This conclusion is consistent with the cost of capital argument presented earlier. However, since one purpose of this SIFT study was to analyze the manner in which the executives coped with variance as a risk measure, this calculation was not given to the executives.

This choice of 10 percent was employed on the grounds of expediency. Having faced an evaluation of projects in the (A) case using a weighted cost of capital (which includes a risk premium), most executives in the experiments seemed to respect the idea of cost of capital. In the (A) case, the projects were discussed individually with no regard for portfolio risk. In order to minimize preparation time, the necessary instruction required to explain why a risk-free rate should be used in the mean-variance context was eliminated. Instead, the time was spent explaining the concept of variance. In fact, a lower discount rate would change the relative ranking of some of the projects on the single goal of net present value. Rather than enter this issue, the executives were given the same NPV figures in the SIFT portfolio model and in (B) case which they had seen previously.

Appendixes 6A and 6B present a sample scenario which could introduce managers to the portfolio simulation concepts we have emphasized in this book. Appendix 6C, as noted, shows the use of the SIFT program with these hypothetical data.

As part of the evaluation of this model and to learn more about the process of decision-making by managers, these hypothetical results and the model were made available under laboratory conditions to a large number of executives. A description of the experiment, the subjects and the results of the study are contained in Chapter 7.

[d]See, for example, Bierman and Haas (1973) and Keeley and Westerfield (1972).

Appendix 6A:
Coulter Corporation (A)

Coulter Corporation had been formed in 1948 as a diversified manufacturer of specialty machine equipment for a number of industries. Through imaginative use of product innovation and excellent service, the firm progressed to a moderate sized business. The equity of the firm was diversified among a number of shareholders, and shares were traded on the Midwest Stock Exchange. Relationships with banks and various creditors of the firm near its headquarters in Rock Island, Illinois, had been favorable. Recent financial statements are shown in Table 6A-1.

The firm had been founded by Mr. Robert Coulter and was currently managed by his 46-year-old son, James. James had extensive business experience working for a competitor prior to joining his father's business, and had run the Coulter Corporation with what generally was judged to be successful results for the past six years. His assistant, Mr. Ronald Adams, recently had been assigned to develop a method by which the firm could evaluate proposed projects. Mr. Coulter had always appraised projects on a discounted cash flow basis, usually looking at the results in the context of the project's net present value. He thought that a fair cost of capital for the firm was around 10 percent. On the other hand, he recognized that there were interdependencies among projects, as well as attributes for projects which were very difficult to quantify in a present value context. He hoped Mr. Adams would be able to aid him in resolving this problem, and had asked him to review the firm's budgeting procedures.

Proposed Financing

Mr. Coulter intended to raise additional equity in 1973 of $5 million from the public sale of 67,000 shares at $75 per share. He felt this number of shares represented the maximum dilution he wished to absorb. Relationships with a variety of private lenders and institutional financiers had convinced him that debt had been used too little by the firm, and he could expand debt in line with this equity commitment. Contingent on the equity financing, he had confirmed a $2 to $3 million, 30-year term loan with 3 percent sinking fund payments commencing in 1975. Accordingly, he felt that a fair limit on total project commitments in the coming three years would be $10 to $12 million, given projected operating cash flows from current operations and other short-term financing options he might call upon. He was aware that additional equity could be raised in the future, but was reluctant to raise equity at other than at three to five-year intervals because of earnings per share dilution and the cost of

This case was prepared for class discussion by E. Eugene Carter, 1972.

Table 6A-1
Coulter Corporation (A)–Income Statement (Thousands)

	1970	1971	1972 (projected)
Sales	$8,800	$9,900	$10,500
Operating and Administrative	7,800	8,200	8,600
Operating Income	1,000	1,700	1,900
Taxes	500	850	950
Net Income	500	850	950
Dividends	150	150	200
Addition to Retained Earnings	350	700	750
Earnings per share (200,000 shares)	$ 2.50	$ 4.25	$ 4.75**
Dividends per share	.75	.75	1.00
Depreciation (tax)	$ 300	270	410
Depreciation (book)	200	200	230
Tax Payments	450	810	860
Operating Cash Flow* (after Dividends)	$ 600	$ 940	$ 1,070
New Plant Outlays	120	170	200

*Operating Income (for 1972, $1,900) + book depreciation ($230) − tax payments ($860) − dividends ($200) = $1,070.

**Mr. Coulter believed that the market was aware that an equity issue was imminent, although the current price (mid-$70's) gave a very high multiple in light of the diluted 1972 EPS of $3.41 after his proposed issue of 67,000 shares to net $5 million to the firm.

underwriting. Although he was committed to raising equity in 1973 and knew that the debt financing would be available next year or staggered over the coming years, he was uncertain what budget limit he should impose for evaluating projects in the first year, or for several coming years. He knew that even if the budget limit were not exceeded, the strain on management of the company would be substantial, and there was risk of indigestion from the commitment to such a large variety of projects as were feasible. This risk was increased if all the commitments to projects were made in the first year of his planning period, 1973.

Projects Under Consideration for 1973

Mr. Coulter knew that one "project" to which the firm already was committed was the corporation itself, and he had forecast earnings, sales, and cash flow for

Table 6A-1 (cont.)
Coulter Corporation (A)–Balance Sheet (Thousands)

Assets	1970	1971	1972 (projected)
Cash	$ 60	$ 40	$ 50
Marketable Securities	1,200	1,300	1,280
Receivables	1,740	3,020	3,300
Inventory	1,640	1,750	2,020
Total Current Assets	$4,640	$6,110	$6,650
Plant and Equipment	$7,000	$7,170	$7,370
Less Accumulated Depreciation	(4,000)	(4,200)	(4,430)
Net Plant and Equipment	3,000	2,970	2,940
Total Assets	7,640	9,080	9,590
Liabilities and Net Worth			
Accounts Payable	$ 900	$1,200	$1,130
Deferred Taxes Payable	800	840	930
Short-Term Loan	540	860	480
Total Current Liabilities	$2,240	$2,980	$2,540
Long-Term Debt @ 7%	800	800	1,000
Total Liabilities	3,040	3,780	3,540
Common Stock (200,000 shares, $5 par)	1,000	1,000	1,000
Retained Earnings	3,600	4,300	5,050
Total Liabilities and Net Worth	7,640	9,080	9,590

the coming years (Project 1). The other projects under consideration included investment in new product lines (Projects 2-4, 12), machinery replacement (Projects 5-6), a new headquarters building (Project 7), a major plant expansion (Project 8), the building of an entirely new plant on the West Coast (Projects 9 and 10), four acquisitions (Projects 11, 13, 14, 20), the purchase or leasing of a new truck fleet (Projects 15 and 16), and the expansion of a product lease program for customers (Project 17). Other projects included a new computer system to improve payroll and billing processing (Project 18), and a smokestack precipitator requested by the Mayor's office (Project 19). A general description of each of the projects is shown in Table 6A-2.

Project Simulation Results

Mr. Coulter indicated to Mr. Adams his concern about a number of criteria for any project. While he had studied material which convinced him that he should

Table 6A-2

Coulter Corporation (A)–Project Descriptions

Project

1   The corporation with no changes. Based on expected sales, operating expense, required investment and depreciation policies, this project assumes a continuation of current operations.

2   A new product with substantial sales possibilities based on an extension of current operations.

3   A new product similar to the above, but larger in scope.

4   A new product with broader sales possibilities than an extension of current operations (Projects 2 and 3).

5   Investment in new machinery which will modernize certain operations of the company. Revenues from the investment are savings in operating costs which would otherwise have been incurred. These operating expenses are based on the projected levels of operating expenses in the company with no changes in product lines.

6   Machinery replacement of substantially greater intensity than Project 5.

7   A new headquarters building. Revenues are based on intangible estimates of expected benefits to be derived from the building.

8   Major plant expansion useful if the new products (Projects 2, 3, and 4) are undertaken. The benefits from this plant can be realized primarily only with a total sales level above $13 million. Hence, without the three new projects, the plant would be marginal. Projections for this plant include the three new products in sales and operating expenses.

9   An entirely new plant located on the West Coast. Benefits accrue to the company with the three new projects included.

10   The new plant on the West Coast but excluding the three proposed projects and the expected operational savings from them.

11   Acquisition of a new business peripherally related to Coulter's current operation. It involves prefabrication of components for a major appliance manufacturer. Coulter was interested in this project to allow diversification beyond the machine tool business which was heavily sensitive to the business cycle. The business had a book value of over $750,000, and would cost $1,000,000. Sales were expected to be around $1,200,000, with a 10 percent growth rate forecast. The acquisition is made under the accounting regulations for a "pooling" in which there is no amortization of good will (the difference in the purchase price and the book value of the firm). Equity required under the "pooling" arrangement will be used to reduce the amount of additional equity financing proposed for Coulter.

12   Addition of new product line to fill a currently profitable niche in the market. Trade sources indicate that this niche will virtually disappear in five years as competition from other companies weakens Coulter's market position.

13   Acquisition involving direct commitment to fabricating small home appliances for direct sales to the consumer. The business had a substantial history, and again would enable Coulter to diversify itself. Asset value was $950,000 with an agreed-upon purchase price of around $1,500,000. If the expected growth in sales of the business is realized, additional investment in the plant of $275,000 will be required in the third year of operation. This acquisition will be shown as a "pooling of interest" transaction.

14   Pooling acquisition of new business dealing in replacement parts for Coulter and competitors' machinery. This operation is known to be countercyclical to the rest of Coulter's business.

Table 6A-2 (cont.)

Project	
15	Purchase of a new truck fleet which will be used for substantial distribution of the company's products. Since a large share of the distribution is accomplished within the Midwestern area, the firm wished to consider a truck fleet. In addition, the truck fleet will be used for delivery of raw materials to the firm from its various suppliers in return for discounts on purchase costs.
16	The truck fleet discussed as Project 15, but under a leasing arrangement proposed by a major leasing corporation. The firm would be committed to a full pay-out lease (which guaranteed that the leasing company would recover the full cost of the fleet). Operating costs will be borne by Coulter Corporation.
17	Commitment of funds for receivables to enable customers to finance purchases. Competitive pressure in the industry, especially in times of economic recession, had led to the serious consideration of this financing. Although new sales were possible, the company intended to experiment solely with one product line, currently accounting for 20 percent of the firm's sales projections. It was estimated that 40 percent of the existing customers for that product line would convert to the lease financing. Leases for the products would be noncancellable for the estimated ten-year life of each product, with yearly payments by customers of 15 percent of the basic purchase price. Additional sales forecasts together with operating costs for the machines are included in the analysis.
18	Software and hardware installation of a new computer system to process payroll and billing. Management was confident of the serviceability of the new system, and of the cost figures.
19	Smokestack precipitator for the company's main plant in Rock Island. There had been some public pressure in the newspapers for cleaning up this system. Maintenance would be nominal on the project.
20	Pooling acquisition of new business similar to Coulter Corporation but on smaller scale.

be interested in the net present value of a project, he also was concerned with the level and growth rate in earnings and sales over the following three years. He thought Coulter Corporation might apply for listing on the American Stock Exchange, and believed recent earnings would influence analysts in their reaction to the stock. Accordingly, he had asked Mr. Adams to prepare computer simulation results showing probable ranges of earnings per share and sales for each of the proposed projects. In addition he wished to avoid critical cash flow problems. He was aware that some projects might create a heavy cash drain upon the firm not only in their initial year of investment but in subsequent years. Hence, he also asked for simulation results on the cash flow of each project for the coming three years.

Mr. Adams showed Mr. Coulter the simulation results of one of the projects the Coulter Corporation was considering. A description of the project and the partial results of a 50-trial simulation are shown in Tables 6A-3 and 6A-4. Mr. Coulter was pleased to see that it was possible to have simulation results on criteria other than net present value. Looking at the results for this project, he saw a wide dispersion of returns in operating cash flow in the first year.

Table 6A-3
Coulter Corporation (A)–Simulation Model for Project 2

This new product will have immediate tooling cost and machinery cost of $500,000. In the first year, $80,000 will be expensed with the balance depreciated over eight years.

Projected sales of this new product are $200,000 in Year 1, with a range from $190,000 to $210,000 with uniform probability over this interval. For Year 2, sales are expected to be $400,000 plus an increase in sales based on the sales for the first year times the growth rate in the Gross National Product. This figure is subject to a 2 percent variation in either direction on the basis of forecast made by the company. Sales in future years are based on an expected growth rate of 3 percent on the prior year's sales, plus an increment based on 1/10th of the increase in the percentage growth in GNP. From Year 9 onward, sales will decrease at 10 percent per year from the prior years' sales because of the product life cycle. After Year 14, the product will have essentially no sales.

Operating expenses for the product are a fixed cost of $75,000 plus distribution based on the level of sales. These costs are forecast with a 15 percent variation based on management's confidence in the estimates.

Table 6A-4
Coulter Corporation (A)–Simulation Results, Project 2

Trial	Net Present Value (000's)	Cash Flow (000's)			Sales (000's)			Earnings per share (267,000 shares)		
		Year 1 (1973)	Year 2 (1974)	Year 3 (1975)	Year 1 (1973)	Year 2 (1974)	Year 3 (1975)	Year 1 (1973)	Year 2 (1974)	Year 3 (1975)
1	$148	$120	$ 92	$110	$205	$401	$438	($.07)	$.65	$.77
2	162	150	110	143	208	407	448	(.06)	.78	.89
3	138	80	73	65	195	399	425	(.08)	.38	.51
4	130	61	43	53	193	396	422	(.09)	.50	.62
5	118	40	23	41	185	392	408	(.10)	.16	.31
6	123	52	38	37	193	393	415	(.09)	.22	.33
7	146	131	93	113	207	405	436	(.08)	.73	.83
8	148	143	89	106	208	409	437	(.08)	.83	.96
9	153	163	92	86	209	410	443	(.07)	.63	.74
.										
.										
.										
45	160	160	90	108	215	410	443	(.06)	.88	1.05
46	149	114	104	122	209	403	438	(.07)	.73	.96
47	143	120	115	132	203	405	440	(.07)	.54	.72
48	158	140	96	93	206	407	436	(.08)	.73	.96
49	140	90	71	80	201	402	431	(.08)	.50	.61
50	143	99	92	106	203	401	433	(.08)	.61	.80
Average	140	90	70	80	200	400	430	(.08)	.50	.60

Likewise, he saw the impact on earnings from the project would be negative in the first year because of large expensed charges. Finally, he noted that the net present value of the project usually was favorable at the 10 percent discount rate which he had told Mr. Adams to employ. On the other hand, he realized that he could not make sense out of 10 standards per project, 20 projects, and a wide dispersion on each standard. He indicated to Mr. Adams that he seemed to be drowning in numbers.

Summary Statistics for Project Evaluation

Mr. Adams then explained to Mr. Coulter that the distribution of outcomes from a simulation analysis could be shown in various ways. For any given criterion, one could construct a cumulative plot of the distribution, a bar chart of frequency intervals, or a standard frequency distribution. For the project discussed previously, a sample of each of these three forms of output for the net present value is presented in Figure 6A-1. Mr. Adams also pointed out that there were a number of summary statistics which could be used to describe some of the features of any distribution. These summary statistics were divided into two categories: measures of central tendency and measures of dispersion. In the former category were such measures as the mean of the trials (the arithmetic average), the median (that return which has 50 percent of outcomes above it and 50 percent below it), and the mode (the most frequent return or returns). In the case of a symmetrical distribution, the mean, median and mode might all coincide. For nonsymmetrical distributions, there could be different figures for each of these "averages." Since the mean was one of the most easily understood figures, Mr. Coulter indicated it would be the statistic he would focus upon.

In the area of dispersion, Mr. Adams explained that a very common measure of dispersion was the range, as from the highest to the lowest return. However, this measure was subject to the vagaries of possible extreme values. Another range, called the interquartile range, can be computed. This is the range between the highest and lowest quartile. The highest quartile is defined as the return which has 25 percent of the returns above and 75 percent below it. The lowest quartile has 25 percent of the returns below and 75 percent above it. Thus, 50 percent of all outcomes are between the highest and lowest quartile. In a Normal, or bell-shaped curve, such as shown in Figure 6A-2, the *standard deviation* is a good measure of dispersion. From this standard deviation, one could compute the probabilities with which returns would occur in certain ranges. Thus, from the mean minus one standard deviation to the mean plus one standard deviation, .65 of the possible returns should occur in a simulation trial. Similarly, one could be 65 percent "confident" that the actual return from the investment project would be within that range. From the mean minus two standard deviations to the mean plus two standard deviations for a Normal curve, .95 of the probable returns were included. Hence, one could use a

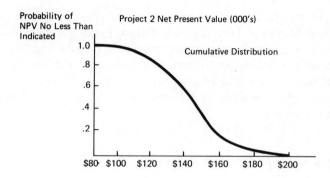

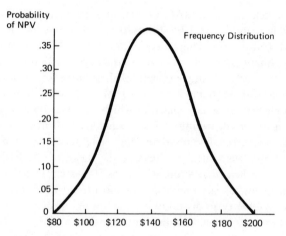

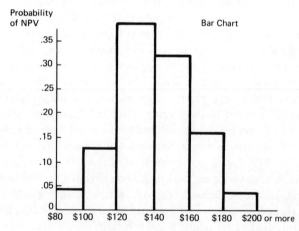

Figure 6A-1. Coulter Corporation (A)–Project 2 Net Present Value (000's)

Normal Curve

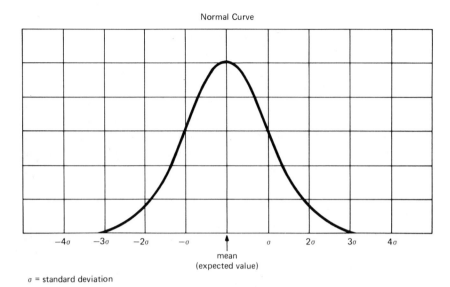

σ = standard deviation

Figure 6A-2. Coulter Corporation (A)–Normal Curve.

measure of the mean plus or minus some constant times the standard deviation to derive any sort of confidence interval. For example, one could be sure with 50 percent confidence that the mean plus or minus .675 times the standard deviation would include the actual return.

Mr. Coulter recalled that Mr. Adams had previously emphasized that in the case of a non-Normal curve, the measurement of a mean plus or minus the standard deviation did not have the same statistical implications as it would under the Normal distribution. For this reason, he knew that a final distribution of returns substantially different from the Normal might not have the same statistical properties which he was counting upon. However, he still believed that the standard deviation was a good measure of the dispersion of possible returns. He believed that the greater the standard deviation, the greater the volatility of the project.

The Problems of Portfolio Evaluation

While Mr. Coulter vaguely understood what Mr. Adams was talking about, and saw that the summary statistic measures could help him evaluate the portfolio implications of the projects under consideration, he was unsure just how many numbers he could feasibly add together to develop portfolio statistics. In addition, he was uncertain how he should trade off the alternate criteria. Thus, was he to sacrifice some net present value to avoid having earnings per share decline in any year? How much of a sales growth factor should he demand before he looked at the net present value? What were the revelant criteria or blending of criteria which he should use in his evaluation? When he saw the results of the summary statistics for the 20 projects for the 10 criteria, (Tables 6A-5 through 6A-8), he was even more at a loss as to how to select projects.

From the start, he recognized that there were combinations of projects which could not be made. Furthermore, since some projects were combinations of other projects, he would not want to have both the combined project and one or more of the components which made up the combined projects in a portfolio. His list of illegal combinations was as follows:

Illegal Combinations

2,8	4,8	With any of Projects 2,3 or 4, Projects 8,9, and 10 should not be used in the analysis. Since Projects 8 and 9 showed the effects of Projects 2,3 and 4, to include them again would be double counting.
2,9	4,9	
2,10	4,10	
3,8		
3,9		
3,10		
9,10		Likewise, only one profile of the new plant could possibly be included (Project 9 or 10).
8,9		The combined manufacture of three new projects would be either in the old plant (Project 8) or the new plant (9), not both.
5,6		Plant modernization would take place on one of two levels (Projects 5 and 6), but not both.
15,16		The truck fleet would be either bought (Project 15) or leased (Project 16), but not both.

111

Table 6A-5

Coulter Corporation (A)–Project Returns and Entry Costs

Project	Entry Cost (000's)	Net Present Value* (000's)	Profitability Index**	Rate of Return
1	0	1,750 (190)	∞	10%
2	500	140 (19)	1.28	13.0
3	1,200	93 (20)	1.08	11.1
4	700	831 (30)	2.19	18.9
5	1,000	80 (20)	1.08	11.9
6	2,000	109 (35)	1.05	11.2
7	750	3 (2)	1.00	10.1
8	2,900	1,072 (380)	1.37	17.1
9	3,400	1,590 (500)	1.47	17.9
10	1,000	298 (200)	1.30	14.8
11	950	−73 (80)	.92	7.1
12	1,00	−92 (31)	.91	4.8
13	1,500	111 (50)	1.07	11.0
14	1,750	90 (26)	1.05	10.7
15	400	125 (50)	1.31	16.7
16	0	234 (30)	∞	35.6***
17	720	232 (40)	1.32	20.0
18	60	34 (15)	1.56	34.2
19	130	−100 (80)	.23	−
20	400	−60 (7)	.85	4.1

*Figure in parentheses beside Net Present Value is the Standard Deviation of the expected Net Present Value.

**Ratio of present value of inflows (NPV plus Entry Cost) to Entry Cost. For Project 3, this figure is ($93 + $1,200)/$1,200 = 1.08.

***Rate of return using present value of yearly lease payments as the investment.

Table 6A-6
Coulter Corporation (A)—Three-Year Cash Flow (000's)
Mean (Standard Deviation)

Project	Year 1 (1973)	Year 2 (1974)	Year 3 (1975)
1	$870 ($75)	$960 ($80)	$990 ($82)
2	90 (60)	70 (50)	80 (60)
3	204 (130)	50 (6)	70 (8)
4	120 (65)	70 (8)	80 (10)
5	250 (30)	120 (10)	140 (18)
6	700 (90)	180 (6)	190 (6)
7	145 (80)	40 (8)	45 (8)
8	550 (240)	450 (35)	520 (40)
9	620 (275)	500 (40)	625 (65)
10	150 (52)	85 (8)	90 (10)
11	170 (45)	250 (18)	270 (22)
12	500 (40)	300 (18)	100 (8)
13	200 (120)	240 (4)	−40 (5)
14	100 (50)	150 (18)	180 (25)
15	40 (18)	80 (8)	90 (10)
16	50 (16)	52 (3)	55 (3)
17	540 (40)	30 (7)	50 (8)
18	30 (5)	35 (4)	38 (4)
19	0 (10)	0 (0)	0 (0)
20	50 (15)	75 (8)	225 (18)

Table 6A-7
Coulter Corporation (A)–Three-Year Sales (000's)
Mean (Standard Deviation)

Project	Year 1 (1973)		Year 2 (1974)		Year 3 (1975)	
1	$11030	($109)	$12500	($120)	$13900	($135)
2	200	(8)	400	(5)	430	(6)
3	105	(3)	300	(6)	310	(7)
4	430	(20)	800	(20)	840	(25)
5	0	(0)	0	(0)	0	(0)
6	0	(0)	0	(0)	0	(0)
7	0	(0)	0	(0)	0	(0)
8	735	(90)	1800	(220)	2000	(280)
9	1361	(180)	2380	(320)	2600	(360)
10	628	(35)	700	(50)	1000	(70)
11	1200	(120)	1320	(130)	1450	(150)
12	2000	(140)	1100	(75)	500	(25)
13	1000	(58)	1200	(66)	1300	(78)
14	1200	(58)	1450	(66)	1600	(78)
15	0	(0)	0	(0)	0	(0)
16	0	(0)	0	(0)	0	(0)
17	130	(5)	140	(6)	160	(7)
18	0	(0)	0	(0)	0	(0)
19	0	(0)	0	(0)	0	(0)
20	450	(15)	600	(30)	1000	(52)

Table 6A-8
Coulter Corporation (A)–Three-Year Earnings per Share
Mean (Standard Deviation)

Project	Year 1 (1973)	Year 2 (1974)	Year 3 (1975)
1	$3.50 ($.20)	$3.60 ($.22)	$3.72 ($.28)
2	−.08 (.10)	.50 (.60)	.60 (.60)
3	−1.10 (.90)	.50 (.70)	.60 (.70)
4	−.30 (.60)	.20 (.80)	.30 (.80)
5	−.10 (.01)	.21 (.02)	.26 (.05)
6	−.41 (.60)	.30 (.01)	.32 (.02)
7	−.20 (.20)	.13 (.01)	.13 (.02)
8	−1.80 (.80)	1.12 (.50)	1.40 (.58)
9	−1.90 (.80)	1.30 (.68)	1.48 (.72)
10	−.60 (.08)	.52 (.28)	.54 (.32)
11	.75 (.10)	.80 (.05)	.90 (.05)
12	.90 (.20)	.40 (.10)	.20 (.05)
13	.10 (.02)	.15 (.01)	.18 (.01)
14	.07 (.02)	.12 (.01)	.15 (.01)
15	.01 (.01)	.02 (.01)	.02 (.01)
16	.01 (.01)	.01 (.03)	.01 (.02)
17	−.05 (.80)	.01 (.01)	.02 (.01)
18	.02 (.02)	.03 (.01)	.03 (.01)
19	−.02 (.01)	−.01 (.01)	−.01 (.01)
20	.20 (.04)	.15 (.03)	.60 (.10)

Appendix 6B:
Coulter Corporation (B)

Portfolio Aspects of Simulation

The idea of looking at a standard deviation appealed to Mr. Coulter, since it gave him an idea of how likely he was to have a return, an earnings per share figure, or some other variable. He would use the standard deviation to see how confident he was of the earnings, cash flow, or the like being above some critical value. Often he was concerned with the probability of doing as well with a project as he expected to do without the project. If that was true, how large was the chance that the firm's net present value with the project would be below what he expected without the project?

Although it was possible to express risk (using standard deviation) for a single project for a variety of criteria, the interdependency among the projects made risk evaluation more complex. Mr. Coulter assumed that he could simply add the standard deviations for two projects as he had done with their mean values. In this way, any portfolio of projects would be simply the sum of the statistics for the respective projects contained in the portfolio.

After he indicated this method to Mr. Adams, it was explained to him that the standard deviation of a portfolio was not the same as the simple addition of the standard deviations of the projects in the portfolio. Mr. Adams explained this inconsistency to him by an example of two projects. If the projects were both in the same industry, they might be expected to have outcomes which were similar. Thus, spreading his money so that he had funds in each project would not change the deviation in the return per dollar invested. On the other hand, if the projects were in different industries, there would be a large element of risk reduction involved. Project A might have an outcome above its expected rate when Project B would be above or below its expected outcome. Hence, the deviation in return per dollar invested would be lower than the simple sum of the project deviation. Finally, if the projects were negatively related in the systematic deviation from the expected return, then it would be possible to lessen the standard deviation even more, for a high return on Project A would coincide with a low return on Project B, and vice versa. Hence, any possible outcome would be very close to the simple expected value of the return of the portfolio. Mr. Coulter immediately recognized the logic as similar to the discussions he had heard relating to investment diversification for a private investor.

Mr. Coulter recalled the term "correlation," and Mr. Adams noted that this was the concept which would determine the portfolio standard deviation. The coefficient of correlation was a measure of the relationship between two projects

This case was prepared for class discussion by E. Eugene Carter, 1972.

for a given criterion. If the two projects were completely independent, the correlation between them would be zero. If they were heavily dependent on the same industry characteristics, then the measure of correlation would be positive, up to a maximum of 1.00. Only rarely would there be projects of direct dependence with a negative correlation coefficient, although Mr. Adams stressed that this was possible. A detailed memorandum explaining these concepts and showing the calculation of a portfolio standard deviation for some of the proposed corporate projects was sent to Mr. Coulter, and is shown in Attachment 1.

Calculation of Correlations

Although cognizant of the value of correlation coefficients to compute the final standard deviation of any portfolio of projects, Mr. Coulter indicated to Mr. Adams that he was not at all sure that he could specify the correlation between projects. Mr. Adams pointed out to him that it was possible for the correlation to be computed as a byproduct of the computer simulation. He explained to Mr. Coulter that if the results for any project for a given trial were saved in the computer, then the return for that project for that trial could be compared to the return of each of the other projects for that trial. From this comparison over the total number of trials used in the computer simulation calculation, he indicated it was possible to compute the correlation between each pair of projects. It was from such computations for a large-scale simulation that Mr. Adams prepared the correlation tables for the proposed projects for the criteria Mr. Coulter wished (shown in Tables 6B.1-6B.10). Because the correlation between Project A and Project B is always the same as the correlation between Project B and Project A, Mr. Adams merely presented the upper triangle of each table.

Conclusion

At this point, Mr. Coulter decided to begin his portfolio evaluation. However, he realized he needed to think about the criteria. How was he to trade off sales, earnings, cash flow and net present value? What was the basic target he should seek? How should he consider the possible riskiness of projects?

A brief look at Tables 6B.1-6B.10 convinced him that he had no way to compare the projects meaningfully since the number of figures was so large. He thought a general pattern of rating projects on risk might be helpful. This might take the form of evaluating them on whether they were maintenance of existing operations, expansion of existing operations, or diversification proposals. Clearly there were major issues of corporate strategy involved. In addition, the expenditure of all the money in late 1972 and 1973 would seriously limit the cash available in later years, other than what the existing operations and the new projects generated, and funds from even more financing. Mr. Coulter recognized there were few possibilities to postpone the projects, and he had a very limited feeling for what projects conceivably might appear in future years. How could he evaluate this problem? He called Mr. Adams' office to ask him about these points, and learned that Adams was on a one-week field trip to the firm's Wichita office.

Attachment 1

Coulter Corporation (B)

To: James Coulter
From: Ron Adams
Subject: Portfolio Evaluation of Projects

Consider the problem of sample projects, Project A and Project B. The standard deviation of a portfolio of these projects is dependent upon the relationship between them. Indeed, if the projects are perfectly correlated, then the standard deviation is related only to the individual standard deviations. A measure of correlation is ρ (the Greek letter rho), the coefficient of correlation. In the case of perfect positive correlation ($\rho=1$), when Project A has a high return, Project B also has a high return, and vice versa. The standard deviation of the portfolio ($\sigma_{\text{Portfolio}}$) of the two projects in this case is equal to

$$\sigma_{\text{Portfolio}} = \sigma_A + \sigma_B.$$

The correlation coefficient (p) is a measure of the relationship between two projects. It will range from -1 to $+1$. If two projects are completely independent, the correlation between them is zero. On the other hand, if the outcome of one project is statistically related to the other, then there will be a nonzero correlation measure between them. If, when one project tends to be above its mean for a given criterion, the other is also above its mean, then the coefficient of correlation will be positive. If the projects offset each other in that above average outcome on one project typically will be found with a below average outcome on the other project, then the coefficient of correlation will be negative. The final standard deviation of a portfolio is computed using the *variance* of projects, which is the square of the standard deviation (σ_A^2), and is:

$$\sigma_{\text{Portfolio}} = \sqrt{\sigma_A^2 + \sigma_B^2 + 2\rho\,\sigma_A\,\sigma_B}.$$

That is, the standard deviation of the portfolio is equal to the square root of the sum of the individual variances plus twice the correlation coefficient times the product of the two standard deviations. This formula could be generalized to a portfolio of more than two projects simply by adding the other variances and twice the correlation coefficients times the products of additional combinations of standard deviations.

A simple equivalent of the correlation coefficient times the product of the two standard deviations for any two projects under consideration is the covariance. The covariance between Project A and Project B (written as σ_{AB}) is the same as the correlation coefficient multiplied by the two standard deviations, or

$$\sigma_{AB} = \rho \sigma_A \sigma_B.$$

Hence, the standard deviation of a portfolio of projects is the square root of the sum of the variances plus twice the sum of the covariances between all projects. This standard deviation for the portfolio has the same meaning as for a project. For example, given the assumption of Normality, one can be 65 percent confident that the net present value for the portfolio of Projects 2, 6, and 15 will be in the range of the expected value ($323) minus one standard deviation up to the expected value plus one standard deviation.

All that is really needed is (1) a feeling of how the standard deviation of a portfolio can be calculated and (2) an awareness of the idea of confidence limits created by use of the concept.

Table 6B-1
Coulter Corporation (B)—S1 Correlation Table*
(Correlation Among 1st Yr. Sales)

	1	2	3	4	5	6	7	8	9	10
1		.8	.9	.75	0	0	0	.85	.91	.94
2			.9	.8	0	0	0	X	X	X
3				.69	0	0	0	X	X	X
4					0	0	0	X	X	X
5						X	0	0	0	0
6							0	0	0	0
7								0	0	0
8									X	.9
9										X
10										
11										
12										
13										
14										
15										
16										
17										
18										
19										
20										

	11	12	13	14	15	16	17	18	19	20
1	-.2	.6	.2	-.5	0	0	.7	0	0	.6
2	-.35	.6	.3	-.4	0	0	.65	0	0	.5
3	-.18	.7	.45	-.6	0	0	.5	0	0	.4
4	-.19	.6	.4	-.5	0	0	.69	0	0	.7
5	0	0	0	0	0	0	0	0	0	0
6	0	0	0	0	0	0	0	0	0	0
7	0	0	0	0	0	0	0	0	0	0
8	-.3	.6	.6	-.5	0	0	.7	0	0	.62
9	-.28	.72	.62	-.35	0	0	.72	0	0	.65
10	-.4	.75	.35	-.55	0	0	.7	0	0	.48
11		X	.45	-.15	0	0	.28	0	0	.3
12			.5	-.6	0	0	.2	0	0	.7
13				X	0	0	.26	0	0	.3
14					0	0	.18	0	0	-.4
15						X	0	0	0	0
16							0	0	0	0
17								0	0	45
18									0	0
19										0
20										

*An X is inserted where there are illegal project combinations.

Table 6B-2
Coulter Corporation (B)–S2 Correlation Table
(Correlation Among 2nd Yr. Sales)

	1	2	3	4	5	6	7	8	9	10
1		.83	.9	.78	0	0	0	.82	.9	.9
2			.9	.8	0	0	0	X	X	X
3				.59	0	0	0	X	X	X
4					0	0	0	X	X	X
5						X	0	0	0	0
6							0	0	0	0
7								0	0	0
8									X	.9
9										X
10										
11										
12										
13										
14										
15										
16										
17										
18										
19										
20										

	11	12	13	14	15	16	17	18	19	20
1	−.25	.5	.2	−.36	0	0	.6	0	0	.55
2	−.3	.5	.3	−.38	0	0	.65	0	0	.65
3	−.2	.6	.45	−.45	0	0	.5	0	0	.55
4	−.18	.7	.4	−.4	0	0	.6	0	0	.65
5	0	0	0	0	0	0	0	0	0	0
6	0	0	0	0	0	0	0	0	0	0
7	0	0	0	0	0	0	0	0	0	0
8	−.3	.65	.6	−.6	0	0	.65	0	0	.7
9	−.25	.58	.6	−.6	0	0	.7	0	0	.4
10	−.4	.6	.2	−.36	0	0	.7	0	0	.6
11		X	.43	.2	0	0	.2	0	0	.3
12			.5	−.55	0	0	.15	0	0	.62
13				X	0	0	.2	0	0	.3
14					0	0	.2	0	0	−.5
15						X	0	0	0	0
16							0	0	0	0
17								0	0	.45
18									0	0
19										0
20										

Table 6B-3
Coulter Corporation (B)—S3 Correlation Table
(Correlation Among 3rd. Yr. Sales)

	1	2	3	4	5	6	7	8	9	10
1		.8	.85	.7	0	0	0	.75	.8	.8
2			.8	.7	0	0	0	X	X	X
3				.5	0	0	0	X	X	X
4					0	0	0	X	X	X
5						X	0	0	0	0
6							0	0	0	0
7								0	0	0
8									X	.9
9										X
10										
11										
12										
13										
14										
15										
16										
17										
18										
19										
20										

	11	12	13	14	15	16	17	18	19	20
1	−.2	.7	.2	−.35	0	0	.55	0	0	.7
2	−.2	.8	.2	−.3	0	0	.6	0	0	.6
3	−.1	.5	.4	−.4	0	0	.5	0	0	.5
4	−.18	.6	.4	−.4	0	0	.5	0	0	.7
5	0	0	0	0	0	0	0	0	0	0
6	0	0	0	0	0	0	0	0	0	0
7	0	0	0	0	0	0	0	0	0	0
8	−.3	.6	.6	−.6	0	0	.6	0	0	.5
9	−.2	.55	.6	−.6	0	0	.6	0	0	.4
10	−.4	.65	.2	−.4	0	0	.7	0	0	.5
11		X	.4	.15	0	0	.2	0	0	.3
12			.5	−.6	0	0	.2	0	0	.5
13				X	0	0	.2	0	0	.45
14					0	0	.2	0	0	−.55
15						X	0	0	0	0
16							0	0	0	0
17								0	0	.45
18									0	0
19										0
20										

Table 6B-4
Coulter Corporation (B)–CF1 Correlation Table
(Correlation Among 1st Yr. Cash Flows)

	1	2	3	4	5	6	7	8	9	10
1		.2	.2	.2	.1	.1	.1	.3	.1	.1
2			.7	.6	.5	.5	.1	X	X	X
3				.6	.4	.6	.1	X	X	X
4					.5	.5	.1	X	X	X
5						X	.1	.6	.6	.2
6							.1	.6	.5	.1
7								.1	.1	.1
8									X	.6
9										X
10										
11										
12										
13										
14										
15										
16										
17										
18										
19										
20										

	11	12	13	14	15	16	17	18	19	20
1	.1	.8	-.1	-.5	.1	.7	.1	.1	.1	0.7
2	.5	.7	.4	-.5	.4	.2	.3	.2	.1	.6
3	.5	.6	.5	-.4	.5	.1	.3	.2	.1	.4
4	.4	.5	.3	-.6	.4	.1	.3	.1	.1	.5
5	.8	.55	.3	-.6	.6	.2	.3	.1	.2	.5
6	.2	.65	.4	-.6	.7	.1	.2	.2	.2	.4
7	.2	.45	.1	-.1	.1	.1	.1	.1	.1	.5
8	.2	.8	.3	-.4	.6	.1	.4	.3	.1	.6
9	.3	.65	.3	-.4	.6	.1	.4	.3	.1	.5
10	.1	.52	.2	-.6	.2	.1	.3	.4	.1	.4
11		X	.2	.1	.2	.1	.3	.4	.1	.3
12			.2	-.4	.2	.1	.3	.3	.2	.6
13				X	.2	.1	.2	.3	.2	.3
14					.2	.1	.2	.4	.1	-.5
15						X	.5	.6	.4	.5
16							.1	.1	.1	.2
17								.3	.6	.7
18									.1	.2
19										.3
20										

Table 6B-5
Coulter Corporation (B)–CF2 Correlation Table
(Correlation Among 2nd Yr. Cash Flows)

	1	2	3	4	5	6	7	8	9	10
1		.5	.3	.6	.7	.8	.6	.5	.4	.5
2			.8	.7	.7	.6	.5	X	X	X
3				.8	.8	.6	.4	X	X	X
4					.9	.5	.6	X	X	X
5						X	.5	.6	.5	.6
6							.4	.6	.3	.5
7								.5	.4	.6
8									X	.5
9										X
10										
11										
12										
13										
14										
15										
16										
17										
18										
19										
20										

	11	12	13	14	15	16	17	18	19	20
1	.6	.6	.8	−.6	.7	.3	.6	.5	.2	.4
2	.6	.6	.5	−.5	.6	.1	.5	.4	.2	.5
3	.5	.5	.6	−.4	.5	.1	.4	.5	.3	.4
4	.4	.6	.7	−.3	.3	.1	.3	.6	.1	.5
5	.6	.6	.6	−.4	.3	.2	.2	.5	.1	.6
6	.5	.5	.5	−.5	.4	.2	.1	.3	.2	.7
7	.4	.4	.3	−.6	.6	.2	.3	.4	.1	.3
8	.4	.7	.4	−.6	.7	.1	.4	.5	.2	.4
9	.5	.5	.2	−.5	.4	.3	.5	.4	.1	.5
10	.6	.6	.1	−.45	.3	.2	.4	.3	.1	.4
11		X	.6	.1	.4	.2	.5	.6	.2	.3
12			.6	−.5	.4	.2	.5	.6	.3	.5
13				X	.2	.2	.5	.5	.1	.3
14					.2	.2	.5	.6	.1	−.4
15						X	.4	.5	.2	.5
16							.2	.2	.6	.2
17								.3	.3	.65
18									.1	.2
19										.3
20										

Table 6B-6

Coulter Corporation (B)–CF3 Correlation Table

(Correlation Among 3rd Yr. Cash Flows)

	1	2	3	4	5	6	7	8	9	10
1		.6	.3	.4	.4	.8	.5	.4	.5	.6
2			.6	.7	.8	.6	.5	X	X	X
3				.6	.8	.6	.5	X	X	X
4					.9	.5	.5	X	X	X
5						X	.6	.6	.7	.8
6							.4	.5	.6	.6
7								.6	.3	.7
8									X	.8
9										X
10										
11										
12										
13										
14										
15										
16										
17										
18										
19										
20										

	11	12	13	14	15	16	17	18	19	20
1	.7	.7	.6	−.6	.8	.3	.5	.4	.1	.4
2	.7	.7	.6	−.5	.7	.2	.3	.2	.2	.5
3	.7	.7	.6	−.6	.6	.2	.6	.3	.3	.4
4	.7	.7	.5	−.5	.5	.1	.4	.4	.2	.4
5	.6	.6	.4	−.5	.3	.1	.5	.5	.3	.5
6	.5	.5	.5	−.6	.2	.1	.4	.6	.2	.3
7	.5	.5	.5	−.4	.4	.1	.2	.7	.1	.6
8	.4	.7	.5	−.4	.6	.2	.3	.8	.1	.5
9	.3	.6	.5	−.6	.7	.2	.4	.9	.2	.7
10	.6	.5	.5	−.6	.5	.2	.5	.5	.3	.7
11		X	.5	.15	.6	.2	.6	.6	.2	.3
12			.5	−.5	.6	.2	.6	.6	.2	.6
13				X	.5	.8	.5	.4	.1	.4
14					.4	.8	.4	.3	.1	−.5
15						X	.3	.2	.1	.3
16							.2	.2	.6	.2
17								.3	.1	.4
18									.1	.5
19										.2
20										

Table 6B-7
Coulter Corporation (B)—EPS1 Correlation Table
(Correlation Among 1st Yr. E.P.S.)

	1	2	3	4	5	6	7	8	9	10
1		.2	.1	−.1	−.2	−.3	.2	.2	.2	.3
2			.7	.6	.1	.3	.4	X	X	X
3				.7	.3	.3	.3	X	X	X
4					.4	.3	.5	X	X	X
5						X	.3	.4	.6	.5
6							.3	.4	.5	.4
7								.2	.2	.2
8									X	.5
9										X
10										
11										
12										
13										
14										
15										
16										
17										
18										
19										
20										

	11	12	13	14	15	16	17	18	19	20
1	.8	.8	.7	−.6	.5	.6	−.3	.2	.2	.4
2	.4	.5	.6	−.7	.6	.3	.7	.1	.2	.5
3	.6	.4	.3	−.6	.5	.2	.7	.1	.3	.6
4	.5	.7	.5	−.4	.4	.3	.7	.1	.4	.7
5	−.2	.6	−.4	−.4	.3	.5	.6	.1	.3	.5
6	−.3	.5	−.5	−.5	.2	.5	.7	.2	.4	.4
7	−.2	.4	−.3	−.3	.2	.5	.8	.2	.6	.3
8	.2	.7	−.2	−.2	.4	.5	.7	.3	.6	.6
9	.3	.6	.3	−.3	.6	.5	.7	.2	.4	.4
10	.3	.8	.4	−.4	.6	.5	.7	.3	.4	.4
11		X	.3	.2	.2	.3	−.2	.6	−.3	.2
12			.3	−.5	.2	.3	−.1	.5	−.3	.6
13				X	.3	.3	−.1	.4	−.2	.4
14					.3	.3	−.2	.6	−.2	−.5
15						X	−.2	.7	.6	.5
16							−.1	.6	.6	.5
17								.7	.7	.7
18									−.1	.2
19										.2
20										

Table 6B-8
Coulter Corporation (B)—EPS2 Correlation Table
(Correlation Among 2nd Yr. E.P.S.)

	1	2	3	4	5	6	7	8	9	10
1		.3	.1	.3	.4	.5	.2	.2	.3	.3
2			.6	.6	.1	.3	.3	X	X	X
3				.7	.3	.4	.4	X	X	X
4					.4	.5	.3	X	X	X
5						X	.3	.4	.5	.5
6							.3	.4	.5	.4
7								.2	.2	.3
8									X	.5
9										X
10										
11										
12										
13										
14										
15										
16										
17										
18										
19										
20										

	11	12	13	14	15	16	17	18	19	20
1	.8	.9	.7	−.6	.5	.6	−.2	.2	.2	.4
2	.4	.4	.6	−.6	.5	.2	.6	.1	.2	.5
3	.6	.5	.3	−.6	.4	.3	.5	.1	.2	.5
4	.5	.6	.5	−.4	.3	.3	.6	.1	.2	.4
5	−.1	.5	−.3	−.2	.2	.5	.5	.1	.2	.6
6	−.2	.7	−.5	−.5	.2	.4	.6	.1	.4	.7
7	−.1	.3	−.2	−.2	.2	.4	.5	.1	.3	.3
8	.1	.5	−.1	−.3	.3	.4	.6	.3	.3	.4
9	.4	.5	.1	−.5	.5	.4	.3	.4	.2	.5
10	.5	.5	.2	−.5	.2	.5	.4	.5	.2	.4
11		X	.3	.2	.3	.4	.2	.3	−.2	.4
12			.3	−.4	.4	.6	.3	.2	−.2	.5
13				X	.5	.4	.4	.4	.3	.4
14					.5	.3	.2	.3	.2	−.3
15						X	.3	.2	.2	.2
16							.4	.5	.1	.2
17								.4	.2	.7
18									.2	.4
19										.2
20										

Table 6B-9
Coulter Corporation (B)–EPS3 Correlation Table
(Correlation Among 3rd Yr. E.P.S.)

	1	2	3	4	5	6	7	8	9	10
1		.3	.1	.3	.4	.5	.2	.2	.3	.3
2			.6	.6	.1	.3	.3	X	X	X
3				.7	.3	.4	.4	X	X	X
4					.4	.5	.3	X	X	X
5						X	.3	.4	.5	.5
6							.3	.4	.5	.4
7								.2	.2	.3
8									X	.5
9										X
10										
11										
12										
13										
14										
15										
16										
17										
18										
19										
20										

	11	12	13	14	15	16	17	18	19	20
1	.8	.5	.7	−.6	.5	.6	−.2	.2	.2	.4
2	.4	.6	.6	−.6	.5	.2	.6	.1	.2	.7
3	.6	.5	.3	−.6	.4	.3	.3	.1	.3	.5
4	.5	.7	.5	−.6	.3	.3	.3	.1	.4	.6
5	−.1	.8	−.3	−.4	.2	.5	.5	.1	.2	.7
6	−.2	.7	−.5	−.5	.2	.4	.6	.1	.2	.4
7	−.1	.3	−.2	−.2	.2	.4	.5	.1	.2	.3
8	.1	.5	−.1	−.5	.2	.4	.6	.3	.2	.4
9	.4	.8	.1	−.5	.5	.4	.3	.4	.3	.5
10	.5	.6	.2	−.5	.2	.5	.4	.5	.2	.7
11		X	.3	.15	.3	.4	.2	.3	.2	.4
12			.3	−.4	.4	.6	.3	.2	.2	.5
13				X	.5	.4	.4	.4	.3	.4
14					.5	.3	.2	.3	.3	−.3
15						X	.3	.2	.4	.2
16							.4	.5	.2	.2
17								.4	.3	.4
18									.3	.4
19										.2
20										

Table 6B-10
Coulter Corporation (B)–NPV Correlation Table
(Correlation Among NPV's)

	1	2	3	4	5	6	7	8	9	10
1		.5	.7	.9	.8	.6	.7	.4	.3	.6
2			.9	.8	.7	.6	.7	X	X	X
3				.7	.6	.5	.6	X	X	X
4					.5	.5	.8	X	X	X
5						X	.7	.5	.3	.6
6							.6	.5	.4	.6
7								.4	.6	.7
8									X	.6
9										X
10										
11										
12										
13										
14										
15										
16										
17										
18										
19										
20										

	11	12	13	14	15	16	17	18	19	20
1	.2	.6	.3	−.3	.7	.8	.7	.6	.3	.6
2	.2	.8	.2	−.3	.6	.7	.6	.6	.3	.6
3	.2	.6	.3	−.6	.5	.7	.5	.6	.2	.7
4	.2	.7	.2	−.3	.6	.7	.4	.6	.2	.7
5	.4	.5	.3	−.3	.7	.7	.5	.3	.2	.6
6	.6	.5	.3	−.4	.6	.3	.5	.4	.2	.6
7	.4	.4	.3	−.5	.3	.4	.4	.4	.2	.3
8	.2	.8	.3	−.3	.4	.5	.3	.8	.3	.6
9	.2	.5	.3	−.3	.4	.5	.4	.8	.4	.5
10	.4	.6	.7	−.6	.4	.6	.3	.4	.3	.4
11		X	.2	.1	.3	.3	.3	.3	.3	.3
12			.2	−.3	.3	.3	.3	.3	.3	.4
13				X	.2	.2	.2	.2	.2	.3
14					.2	.2	.2	.2	.2	−.6
15						X	.4	.7	.2	.3
16							.6	.6	.2	.3
17								.7	.2	.6
18									.2	.5
19										.2
20										

Appendix 6C:
Sample Runs of SIFT

In Chapter 6, the opening message received from SIFT by the manager was shown. Here, additional output as a manager interacts with the model is presented. His/her responses to questions asked by the computer are circled. The boxed explanatory comments elaborate on the process as the model operates.

WHICH CONFIDENCE LEVEL ? (1 = 99/1%, 2 = 95/5%, 3 = 90/10%, 4 = 75/25%)

? ②

PORTFOLIO CONTAINS PROJECTS

1

> The initial portfolio contains only the firm.

BUDGET REMAINING $8000   DEBT RAISED $00

CRITERION	YEAR	MEAN	STD. DEV.	95% LEVEL	5% LEVEL
SALES	1	11030	109	10851	11209
SALES	2	12500	120	12303	12697
SALES	3	13900	135	13678	14122
CASH FLOW	1	870	75	747	993
CASH FLOW	2	960	80	828	1092
CASH FLOW	3	990	82	855	1125
E.P.S.	1	3.5	0.2	3.17	3.83
E.P.S.	2	3.6	0.22	3.24	3.96
E.P.S.	3	3.72	0.28	3.26	4.18
NPV		1750	198	1437	2063

OPTION ? ⓔⓒ   EC = list of project entry cost

0

PROJECT	ENTRY COST	STATUS
1	0	IN
2	500	OUT
3	1200	OUT
4	700	OUT
5	1000	OUT
6	2000	OUT
7	750	OUT
8	2900	OUT
9	3400	OUT
10	1000	OUT
11	950	OUT
12	1000	OUT
13	1500	OUT
14	1750	OUT
15	400	OUT
16	0	OUT
17	720	OUT
18	60	OUT
19	130	OUT
20	400	OUT

> Indicates the project is contained in the current portfolio.

BUDGET REMAINING $8000   DEBT RAISED $00

OPTION ? ⓘⓟ   IP = list of illegal project combinations

0

ILLEGAL PROJECT COMBINATIONS

2, 10
3, 10
4, 10
9, 10
8, 9
5, 6
2, 8
3, 8
4, 8
2, 9
3, 9
4, 9
15, 16

OPTION ? (MR)   MR = rank projects by mean values
0

"Why?" and the answer are not necessary for the simulation. They are only for information purposes.

WHY ? (TO SELECT A PROJECT WHICH INCREASES EPS IN YEAR 3)

CRITERION ? (EPS3)

PROJECT STATUS (IN, OUT, BOTH) ? (OUT)

RANKING ORDER (INC, DEC) ? (DEC)

List 6 projects not in the portfolio which will have highest impact upon expected 3rd Year Earnings per Share.

MAXIMUM NUMBER PRINTED ? (6)

IF PROJECT IS IN CURRENT PORTFOLIO, THE MEAN AND STANDARD DEVIATION LISTED BELOW SHOW EFFECTS OF DELETING IT.

CRITERION-EARNINGS PER SHARE IN YEAR 3 (EP53)

PROJECT	CHANGE IN MEAN	CHANGE IN STD. DEV.	STATUS	ENTRY COST
9	1.48	0.57	OUT	3400
8	1.4	0.41	OUT	2900
11	0.9	0.04	OUT	950
20	0.6	0.05	OUT	400
3	0.6	0.5	OUT	1200
2	0.6	0.45	OUT	500

BUDGET REMAINING $8000   DEBT RAISED $00

OPTION ? (C)   C = Combine (or compare)
0

INPUT PROJECT NUMBERS (-0-(ZERO) FOR CURRENT PORTFOLIO)
? (9)
? (0)

Shows the effect of adding Project 9 to the portfolio.

COMBINATION OF PROJECT 9 AND CURRENT PORTFOLIO

CRITERION	YEAR	MEAN	CHANGE	STD. DEV.	CHANGE
SALES	1	12391	1361	283	174
SALES	2	14880	2380	431	311
SALES	3	16500	2600	475	340
CASH FLOW	1	1490	620	292	217
CASH FLOW	2	1460	500	103	23
CASH FLOW	3	1615	625	128	46
E.P.S.	1	1.6	-1.9	0.86	0.66
E.P.S.	2	4.9	1.3	0.77	0.55
E.P.S.	3	5.2	1.48	0.85	0.57
NPV		3340	1590	586	396

OPTION ? A   A = Add
0

WHY ? (TO ADD PROJECT 9 TO PORTFOLIO)

WHICH PROJECT IS ADDED ? (9)
BUDGET REMAINING $4600   DEBT RAISED $00

OPTION ? (MR)
0

WHY ? (TO SELECT A PROJECT WHICH INCREASES EPS IN YEAR 3)

CRITERION ? (EPS3)

PROJECT STATUS (IN, OUT, BOTH) ? (OUT)

RANKING ORDER (INC, DEC) ? (DEC)

MAXIMUM NUMBER PRINTED ?(5)

IF PROJECT IS IN CURRENT PORTFOLIO, THE MEAN AND STANDARD DEVIATION
LISTED BELOW SHOW EFFECTS OF DELETING IT.

CRITERION-EARNINGS PER SHARE IN YEAR 3 (EPS3)

PROJECT	CHANGE IN MEAN	CHANGE IN STD. DEV.	STATUS	ENTRY COST
11	0.9	0.03	OUT	950
20	0.6	0.06	OUT	400
6	0.32	0.01	OUT	2000
5	0.26	0.03	OUT	1000
12	0.2	0.04	OUT	1000

BUDGET REMAINING $4600   DEBT RAISED $00

OPTION ?(A)
0

Notice Projects 6, 5 and 12
are shown, rather than 8, 3
and 2, which are illegal
given the presence of Project 9. Also, note change
in standard deviation impact of Projects 11 and 20
because of the different
portfolio.

WHY? (TO FURTHER INCREASE EPS IN YEAR 3)

WHICH PROJECT IS ADDED ? (11)
BUDGET REMAINING $3650   DEBT RAISED $00

OPTION ?(P) | P = Portfolio information |
0

WHICH CONFIDENCE LEVEL? (1 = 99/1%, 2 = 95/5%, 3 = 90/10%, 4 = 75/25%)
?(2)

PORTFOLIO CONTAINS PROJECTS
  1
  9
  11

BUDGET REMAINING $3650   DEBT RAISED $00

CRITERION	YEAR	MEAN	STD. DEV.	95% LEVEL	5% LEVEL
SALES	1	13591	278	13134	14048
SALES	2	16200	417	15513	16887
SALES	3	17950	467	17181	18719
CASH FLOW	1	1660	309	1152	2168
CASH FLOW	2	1710	115	1520	1900
CASH FLOW	3	1885	142	1652	2118
E.P.S.	1	2.35	0.91	0.85	3.85
E.P.S.	2	5.7	0.8	4.38	7.02
E.P.S.	3	6.1	0.88	4.66	7.54
NPV		3267	610	2264	4270

OPTION ? (VR) | VR = Variance ranking |
0

WHY? (TO DECREASE VARIANCE IN YEAR 1 EPS)

CRITERION ? (EPS1)

PROJECT STATUS (IN, OUT, BOTH) ? (OUT)

RANKING ORDER (INC, DEC) ? (INC)

MAXIMUM NUMBER PRINTED ? (4)

CRITERION-EARNINGS PER SHARE IN YEAR 1 (EPS1)

To find external projects which will reduce variance, the manager wants projects with the smallest s.d. impact, preferably negative. In this example, Project 14 would be most suited to this purpose.

PROJECT	CHANGE IN MEAN	CHANGE IN STD. DEV.	STATUS	ENTRY COST
14	0.06	−0.01	OUT	1750
19	−0.02	0	OUT	130
5	−0.1	0	OUT	1000
18	0.02	0.01	OUT	60

BUDGET REMAINING $3650   DEBT RAISED $00

OPTION ? (D)
0

WHY? (TO REMOVE PROJECT 11)

WHICH PROJECT IS DELETED ? (11)

BUDGET REMAINING $4600   DEBT RAISED $00

OPTION ? (SP) | SP = Short portfolio output |
0

CRITERION ? (EPS3)

WHICH CONFIDENCE LEVEL ? (1 = 99/1%, 2 = 95/5%, 3 = 90/10%, 4 = 75/25%)
? (4)

CRITERION	YEAR	MEAN	STD. DEV.	75% LEVEL	25% LEVEL
E.P.S.	3	5.2	0.85	4.63	5.77

OPTION ? (NP) | NP = New portfolio |
0

HOW MANY PROJECTS TO BE IN YOUR PORTFOLIO IN
ADDITION TO PROJECT 1 ?
? (4)

INPUT PROJECT NUMBERS
? (11)
? (20)
? (6)
? (5)

ILLEGAL PROJECT COMBINATION 5 AND 6
PROJECT 5 REJECTED
? (9)

Project additions which are illegal in light of present portfolio of projects are rejected. The manager then has the opportunity to replace the rejected project with a legal alternative.

BUDGET REMAINING $1250   DEBT RAISED $750

OPTION ? Ⓒ
0

INPUT PROJECT NUMBERS (–0–(ZERO) FOR CURRENT PORTFOLIO)
? ③
? ⑱

> Shows results of combining two projects with each other.

COMBINATION OF PROJECT 3 AND PROJECT 18

WHICH CONFIDENCE LEVEL ? (1 = 99/1%, 2 = 95/5%, 3 = 90/10%, 4 = 75/25%)
? ③

CRITERION	YEAR	MEAN	STD. DEV.	90% LEVEL	10% LEVEL
SALES	1	105	3	101	109
SALES	2	300	6	292	308
SALES	3	310	7	301	319
CASH FLOW	1	234	131	66	402
CASH FLOW	2	85	9	74	96
CASH FLOW	3	108	10	95	121
E.P.S.	1	−1.08	0.9	−2.24	0.08
E.P.S.	2	0.53	0.7	−0.37	1.43
E.P.S.	3	0.63	0.7	−0.27	1.53
NPV		127	40	75	179

OPTION ? Ⓒ
0

INPUT PROJECT NUMBERS (–0–(ZERO) FOR CURRENT PORTFOLIO)
? ⓪
? ①

> The compare option permits the manager to examine his portfolio performance relative to the on-going firm.

EFFECT OF PROPOSED PORTFOLIO COMPARED TO ON GOING FIRM (I.E. PROJECT 1)

CRITERION	YEAR	MEAN	STD. DEV.	PROBABILITY OF REMAINING ABOVE PROJECT 1 PERFORMANCE
SALES	1	14041	290	100%
SALES	2	16800	435	100%
SALES	3	18950	501	100%
CASH FLOW	1	2384	372	100%
CASH FLOW	2	1939	124	100%
CASH FLOW	3	2274	158	100%
E.P.S.	1	2.04	1.27	13%
E.P.S.	2	6.05	0.83	100%
E.P.S.	3	6.92	0.95	100%
NPV		3316	635	99%

OPTION ? Ⓒ
  0

INPUT PROJECT NUMBERS (−0−(ZERO) FOR CURRENT PORTFOLIO)
  ? ⓪
  ? ⑪

COMBINATION OF PROJECT 11 AND CURRENT PORTFOLIO

PROJECT 11 IN EXISTING PORTFOLIO. EFFECTS OF DELETING ARE SHOWN.

CRITERION	YEAR	MEAN	CHANGE	STD. DEV.	CHANGE
SALES	1	12841	−1200	293	3
SALES	2	15480	−1320	445	11
SALES	3	17500	−1450	503	3
CASH FLOW	1	2240	−144	356	−17
CASH FLOW	2	1715	−224	112	−13
CASH FLOW	3	2030	−244	144	−14
E.P.S.	1	1.39	−0.65	1.25	−0.02
E.P.S.	2	5.35	−0.7	0.8	−0.03
E.P.S.	3	6.12	−0.8	0.92	−0.03
NPV		3389	73	610	−25

OPTION ? (END)
  0
FINAL PORTFOLIO

USER; JG
WHICH CONFIDENCE LEVEL? (1 = 99/1%, 2 = 95/5%, 3 = 90/10%, 4 = 75/25%)
  ? 3

PORTFOLIO CONTAINS PROJECTS
  1
  6
  9
  11
  20

Note EPS figures include interest charges for debt as well as the firm's operating results.

BUDGET REMAINING $1259   DEBT RAISED $750

CRITERION	YEAR	MEAN	STD. DEV.	90% LEVEL	10% LEVEL
SALES	1	14041	290	13670	14412
SALES	2	16800	435	16242	17358
SALES	3	18950	501	18308	19592
CASH FLOW	1	2384	372	1906	2862
CASH FLOW	2	1939	124	1779	2098
CASH FLOW	3	2274	158	2071	2477
E.P.S.	1	2.04	1.27	0.41	3.67
E.P.S.	2	6.05	0.83	4.99	7.11
E.P.S.	3	6.92	0.95	5.7	8.14
NPV		3316	635	2502	4139

DO YOU FEEL YOU MET THE OBJECTIVES YOU INDICATED AT THE BEGINNING OF THIS EXERCISE? (YES)

ON THE NEXT THREE LINES EXPLAIN WHY

? EPS IN YEAR THREE
? HAS BEEN INCREASED
? TO 6.92

7

The Model in Use: Executives and SIFT

We are accustomed to making the assumption that the world is a shared awareness of all normal people. Such is not the case. World is a construction of each person in relation to life. That there is much overlap between my world and yours is not denied, but this is far different from saying that they are identical. It is impossible to write general descriptions of world just as it is impossible to write general translations of dream symbols, and for the same reason.

J.F.T. Bugenthal

This chapter represents a small digression from the main body of the book, inasmuch as it is not concerned with teaching "corporate capital budgeting" but rather with a report on how executives behave when given an interactive computer model and portfolio risk analysis simulation. What criteria do they find important? What goals do they seek? What risks do they consider?

In this chapter, we will be seeking evidence bearing on five issues:

First, are there different goals and attitudes toward risk depending on the professional background of the participant?

Second, are there different goals and attitudes toward risk depending on the regional background of the participant?

Third, if there are multiple goals in the mind of the executive, how does (s)he filter projects in the capital budgeting setting? Does (s)he effectively find projects which realize his/her primary goals?

Fourth, how does (s)he cope with risk? When given the information and the tools (e.g., computer assisted analysis), does (s)he attempt to deal with risk in an explicit form?

Fifth, with different project rankings under rate of return and present value criteria, the evaluation of leases, and the importance of looking at rate of return or present value in a portfolio context rather than simply adding projects, does the executive react to these financial subtleties in a consistent and logical manner?

The Subject Group

The men and women in this experiment were typically 30 to to 45 years old, with a minimum of eight years of managerial experience. About 40 percent were non-United States citizens working in other lands. Some were military career officers in the United States Navy and Air Force. Many were from small firms, but the majority were from major corporations. All had been selected by their companies to attend a fourteen-week executive development program, and had completed eleven weeks of that program at the time of this exercise.

After reviewing each of the (A) and the (B) cases, the participants were asked to complete a questionnaire. This questionnaire asked them to indicate the projects they would like to have in their final portfolio, the reasons for that portfolio, and their goals. They also were asked to indicate the time spent on the assignment. For the (B) case, the same questions were asked together with time spent on the computer in the event they used it. In addition, they were asked to attach their computer output to the questionnaire.

Evaluation of Data

The participants' responses to the questionnaire were coded on a variety of characteristics. Responses to the questions about what caused them to select certain projects ranged from casual to thoughtful to highly detailed. Often, they would be of the form, "I wanted to maximize earnings by the third year subject to a reasonable growth in sales, and not too much risk in cash." These responses were codified into Goals, Constraints, and Risk considerations. *Goals* were identified as the major factor in which there was an optimization process. There could be more than one major goal for a subject. However, often the multiple attributes of the decision were included as "a reasonable growth in sales," for example, and such a codification was taken as a *Constraint*, where the objective was to meet some minimal level of achievement. Beyond that level, it was assumed that the criterion was not of paramount importance. Finally, the aspect of *Risk* was considered important if the executive (1) specifically noted detailed standard deviation considerations in the questionnaire, (2) mentioned "risk" or a synonym in his response, or (3) emphasized "diversified," "broadly based," or synonyms in describing the portfolio.

An alternative to this approach is specifically to ask each respondent whether factor X was considered in the decision. This approach seems to stimulate a respondent either to say that factor was studied or to justify ignoring it. Furthermore, it may encourage a participant to think about such a factor when it was not considered. On the other hand, the choice followed here of interpreting the responses is also hazardous. There may be a loss of information (some managers very concerned with a factor may have forgotten to mention it) as well as a bias of interpretation. Subject to the considerations mentioned above, it is hoped this bias is minimal. Furthermore, in most cases, the responses were surprisingly direct and ordered. That is, the explanation for behavior when included coincided with the original objectives noted.

Separating goals and constraints in such a setting is not trivial. There could be multiple responses in each of these categories. There might be situations in which there was a criterion named simultaneously as a goal and as a constraint (e.g., maximize third-year earnings per share without having a loss in any year). As the interpretation of the results below will indicate, however, the responses as categorized did tend to make sense given the outcomes presented.

Projects included were tabulated for both (A) and (B) runs by backgrounds of the participants. Backgrounds were segmented into United States, British Commonwealth, European, and other. The justification for segmenting the Commonwealth into a separate group including Australia, Great Britiain and India is that much of the educational experience and business practice is of common form in the Commonwealth. Such a segmentation seems justifiable given the group size and the common experience of business careers.

The computer printouts were evaluated along each of four major criteria (present value, earnings per share, cash flow, and sales) and then stratified by no computer usage (0) for that criteria, low usage (1-3), moderate usage (4-6), or heavy usage (7-9). The purpose of computer usage and the amount used were inferred from the computer output. Since the participant repeatedly had to request a particular criterion on which (s)he wished to have results returned, the number of iterations and the criterion were well defined. Given usage, the four levels of intensity was derived after sampling of output. Earlier runs were deleted from this rough calculation since it was felt that some participants would be mainly concerned with discovering the operation of the system rather than with seeking a portfolio.

All of these results were punched on Hollerith cards, and then tabulated. Since all the variables were designed to be either 0 or 1, with the exception of computer usage, the results were keyed for standard proportionate evaluations in 2 X 2 contingency tables.

Tests of Significance

In evaluating the data, conclusions will often be based on statistical tests for the differences in proportions of various classifications of the executives participating in the experiment. These *significance tests* are based on 10, 5, and 1 percent probabilities of the difference occurring simply by chance. That is, if a footnote states that the results are "significant at the 5 percent level," the probability of that result occurring when there is *no* difference in fact is less than 1 out of 20. There will also be reference to "one" or "two-tailed tests of significance." When a particular hypothetical relationship or expectation is indicated, the one-tailed test of significance will be used. Here, the significance level refers to the "accidental" or "random" chance of the outcome having the "greater-than" or "less-than" relationship which was expected. Again, the significance will be at the 10, 5, or 1 percent level as is appropriate. The two-tailed test will be used when we are interested in observing if a statistically different proportion occurs in the two subgroups *without* prior expectation as to which proportion is larger. Those readers interested in more detailed explanation of these concepts are referred to one of the statistical sources mentioned below, or any other introductory statistics textbook.

The results described below were evaluated by using a Chi-square test with one degree of freedom in a 2 × 2 contingency table, and the calculations adjusted for continuity. With both large samples and interval groupings, this procedure is equivalent to the use of the Z (Normal deviate) distribution. The adjustment consists of adding 1/2 to the smaller proportion's raw number and 1/2 subtracted from the larger proportion's raw number. The proportions are then recomputed, and

$$Z = \frac{P_A - P_B}{\sqrt{\hat{P}\hat{Q}\left[\dfrac{1}{N_A} + \dfrac{1}{N_B}\right]}}$$

ignoring the sign of Z, P_A and P_B are the proportions of the attribute in Sample A and Sample B, respectively. $\hat{P}$ and $\hat{Q}$ are the proportions of the observations *with* and *without* that characteristic in the total sample, respectively ($\hat{Q} = 1 - \hat{P}$). N_A and N_B are the number of observations in the two samples.

Both the Chi-square and the Z tests are approximations. It has been shown that exact tests for samples of smaller size yield different results.[a] Tables used for a small A or B sample (less than 20) or an A or B sample between 20 and 40 observations where the smallest absolute observation was less than 5 are from D.J. Finney, et al. *Tables for Testing Significance in a 2 x 2 Contingency Table* (1963) following the procedure of Snedecor and Cochran (1967), page 221.

Professional Background and Project Selection

Dearborn and Simon (1958) and others have presented evidence that professional identification with a particular area of business specialization is a factor influencing the manner in which an individual views a business problem. Given the laboratory setting of these experiments, it may be possible to find whether the departmental identification effect found by Dearborn and Simon was repeated in the goals and attitudes toward risk of this group of managers.

Accepting these results, one can hypothesize that (*H*1) *finance* professionals will have a higher interest than other groups in rate of return and earnings per share, together with considerations of risk in those two factors. One may also hypothesize (*H*1 *A*) that *marketing* professionals will have a greater interest in sales and risk in sales than other professionals.

[a]R.A. Fisher (1941), paragraph 21.02.

These results are presented in Table 7-1. For all groups, earnings per share (.92) were dominant with some concern for rate of return (.38). In terms of goals, sales and cash flow were rarely considered.

The finance group placed more emphasis on rate of return, as hypothesized. This emphasis was significantly higher (at the 10 percent level) than that considered by both the marketing and general management executive. Marketing executives were somewhat lower in rate of return evaluations compared to the other groups, but were *not* significantly different from the others in their appraisal of the importance of sales as a goal. In fact, the marketing group had a slightly lower proportion (.17) selecting sales as a major goal than any other subgroup.

In terms of risk, 57 percent of all executives indicated a concern for risk in the area of earnings per share, and 33 percent noted a concern for risk in rate of return. An executive considering risk in one category is not necessarily a person

Table 7-1
Professional Background, Goals, and Risk Evaluation

	Finance (N=20)	Marketing (N=12)	Production (N=22)	General Management (N=48)	Total (N=102)
Goals					
Rate of Return	.55*	.25*	.46	.31*	.38
Sales	.20	.17	.23	.21	.21
Earnings Per Share	.85	1.00	.91	.94	.92
Cash Flow	.15	.17	.14	.13	.14
Other	.10	–	.09	.02	.05
Risk					
Rate of Return	.30	.17	.36	.38	.33
Sales	.05	.08	.05	.15	.10
Earnings Per Share	.55	.67	.59	.54	.57
Cash Flow	.15	.17	.05**	.31**	.21
Other	–	.08	.05	.02	.03
Average (excluding Other)	.27	.27	.26	.34	.30

Note: Results significantly different at the 10 percent (*) or 5 percent (**) level, one-tailed or two-tailed test as per text.

For example, .55 (11 of 20) Finance professionals selected "rate of return" as a goal. Similarly, .25 (3 of 12) Marketing executives selected rate of return. $H1$ is that Finance professionals will have a greater propensity to select rate of return than other groups. The asterisks indicate this hypothesis is confirmed at the 10 percent level compared to the Marketing and General Management groups. This statement of significance says that there is a 90 percent probability that the Finance group does have a greater propensity to select rate of return as a criterion. Alternatively, one may say there is a 10 percent probability that the difference found could occur by chance if there were, in fact, no difference in goal preference between the group pairs.

who will consider risk in other areas. Overall, more than 80 percent of the participants did consider risk on some dimension as a source of concern. Another way of viewing the data is to note that on any of the four dimensions, there was an average of 30 percent of the participants considering risk on that dimension. There was a significantly lower level in production executives' interest in risk in cash flow compared to general managers on a two-tailed test. The reason for this difference is not apparent. The general managers had a higher average incidence of concern with risk than any of the subgroups although this difference was not statistically significant.

Based on these initial statistics, the hypothesis for departmental identification being associated with differential selection of criteria is supported in the area of finance ($H1$). The expected identification of marketing executives with sales standards was not found ($H1 A$). As will be noted below, however, the nature of the executives and the general management program in which they were enrolled may account for this lack of differentiation.

Projects 2, 3, 4, 8, and 9 in conjunction are projects which could reveal the professionals' ability to decompose a financial problem. The first three projects relate to new products with certain sales possibilities. The latter two projects include major plant realignments which are useful only if the three new projects are all taken in concert. Projects 8 and 9 have rates of return over 17 percent; however, the highest rate of return in these five proposals belongs to Project 4, with a rate of return of nearly 19 percent. Given the nature of the proposals, Projects 8 and 9 are mutually exclusive of Projects 2, 3, or 4. Hence, a person initially selecting projects on the basis of rate of return might well include Project 4, and then find neither Projects 8 or 9 would be permissible. Of course, Projects 8 and 9 involve greater outlays of cash. On the other hand, for those who find rate of return a compelling criterion, there is a need to escape the "trap" of taking Project 4 (with a high rate of return on a relatively small outlay), and losing Project 8 or 9 (with high return on a larger base).

The slightly higher orientation of finance executives to rate of return as a goal is reflected in project selection among these five projects, as shown in Table 7-2. Consistent with the expectation (and finding) that finance professionals are more interested in rate of return calculations, one may also hypothesize ($H2$) that they will be more likely to select a high rate of return project (e.g., Project 4). With this selection, they will lose the opportunity for a larger investment (e.g., Project 8 or 9) with a lower rate of return than Project 4 but a return which is still greater than almost any other project. The inclusion of Projects 2, 3 or 4 in total (.40) is higher than these projects' inclusion for the other professional subgroups.[b] These results are significant at the 5 percent level on a

[b]The figure .40 is less than the simple sum of the three projects' inclusion, since .40 measures the proportion of participants who selected any of these three projects. Projects 8 and 9 are mutually exclusive, and the incidence of inclusion is the sum of the two respective project frequencies. This pattern of analysis will reappear below.

Table 7-2
Professional Background and Project Selection

Project	Finance (N=20)		Marketing (N=12)		Production (N=22)		General Management (N=48)		Total (N=102)	
2	.30		.25		.22		.10		.19	
3	.20	} .40**	.17	} .25	.09	} .27**	.04	} .13**	.10	} .23
4	.35***		.25		.23		.06***		.18	
8	.10	} .45	.17	} .59	.18	} .59	.25	} .56	.20	} .55
9	.35		.42		.41		.31		.35	
7	.25		.17		.25		.17		.20	
11	.75		.92		.77		.75		.78	
13	.40		.67*		.32		.35*		.39	
19	.65		.42***		.91***		.77		.74	
	*					*					

Note: Results significantly different at the 10 percent (*), 5 percent (**), or 1 percent (***) level, one- or two-tailed tests as per text.

Note figure following brackets on Projects 2, 3 and 4 is the proportion of participants who selected one or more of these three projects.

one-tailed test in the case of finance versus general managers. In addition, the specific inclusion of Project 4 is significantly higher, at the 1 percent level, for finance professionals than for general managers. This outcome indicates that the "selective filtration" of rate of return may entrap those having rate of return as a major goal, losing sight of the importance of combining projects. Such an interpretation will find support from later evidence as well; those executives who specifically emphasized rate of return as a goal generally had a greater orientation toward the selection of Projects 2, 3, and 4 than 8 or 9.

Project 7 was an "intangible" project consisting of new executive offices. This project was nominally justified on the basis of "better spirit" of executives because of the improved working environment. All groups seemed to accept this premise with equal incidence of approval. No one challenged directly the assertions relating to its desirability.

Project 11 has a very favorable impact on reported earnings in the earlier years of its life but has a low rate of return (7 percent). In contrast, Project 13 has a higher rate of return (11 percent) but a less favorable impact on earnings per share in any of the early years. These are not mutually exclusive projects. However, the rate of return increment was usually sacrificed for the favorable early impact on earnings per share. Overall, there was a two-to-one preference for Project 11 over Project 13. This reaction is consistent with the goals admitted earlier, and is a pattern which appears consistently across all groups. The marketing group does tend to have more interest in Project 13 than the other groups, on a two-tailed test.

Project 19 involves "social responsibility" or "enlightened self-interest" depending on one's view of business leadership. It is a smokestack precipitator with no rate of return in nominal terms. It has been suggested to the firm by the mayor of the town as an investment the company should consider. Three groups accepted the project overwhelmingly, but a majority of the marketing group rejected the claims for social responsibility. Significant differences on a two-tailed test are starred. Although one might expect production executives (who are largely from engineering backgrounds) to be less sensitive to this issue, in fact they were markedly more receptive. This acceptance may derive from their awareness of the technological feasibility coupled with personal experience in confronting exactly this sort of project. No explanation of the higher rejection by the marketing executives relative to other groups will be attempted.

Hypothesis of professional identification inducing biased project selection was found in the case of financial executives. Different project acceptance among professional groups was also found in the area of "social responsibility" investments, although no explanation can be given with confidence either before or after the relationship is found.

Regional Background and Project Selection

Among the studies of comparative management values of managers from different cultures, England and Lee (1971) used questionnaires to seek differences in values among American, Japanese and Korean managers. The raw scores which resulted could be used to assess not only which goals were most relevant for particular managers, but how the managers from different cultures valued goals. For example, the questionnaire administered by the researchers allowed discrimination among eight goals:

1. high productivity
2. organizational growth
3. organizational efficiency
4. profit maximization
5. organizational stability
6. industry leadership
7. employee welfare
8. social welfare

Goals which were seen to have a "behavioral relevance score," a term developed by England, were suggested as maximization criteria in the context of Simon (1964). A second subset of goals were labelled as an "associative constraint set" by England and Lee. The third set of goals were those of minor importance in this hierarchy.

In the comparison of American and Japanese managers for example, the maximization criteria for American managers were productivity, organizational efficiency and profit maximization. For Japanese managers, the maximization criteria were productivity and organizational growth. If this pattern is repeated in relation to the SIFT model here, one might suggest that some managers stratified by regional background would have a greater concern for sales (organizational growth or industry leadership) than other managers. Another group might emphasize earnings, which would have direct impact on profit maximization in the England and Lee terms.

The "Commonwealth" grouping included the United Kingdom to Australia geographically, on the basis of a common business heritage in practice and in education. One may hypothesize that ($H3$) Americans will be more concerned about earnings per share than other groups, given the "stock market orientation" of this country. Similarly, ($H3A$) Europeans and Commonwealth participants will be more interested in cash flow and sales, standards for the long-range viability of a business, as opposed to EPS, which, given the three-year horizon of the SIFT model, may be regarded as less important.

Although one cannot evaluate this issue with finality, it seems probable that such distinctions are blurring with the internationalization of business experience. This test group, given their backgrounds and the educational program in which they were enrolled, is likely to be less distinctive along these culturally determined lines than managers at large. They are also likely to be representative examples of future executives.

As shown in Table 7-3, Americans were substantially less interested in cash flow than the other groups, as hypothesized. Europeans were less interested in sales as a goal, contrary to the hypothesis.[c] The results found in goals (emphasis on rate of return and earnings per share) in the regional grouping is consistent with that found in the segmentation by professional background. There was no significant deviation by standards of risk evaluation.

In terms of the five projects which involve a rate of return bias (Projects 2, 3, 4, 8, and 9), the Commonwealth participants seemed to have an especially heavy inclination to select one or two of the separate projects and to avoid the higher rate of return on a large asset base from investing in either Project 8 or 9 (Table 7-4). Since there was no a priori assertion of greater interest in rate of return by regional subgrouping, a 2-tailed test is applied and the difference is significant.

On the other hand, this Commonwealth group rejected the intangible argument for the new headquarters building (Project 7) more strongly than the other groups. The pattern indicating preference for earnings in Project 11 over rate of return in Project 13 continued, with the Europeans rejecting the low earnings of Project 13 more frequently than the Americans at the 10 percent

[c]Separate tabulation indicated that the incidence of professional backgrounds when cross-tabulated by regional background was not significantly different from that of the total sample.

146

Table 7-3
Regional Background, Goals, and Risk Evaluation

	U.S. (N=69)	Commonwealth (N=13)	Europe (N=15)
Goals			
Rate of Return	.36	.39	.40
Sales	.22	.31	.07
Earnings Per Share	.90	.92	1.00
Cash Flow	.07***	.23	.33***
Other	.06	.08	–
Risk			
Rate of Return	.33	.31	.27
Sales	.10	.15	–
Earnings Per Share	.55	.62	.47
Cash Flow	.23	.08	.13
Other	.04	–	–
Average (excluding Other)	.30	.29	.22

Note: Results significantly different at the 1 percent level (***), one-tailed test of significance.

Table 7-4
Regional Background and Project Selection

	U.S. (N=69)	Commonwealth (N=13)	Europe (N=15)
Project			
2	.15**	.46**	.07**
3	.06** } .16**	.31** } .54**	.07 } .13*
4	.10***	.46***	.13
8	.18 } .57	.23 } .38	.27 } .74
9	.39	.15	.47
7	.20	.07	.33
11	.72	.85	1.00
13	.43*	.39	.13*
19	.77	.54	.73

Note: Results significantly different at the 10 percent (*), 5 percent (**), or 1 percent (***) level, two-tailed test as per text.

significance level. In terms of social responsibility, the Commonwealth participants were somewhat lower in their interest in the smokestack precipitator (.54) than either the Americans or the Europeans (.77 and .73, respectively).

Such differentials may suggest characteristics of the capital markets and educational programs. The heavy emphasis on simple earnings in some environments was expected ($H3$) to cause this factor to be overemphasized by those respondents (the Americans). This was not observed. Greater interest from non-U.S. participants in cash flow considerations was found in the case of the Europeans as hypothesized ($H3A$). Since many of the Commonwealth participants are from nations where the impact of the environmentalist movement has been less substantial than Western Europe and the United States, one might conceivably explain the lower interest in the smokestack precipitator (Project 19). On balance, there is minor evidence on the differential standards for portfolio selection, for risk, and for project selection when the results are stratified by regional background. There is no evidence that the "rate of return trap" projects found in the Commonwealth results derived from a sharp interest in rate of return as a goal. The differences are not of major importance, in contrast to the England and Lee results.

Again, it is possible that our results may occur because of the selection of participants in this program, or because of the experience in the program itself. Thus, participants may be more international (and more homogeneous) in outlook. Some non-U.S. executives worked for subsidiaries of American corporations. The tone of the eleven weeks of the program may have blended them into a more homogeneous group. Such speculation is not unreasonable for explaining the lack of differences in regional backgrounds.

Portfolio Consistency

The previous tables were based on the full sample of usable responses (102). For the following tables, the results will be based on a subgroup for which detailed independent responses on both the (A) and (B) packages were available. As discussed in Chapter 6, the (B) package provided additional information regarding the covariance among projects on various criteria and permitted optional use of the SIFT computer program to evaluate interrelationships.

The idea of myopia or blockage, in which a strong initial commitment to a project precludes the possibility of rejecting the project subsequently as more evidence becomes available is one explanation for the significant carryover of support for certain projects by some groups. Indifference to negative aspects and risks associated with an accepted project has been noted before in corporate settings [see, for example, Carter (1971)].

Projects 3, 6, and 15 have low incidence of inclusion in the (A) portfolio and even lower in the (B) portfolio. Yet, the proponents of these three projects in (A) have a consistently strong bias toward including them in (B) as well. Project 3 is a new product; Project 6 is a replacement of machinery in the building. There is no particular reason for especially strong loyalties to these projects. Project 15 is a new truck fleet which can also be leased (Project 16). The more frequent decision in both (A) and (B) cases is to lease:

	(A)	(B)
Buy	.35	.20
Lease	.50	.60

The strong carryover in (B) for those who also preferred to buy the trucks in (A) represents a heavy bias against leasing. As will be shown later, there was good reason for this skepticism based on analysis of the data.

In the case of four other projects, the heavy carryover in enthusiasm by the proponents of those projects in the (A) package is matched by a marked movement toward these projects in the (B) portfolio by all participants (Projects 5, 11, 12, and especially Project 20). All of these projects are noted with asterisks in the third column of Table 7-5.

Both Projects 11 and 12 are popular in (B) and both are projects with high earnings per share impact. The absolute level of their incidence increases, and the holdover is significantly large in both cases. Project 20, a simple acquisition with little diversification, is heavily selected in (B). The rate of return of the project is one of the lowest (4.1 percent), but the earnings per share impact in all years is highly favorable. As will be seen later, this project does tend to have basic appeal for those participants interested in earnings per share, and the incidence of earnings per share as a goal increases from (A) to (B), as will be shown in Table 7-6. Such movement also explains the increase in selection of Projects 11 and 12.

In terms of the five projects with interrelationships in rate of return (Projects 2, 3, 4, 8, and 9), the incidence of inclusion of the larger, higher rate of return Projects 8 and 9 is not changed [.55 include one of them in each of the (A) and (B) portfolios] and there is movement away from one or more of the smaller projects.

Project 13, for which a strong rate of return is projected, remains virtually unchanged in frequency of inclusion, largely because of significantly heavy carryover from (A) to (B) (.57). The proposal dealing with social responsibility, Project 19, is strong in both portfolios.

Without detailed discussion of the projects, there is overall evidence of an initial acceptance of a project on limited evidence in the (A) case associated with a disproportionate selecting of the same project in (B). Thus, 13 of the 19 projects have levels of inclusion in (B) portfolio given acceptance in (A) which are significantly greater than the level of inclusion on (B) by those who did not accept the project in (A).

Table 7-5
Portfolio Consistency

	Frequency of Inclusion in (A) Portfolio (N=68)	Frequency of Inclusion in (B) Portfolio (N=68)	Frequency of Inclusion in (B) Given *Not* Included in (A) Portfolio	Frequency of Inclusion in (B) Given Inclusion in (A) Portfolio
Project				
2	.25	.16	.14	.23 (N=17)
3	.15	.09	.03	.40 (N=10) ***
4	.26	.16	.14	.22 (N=18)
5	.59	.66	.43	.83 (N=40) ***
6	.22	.17	.09	.47 (N=15) ***
7	.13	.22	.17	.56 (N=9) **
8	.18	.24	.21	.33 (N=12)
9	.37	.32	.23	.48 (N=25) **
10	.09	.17	.18	.17 (N=6)
11	.44	.75***	.63	.90 (N=30) **
12	.18	.41***	.36	.67 (N=12) *
13	.31	.35	.25	.57 (N=21) **
14	.63	.41**	.32	.46 (N=43)
15	.35	.20*	.11	.38 (N=24) **
16	.50	.60	.47	.74 (N=34) **
17	.41	.30	.13	.54 (N=28) ***
18	.81	.85	.69	.89 (N=55) *
19	.73	.76	.50	.86 (N=50) ***
20	.16	.76**	.72	1.00 (N=11)

Note: Significantly different frequencies of inclusion in the (A) and (B) portfolios (two-tailed test). Significantly greater frequency of inclusion in (B) portfolio given inclusion in (A) portfolio at the 10 percent (*), 5 percent (**), and 1 percent (***) levels (one-tailed test).

Goal Consistency

Generally, there was a major carryover of goals, as would be expected. In each category, the carryover was *no less* than the transfers from other categories (see Table 7-6).

The participants also had a high probability of moving to the EPS standard from other standards. Multiple goals are allowed in both (A) and (B) cases. Rate of return as a goal was somewhat deserted. Of all those participants selecting rate of return on (A), only .74 carried it over to (B). In contrast, 1.00 retained EPS. For sales and cash flow, the carry-over was low, with slightly over half retaining each goal as a major goal on (B) as well. Even for those

Table 7-6
Goal Consistency

		Probable Goal(s) in (B) Case				
		ROR	Sales	EPS	Cash Flow	Other
Goal(s) in (A) Case						
ROR	.63	.74	.21	.93	.23	0
Sales	.31	.33	.57	1.00	.24	0
EPS	.69	.46	.20	1.00	.23	0
Cash Flow	.34	.61	.26	1.00	.52	0
Other	.12	.25	.12	.88	0	.12
(B) Goal(s)		.49	.25	.94	.21	.01

Goals noted in (A) 142
Goals noted in (B) 129

Note: Multiple Goals in both (A) and (B) cases are permitted.

participants who had other, subtle goals (social responsibility, a going business, good public offering), the movement was heavily to EPS by the time the specifics of the (B) case appeared.

Given the availability to use the computer and data which would permit evaluation on many more criteria, one can hypothesize (H4) that *more goals* will be considered. In contrast, other observers would argue that the reason a manager has multiple goals is that he has little confidence in the information or the evaluative procedures on the few goals which are very important to him and that multiple goals are a means of eliminating imprecisions in the system. Accordingly, when a device to handle the important information is made available, one would argue under this theory that *fewer goals* would be mentioned; the executive now has the means to focus on the goals of real importance to him. [See, for example, the Cyert and March (1963) concepts of quasiresolution of conflict, and the idea of multiple goals which are very imprecisely fulfilled and traded-off against each other.] Thus, both explanations seem plausible.

The result is inconclusive; there is no significant difference in the number of goals mentioned in the (A) and (B) cases. These results contrast with Marris (1963), in that the goal to which most participants turn initially is also the goal selected subsequently: earnings per share. This goal so clearly dominates others as a major idea of the participants that the desertion of high rate of return projects for those projects with high earnings impact is readily apparent.

Goal Achievement—EPS

In Tables 7-7 to 7-9, one may consider particular projects which might indicate significance of goal fulfillment *given* certain criteria as a major

Table 7-7
Goal Achievement—Earnings per Share

	(A) Case		(B) Case	
	$P(X \mid -EPS)$	$P(X \mid EPS)$†	$P(X \mid -EPS)$	$P(X \mid EPS)$†
	(N=21)	(N=47)	(N=4)	(N=64)
Project Number (X)				
11	.32	.49	.25	.78**
13	.21	.34	.50	.34
12	.18	.17	0	.44*
20	.05	.21*	.50	.78

†The frequency of project's inclusion in portfolio if a major criterion *was* EPS [$P(X \mid EPS)$] or *was not* EPS [$P(X \mid -EPS)$] .
Note: Results significantly different given EPS as a criterion at the 10 percent (*) and 5 percent (**) levels, one-tailed test.

standard. Calculations based on both the (A) case and the (B) case are shown.

Project 11 has a very favorable EPS impact and Project 13 has a high rate of return and diversification possibilities. As can be seen in Table 7-7, in the (A) case, Project 11 was more frequently selected by both EPS and non-EPS goal groups. Furthermore, there was a more than proportionate inclination on the part of the EPS group to accept this project with high EPS, as expected, although the difference is not statistically significant. Since there was a large overlap between EPS and rate of return groups in the sample, the selection of these projects implies that the EPS and ROR group together selected these projects more than the non-EPS/non-ROR groups did, which is also consistent.

Project 12, which has a 4.8 percent rate of return but good earnings per share impact, shows no difference in frequency of selection in the (A) case. Project 20 is included much more frequently in the EPS-oriented participants' portfolios, reflecting favorable reaction to the high EPS contribution of this low rate of return (4.1 percent) project.

In the (B) case, the small size of the non-EPS groups makes tests of significance difficult. The methodology noted earlier allows such evaluation, however. As far as the acceptance of Project 13 is concerned, there is little difference among groups. Acceptance of the high EPS-impact Project 11 is significantly greater for the EPS group (.78) versus the non-EPS group (.25) on a one-tailed test. Project 12, with a similar high EPS impact also has higher acceptance at the 10 percent level among participants favoring EPS (.44) than among those not particularly concerned with EPS (0). Project 20 continues its general acceptance with the EPS group favoring it more than the non-EPS group.

In terms of the goal fulfillment and consistency for those selecting earnings per share, the key project comparisons indicate consistency. With earnings per share as a goal, there was heavy determination to select projects which met that goal. This fulfillment was achieved even when there were low rates of return on those projects, a selection conflicting with the goal named second most frequently by the same participants.

Goal Achievement—Rate of Return

The exhibits were couched in terms of net present value although results were also presented for the internal rate of return and profitability index. The computer output and the tables accompanying the (B) case were stated exclusively in net present value terms. However, more than *80* percent of the participants referred to *rate of return* rather than net present value when evaluating projects. Such a reaction indicates the difficulty of accepting the meaning of net present value. It is consistent with the expectations of many observers of business, who know the disinclination of a manager to accept a concept foreign to his sensibilities; rate of return *is* a familiar concept based on bond yields or debt rates. Accordingly, one can expect ($H5$) that rate of return will be used as a criterion more than net present value. This behavior can be seen again in the comparisons of the frequencies of inclusion of Projects 5 and 6. These two projects are mutually exclusive projects with *alternate* rankings on rate of return and net present value.

	Rate of Return	Net Present Value	Entry Cost
Project 5	11.9%	$ 80	$1,000
Project 6	11.2%	$109	$2,000

In the (A) case, those having the rate of return as a criterion had a slight preference for either Project 5 or Project 6 than other groups. However all participants consistently favored Project 5 (with a higher rate of return) over Project 6 (with a higher net present value) at the 1 percent level on a one-tailed test based on data in Table 7-8. This result is consistent with their responses being phrased in terms of the rate of return. Because of the differences in entry costs this selection is likewise consistent with their favoring a project with a higher rate of return on a small asset base. In the (B) case, this pattern continues.

In terms of the five projects with a high rate of return on an initial project causing the rejection of much larger projects because of their mutual exclusivity, there is mixed evidence to support an hypothesis ($H2A$) that those participants favoring rate of return were myopic. Projects 8 or 9 were actually selected *more* frequently in (A) by the ROR group and projects 2, 3, or 4 selected *less* often.[d] Their frequency of selection of one or more of the smaller projects (2, 3 and 4)

---

[d]The frequency of Projects 8 or 9 was significantly greater in the ROR portfolio at the 10 percent level in (A) on a two-tailed test, contrary to a hypothesis of myopia.

Table 7-8
Goal Achievement—Rate of Return

Project Number (X)	(A) Case		(B) Case	
	$P(X\mid -ROR)$ (N=25)	$P(X\mid ROR)$† (N=43)	$P(X\mid -ROR)$ (N=35)	$P(X\mid ROR)$† (N=33)
2	.32	.21	.11	.21
3	.12 } .40	.17 } .33	.06 } .14	.12 } .27*
4	.28	.25	.11	.21
8	.09 } .37	.23 } .65*	.27 } .61	.21 } .51
9	.28	.42	.34	.30
5	.52	.62	.62	.70
6	.16	.25	.23	.12
11	.63	.33**	.78	.72
13	.20	.34	.30	.39
12	.31	.09**	.49	.33
20	.23	.12	.88	.63**

†The frequency of a project's inclusion if a major criterion was rate of return $[P(X\mid ROR)]$ or was *not* rate of return $[P(X\mid -ROR)]$.

Note: Results significantly different given ROR as a criterion at the 10 percent (*) and 5 percent (**) level, one- or two-tailed tests as per text.

is higher at the 10 percent level only in the (B) case compared to the nonrate of return group. Furthermore, their selection of the larger projects (with major impact on present value and an overall rate of return greater than any other major project) is likewise *lower* in the (B) case compared to the nonrate of return group. These results are consistent with the myopia of viewing single projects rather than portfolios. Given their standard, this selection would seem subnormal. Thus, the nonrate of return group may have resolved this issue in the (B) case. The other groups apparently did not.

In the (A) case, the projects with high earnings per share impact but low rates of return (notably Projects 11, 12, and 20) tended to be rejected by the rate of return group versus the nonrate of return group. The inclusion of Project 13 with favorable rate of return but rather weak impact on earnings in earlier years was accepted by a greater number of rate of return-oriented subjects, as expected. By the time of the (B) case, the momentum toward earnings per share as a goal by all participants (including those participants also concerned about rate of return) caused the patterns to merge. Nevertheless Project 13 was more heavily accepted by the rate of return group, and Projects 11, 12 and 20 were less frequently accepted by this group than by others. However, all three low return projects had increased their incidence of inclusion in the portfolios of the rate of return group as well, indicating the overlap in earnings per share concern by all participants. Furthermore, there was evidence of a "satisficing" strategy: rate of return might still be important, but it was sacrificed in order to generate the required earnings impact.

Goal Achievement–Sales

Projects 5, 6, 7, 15, 16, 18, and 19 have no impact on sales. They are cost reduction projects which have a favorable performance on criteria such as earnings or rate of return. In the (A) and (B) cases, there seems to be no significant difference in the level of acceptance of these projects between the sales and nonsales groups (Table 7-9). Again, the searching and quasifulfillment of goals described by Cyert and March (1963) is consistent with this outcome, for the sales increase standard is achieved by the inclusion of other projects.

Among the projects which provide substantial sales increase, the picture is different. Projects 11 and 12 have low rates of return (5 and 7 percent respectively), but good sales increases, although Project 12's increase only helps the first year's sales. Project 20 has a low rate of return (4 percent), but high earnings in the third year, and a very high contribution to sales in all years.

Table 7-9
Goal Achievement–Sales Increase

	(A) Case		(B) Case	
	$P(X \mid -S)$	$P(X \mid S)$†	$P(X \mid -S)$	$P(X \mid S)$†
	(N=47)	(N=21)	(N=51)	(N=17)
Project Number (X)				
5	.51	.76	.67	.65
6	.23	.19	.19	.12
7	.15	.10	.24	.18
15	.32	.43	.23	.12
16	.47	.57	.58	.65
18	.83	.76	.84	.88
19	.72	.76	.80	.65
11	.40	.52	.72	.82
12	.19	.14	.37	.53
20	.06	.38**	.70	.94**

†The frequency of a project's inclusion in the portfolio if a major criterion was sales $[P(X \mid S)]$ or was *not* sales $[P(X \mid -S)]$

Note: Results significantly different at the 5 percent (**) and 1 percent level (***), one-tailed test.

In the (A) case, Project 11 is accepted more frequently by sales-oriented groups but Project 12 is accepted slightly less frequently. The differential is significantly different for Project 20 (.06 for the nonsales group versus .38 for the sales group). In the (B) case, these three projects are all included with greater frequency for the sales group vis-à-vis the nonsales group.

These results weakly support the concept of goal fulfillment in the area of sales but much less significantly than in the case of earnings per share or rate of return goal fulfillment. There was no significant avoidance of projects which did not fulfill the goal in any way; projects with zero impact on sales were not significantly different in their inclusion in the portfolios of the sales and nonsales-oriented group. However, in the case of projects with low rates of return but sharp contributions to sales increases, there was greater frequency of inclusion of such projects by the sales group, as hypothesized.

Constraints on Project Selection

Nearly one-third of the participants placed a constraint on cash flow in both the (A) and (B) trials. This constraint was typically expressed as part of their goal statement; e.g., "Maximize earnings per share subject to a minimum of $X in second and third year cash flow," or ". . . with a 90 percent confidence level for a positive cash flow in the third year." Table 7-10 indicates the proportions of executives noting various restrictions on their portfolios in both trials. The rate of return constraint was often expressed as "a return no less than the firm's cost of capital," although this requirement was typically ignored in the case of a particular project when the project was especially desirable on some goal (e.g., earnings per share). The low incidence of earnings per share as a constraint was coincident with the major selection of this factor as a goal; the typical goal was maximum earnings per share, with no regard for any minimum level of earnings.

The emphasis upon cash flow as a constraint is a way for the executive to deal with two major problems: *risk* and *intertemporal portfolio considerations*. A minimum cash flow (perhaps with some confidence level) is an approach to the

Table 7-10
Constraints on Project Selection

	(A) Case (N=68)	(B) Case (N=68)
Rate of Return	.21	.24
Sales	.12	.19
Earnings Per Share	.09	.12
Cash Flow	.32	.32
Other	.09	.13

danger of bankruptcy. In addition, in the view of some executives, a positive cash flow was seen as providing cash for dividends, or as a means to permit additional loans from which to pay dividends. The cash flow constraint was frequently noted as being a safety factor, or a way "to handle the risk of the firm."

Aware that some of the projects might be postponed, the executives noted that there were likely to be other desirable projects which might occur in future years, and they wanted to have some minimum level of cash flow available to invest in these unknown projects and/or to convince the debt or equity markets that funds could be advanced prudently for the firm to accept the new projects. Thus, this emphasis focused upon the firm as a "cash generator" over time, in order to enable the manager to accept projects which might subsequently appear. Since the attributes of these projects were unknown, the executives gambled that reasonable proposals would appear; cash inflow was needed to have available the option of investing in those future proposals.

These uses of a cash flow constraint are both risk evaluations and portfolio considerations over time. One can now turn to the explicit considerations of risk found from examination of the statements of the executives and their choice of projects in portfolio.

**Goal Specification and the
Concern with Risk**

The cross-tabulation in Table 7-11 attempts to determine if there is a positive relationship between time spent on the project evaluation process and the

**Table 7-11
Explicit Concern with Risk**

	(A) Case (N=68)	(B) Case (N=68)	(B) Case Without Computer Usage (N=11)	(B) Case Substantial Computer Usage (N=39)
Concern with Risk in				
Rate of Return	.23	.40**	.36 ⎫	.46 ⎫
Sales	.09	.15	.09 ⎬ .25	.23 ⎬ .44
Earnings Per Share	.24	.59***	.36	.67*
Cash Flow	.13	.26**	.18 ⎭	.38 ⎭

Note: Results significantly different for considerations of risk in the computer and noncomputer group at the 10 percent level (*), 5 percent level (**), or 1 percent level (***), one-tailed test.

selection of a risk profile ($H6$). Given the capability for an evaluation of risk among projects in the (B) case, the number of participants who looked at risk increased dramatically for all criteria. In the (A) case, risk of *projects* could be evaluated, but risk of the portfolio, the only risk of ultimate concern, was not possible.

Another hypothesis is that the computer is associated with greater risk evaluation ($H4A$). To review this question, the sample was segmented into those participants who did not use the computer and those who were relatively heavy computer users. For example, those executives without the computer had only a .36 incidence of concern with risk on earnings per share, while those using the computer had a .67 incidence of concern with this risk. Overall, there was an average incidence of risk evaluation of .25 for those not using the computer versus .44 for those using the computer. The small number of those not using the computer makes the test for significance extremely restrictive in this case. However, there is a probable relationship at the 80 percent level.

Given the ability to evaluate risk, the conclusion is that the computer did help those who employed it. Other studies have previously indicated managers have concern over risk, and this study tends to indicate that *given the opportunity to evaluate risk, the managers considered the information from the computer.*

Risk Evaluation

One may also stratify the group based on content analysis of their standards answered in the questionnaires, where the content evaluation is based on a concern with risk. When participants mentioned "risk" on more than two of the four categories in either (A) or (B), they were considered to be concerned with risk to a high level; the tone of the comments indicated that they were generally risk avoiders. Where risk was not mentioned on any goal in either case, the participant was considered to be unconcerned with risk. This means that the group was divided into three parts. The results shown here are for those at either extreme of the risk evaluation continuum.

Project 13 has some risk-reduction qualities suggested in the verbal description given to the participants. Project 14 is the most significantly diversifying of the projects, although the nature of the diversification is most apparent to those using the computer model. In the (A) case, participants who evidenced risk as a major concern included both projects to a greater degree than other participants (Table 7-12). In the (B) case, again there was favor in the acceptance of Project 13. Those executives who indicated risk was a major concern also had a significantly greater inclusion of Project 14. These results are also consistent with the idea of greater evaluation of risk criteria if the information is available.

Another indicator of the manner in which risk may be evaluated concerns the selection of the confidence intervals for the portfolio results returned to the

Table 7-12
Goal Achievement–Risk Avoidance

	(A) Case		(B) Case	
	$P(X \mid -RA)$	$P(X \mid RA)$†	$P(X \mid -RA)$	$P(X \mid RA)$ †
	(N=35)	(N=15)	(N=17)	(N=29)
Project Number (X)				
13	.28	.40	.29	.38
14	.49	.73*	.12	.52***

†The frequency of project's inclusion in the portfolio of a major concern was risk avoidance [$P(X \mid RA)$] or was not risk avoidance [$P(X \mid -RA)$]

Note: Results significantly different at the 10 percent (*) or 1 percent (***) level, one-tailed test of significance.

users of the SIFT computer program. Participants could request confidence intervals of 25/75 percent, 10/90 percent, 5/95 percent, or 1/99 percent. In reviewing the output of the executives who used this program, the majority clearly preferred the middle ranges of confidence intervals. The lower unit (25/75 percent) was specifically mentioned by some participants as being "too low to be real." The higher unit, in contrast, may seem to have such a remote chance of happening (and, correspondingly, be such a large distance in value from the expected outcome produced at their terminals) as to be meaningless. A significant minority (15 percent) iterated among two or more confidence intervals, selecting certain intervals for some problems and other intervals in alternate situations. For example, many were severely concerned with cash flow figures at the lower limit (a constraint), but were willing to employ a wider confidence range for earnings per share.

Confidence Interval

	25%/75%	10%/90%	5%/95%	1%/99%	Multiple
Incidence	.04	.39	.38	.04	.15

In Chapter 5, we noted that some managers look at risk in a "no worse than we are" option; e.g., "if our firm adds these projects, what is the probability of doing as well as we probably can do without the projects?" Since SIFT permitted the manager to view a portfolio versus the ongoing firm (Project 1) in this light, we can check how many users of the SIFT system requested this output. In fact, 14 percent requested such a comparison. The general orientation seemed to be that the firm was growing, did have the funds, and the task was to find a good package of projects. It seemed to the participants, then, that almost any package would be desirable versus doing nothing *given* that the funds were going to be raised and the attendant dilution in EPS was assured. Hence, the nature of the experiment is biased against a subject's frequent concern with this risk measure.

Leasing versus Purchasing

This topic is one in which the finance profession is divided. Most writers agree that leasing should not increase debt capacity for the ongoing firm; however, many observers feel that the process of adjustment for leasing made by lenders and the investment community may be such as to allow greater debt capacity [see, for example, Vancil and Anthony (1959)]. Most writers agree that leases should be discounted at the after-tax cost of debt [Roenfeldt and Osteryoung (1973)].

Leasing was discussed specifically but briefly in the educational program for the participants. In the table of projects, a truck fleet was proposed which could be owned (Project 15) or leased (Project 16). The rate of return of the leased project was defined using the present value of the lease payments as the investments. If a lessor has relatively low charges to the lessee, then the appeal of this debt-like financing via a lease will provide a high rate of return if the operating cash flow itself provides a return above the implicit lease rate.[e] The overall rate of return of the trucks was 16.7 percent (Project 15). When the low-cost lease financing was included in Project 16, the rate of return was 36.6 percent using this specious calculation. The differential in earnings per share in the first three years was minimal for these two approaches, but the initial cash outlay required was $0 for the leasing proposal versus $400,000 for ownership. Thus, the hypothesis is in evaluating a lease proposal versus a purchase, managers viewing a rate of return, the low cash outlay, or other figures will choose the lease, other things constant ($H7$).

The information was there for the executives to reevaluate the lease proposal. However, no one challenged the calculations in writing or verbally. Large majorities of all groups selected the leasing option, Project 16. This selection was significant at the 1 percent level for all groups except finance. Those participants with backgrounds in finance were somewhat less enthusiastic about leasing. However, this favorable observation is tempered by noting that, even in this

---

[e]For example, if one invests $100 to receive a stream of $20 per year for 10 years, the rate of return is 15 percent. On the other hand, a lease proposal with a lessor's cost of funds at (say) 7 percent requiring lessee payment of $14 for 10 years yields a higher rate of return under this sort of calculation in which the investment and the financing proposals are mistakenly mixed. The financing payments are discounted at the firm's cost of capital (10 percent) to give an "investment" of only $86 instead of $100. Since the inflows are still $20 per year, the "rate of return" is 19 percent. This sort of analysis is *not* unusual when people analyze a lease. It is also frequently seen when people analyze major projects that have initial financing tied to them, as oil tankers.

group, a two-thirds majority of those who select one of these two projects still prefers leasing. No one objected to the budgetary treatment, nor suggested that the lenders imposing nominal debt ceilings ought to consider the lease payments. Hence, these results are consistent with the findings of Vancil and Anthony over a decade ago; many analysts may agree that leases should be considered as part of the debt of the firm, but few seem to emphasize the issue or to challenge many calculations presented about leasing.

	All	Finance	Goal of Rate of Return
	(N=102)	(N=20)	(N=39)
Project 15 (own)	.20	.20	.23
Project 16 (lease)	.59***	.40	.56***

Group versus Individual Decisions

Following the analysis presented above, a new pool of executive participants was available for repeating the entire experiment. For this test, the executives were divided into five to eight person groups. Again, the initial information was presented without the means with which to evaluate portfolio risk considerations. However, the purpose of this test was to compare the decisions of groups versus individuals.

There were 12 groups for which paired comparisons (A evaluation and B evaluation) could be made, and 15 groups for which a portfolio evaluation could be made based on a final, (B) case decision. Hence, because of this small size, statistically significant comparisons of groups stratified by major goals, values, project selection, and attitudes toward risk could not be made. However, the sample of 15 groups could be evaluated against the individual decisions reached in the earlier tests, and those results are as noted.

Project Acceptance

The frequency of projects selected by individuals noted in Table 7-5 was generally repeated in the groups. In a rank correlation test, in which the rank order of frequency of selection of projects was compared for two groups, the correlation coefficient for the individual and group decisions was .86 on the (A) case and .90 on the (B) case, indicating highly similar evaluations and frequency of selection by the participants. Furthermore, there were five projects shown in Table 7-5 with statistically significant changes in their frequency of acceptance on the (A) and (B) tests for individuals. The groups exhibited the same sharp changes in acceptance and in the same directions as the individuals.

Goals

Some observers of business have suggested that the organization wishes to avoid conflict, and hence operates by a quasiresolution of conflict, as noted earlier in this book. If that is true, then we would expect groups of individuals to have more goals as standards for projects. Such a selection is a way of avoiding conflict. When one person feels sales are important, another is concerned with rate of return, a third favors a broadly diversified business active in many fields, and so on, the most obvious compromise is to state all of these views as "group goals." Hence, we hypothesize (*H*8) that groups will have more goals than the individuals.

For the 12 groups on which paired comparisons were possible, the frequency of goal selection in the (*A*) and (*B*) cases paralleled the frequency found with individuals, as shown in Table 7-13. However, there were two major changes. First, the inclusion of the "Other" category in goals is much more frequent in the (*A*) and (*B*) trials for groups versus individuals. Second, the goals per responding unit is increased for groups, averaging 3 goals per unit versus the 2 goals which the individual typically had. Both of these differences are statistically significant.

These two changes suggest one conclusion: *as a means of avoiding conflict, groups apparently tended to list as a goal almost any item any person in the group thought was reasonable whatever the inconsistency with the other goals espoused.* Hence, one person would like to see a sales increase, and that would be listed. Another group member favored steady earnings per share growth, and that would be listed. Thus, as hypothesized, the organizations (i.e., the groups)

Table 7-13
Comparison of Group and Individual Goals

	(A) Case		(B) Case	
	Individuals (N=68)	Groups (N=12)	Individuals (N=68)	Groups (N=12)
Goal				
Rate of Return	.63	.58	.49	.50
Sales	.31	.42	.25	.42
Earnings Per Share	.69	.83	.94	.92
Cash Flow	.34	.42	.21	.50
Other	.12	.75***	.01	.58***
Total Goals	142	36	129	35
Per Unit (N)	2.1	3.0***	1.9	2.9***

Note: Results significantly different at the 1 percent level (***), one-tailed tests.

lived with plural goals, often inconsistent, resolving conflict by saying, "Yes, we think your goal is important," even if that goal was directly offset by other goals. In this situation, however, all the nominal goals could be listed, and the conflict (if it arose) would be apparent only with final portfolio decision. In those decisions, the bargaining which progressed would have been interesting to study, but such observation was not possible.

Lease versus Buy

Although it was not reasonable to separate a "group" with a finance background, it was possible to complete a paired comparison between acceptance of the owned truck fleet (Project 15) versus the leased fleet (Project 16) for the total sample and for the groups selecting rate of return as a goal. The results confirm the emphasis by the participants on the lease option.

| | All | | Goal of Rate of Return | |
| | Individuals | Groups | Individuals | Groups |
	($N = 102$)	($N = 15$)	($N = 39$)	($N = 8$)
Project 15 (own)	.20	.20	.23	.13
Project 16 (lease)	.59	.67	.56	.75

Social Responsibility

The incidence of acceptance of the smokestack precipitator (Project 19) was virtually identical in the (A) case for individuals and for groups, with about 75 percent of each group accepting it. However, in the (B) case, the groups had a lower acceptance (.50 versus .76 for individuals) although the difference is not statistically significant.

*Rate of Return versus Net
Present Value*

Following the pattern of the individuals, the groups favored the higher rate of return project (Project 5) over the project with the higher net present value (Project 6). From a total of 15 groups, 11 chose the higher rate of return project and 1 chose the higher net present value project.

Because of the small sample, no statement of significance could be derived from any cross partition among incidence of the small-dollar-value-high-rate-of-return project versus its opposite, as discussed earlier in the individual case.

Conclusion on the Group Choices

The main confirmation from the group experiments were the similarities in group goal standards, considerations of risk, general project selections, and specific lease, socially responsible, and rate of return project selections. However, of greater interest to the student of organizations is the markedly higher incidence of criteria named as "goals" for the group coupled by the preponderance of vaguely defined "Other" goals. This is consistent with previous studies on group behavior as commented upon earlier in this book.

Conclusions

In reviewing these data, one must be cautious in interpreting any differences. In some cases, the absence of differences may seemingly tend to vitiate previous research of others. Where there are significant differences, one must ask whether there is a spurious relationship or whether there may be meaningful justification for such differences. This study sought to evaluate a variety of items which have been hypothesized to affect management decision making. In adding some evidence to this field, the study is designed *only* as evidential and not judgmental. Data from any single study are far too limited to be definitive. Laboratory experiments suffer from artificiality; field experiments suffer from noncontrollability of exogenous factors and other defects. As George Homans once observed, there are neither good nor bad methods of research, only methods which have certain defects vis-à-vis others with alternative limitations. Within the confines of one laboratory method and these executives, one can find the following conclusions warranted.

First, there was consistent evidence of *multiple goals*, and a tradeoff among those goals. This finding is generally consistent with the findings of Marris (1963) but differs in some respects. Even when the criteria were not simultaneously mentioned as constraints, however, many of the goals seemed to be satisficing goals: a reasonable level of goal fulfillment was achieved and the participant turned to other topics. This behavior is consistent with the idea of a global objective function. It is also consistent with quasifulfillment of goals and quasiresolution of conflict in the terms of Cyert and March (1963). Ignoring risk, the portfolios with maximum expected net present value, rate of return, first year earnings per share, and third year earnings per share were determined. These portfolios were rarely selected by the participants in any subclassification. One can argue, of course, that the participants were unable or uninterested in truly maximizing these criteria. Alternatively, and more reasonably it would seem to this writer, one can say that the ideas of multiple goals, risk, and satisficing mentioned in evaluating their responses to the questionnaires are fully consistent with their behavior. There was a global objective function, perhaps shifting as their knowledge of the problem deepened, and requiring a variety of projects in the portfolios.

Second, a major concern was *risk*. It was considered when the information was available and when the means for evaluation was present. Thus, this study indicates that computers or other devices which allow a manager to evaluate risk are useful. Nothing in the model used by these executives is technologically unfeasible for the corporation; obtaining the data and training the executives to use it are the major restrictions.[f] The data problem is lessened with wider use of computer data bases and retention of historical information from which simulation models can be constructed. Risk was most frequently evaluated on the basis of a 5/95 percent or 10/90 percent confidence interval. General responses to questionnaires indicated a major concern with achieving a no-loss portfolio. Finally, the use of cash flow at some minimum level with a certain lower confidence limit was used by some executives as a way of achieving a suitable risk position vis-à-vis dividends and bankruptcy, as well as assuring available financing for unknown projects which might occur in future years.

Third, *goal fulfillment* seemed generally to be successful, given the idea of multiplicity of goals. Nearly all users of the computer model specifically indicated at the end of their efforts that they believed they achieved their goals. There was consistency of goals from one period to the other. Those participants especially concerned about rate of return or earnings per share had a predictably larger incidence of inclusion of projects excelling on these criteria in their portfolios. Likewise, projects especially weak on these criteria were rejected in higher proportions. In the case of sales-oriented subjects, the rejections of projects not increasing sales was no different from the nonsales-oriented group. However, the sales-oriented group did emphasize those projects significantly boosting sales in all years, indicating a one-sided view of this goal. Such a solution is consistent with satisficing, for it may well be that the sales-increasing projects were selected early to achieve certain growth rates; nonsales-increasing projects were added later for a variety of other reasons.

Fourth, there was *emphasis on earnings per share*, and secondly on rate of return. "Rate of return" was preferred to "net present value." The filtering of this measure induced the selection of a small project with a very high rate of return versus a much larger project with a lower return. The combination of this difficulty with the orientation toward leasing indicates the difficulty of communicating these subtleties to individuals in simple terms. Likewise, the orientation toward reported earnings per share as the main goal reflects a concern with the public marketplace and the evaluative standards of that marketplace.

Fifth, *professional bias* in selection of projects was found in the area of finance. There were no consistent patterns of project selection or standards

---

[f]See especially McSweeney (1972; 1973) for a discussion of how a complex management science model may be successfully employed in a corporation to aid in project selection at the highest levels. Chapter 8 will also review this topic.

Table 7-14
Summary of Eleven Hypotheses and Laboratory Results

*H*1	Finance professionals will favor EPS and rate of return as goals and in risk considerations.	Supported
*H*1*A*	Marketing professionals will favor sales in goal selection and risk considerations.	Rejected
*H*2	Finance professionals will favor rate of return and will be myopic, selecting a small project with a very high rate of return project over a larger block of projects with high returns.	Supported
*H*2*A*	Given rate of return as a goal, participants will favor a small project with a very high rate of return over a larger block of projects with high returns.	Supported
*H*3	United States participants will favor EPS more than others.	Rejected
*H*3*A*	Non-US participants will favor cash flow and sales as goals more than others.	Supported (cash flow)
*H*4	Given a computer, participants will evaluate more goals.	Rejected
*H*4*A*	Given the computer, participants will have more complete evaluation of risk.	Supported
*H*5	Rate of return will be more acceptable than net present value as a standard for project acceptance or rejection.	Supported
*H*6	Given time and information, participants will have more complete evaluation of risk.	Supported
*H*7	Leasing is favored over purchasing given a standard NPV analysis at the cost of capital.	Supported
*H*8	Groups will have more goals than individuals as a form of conflict resolution.	Supported

which differentiated marketing production and general management groups from each other. Such lack of differential may be explained by the "general management" orientation of the program environment and the career designs of nearly all executives sent to it, regardless of the professional backgrounds from which the subjects came.

Sixth, in terms of *regional differences*, there was evidence that Europeans tended to be less concerned with sales and Americans less concerned with cash flow than other groups. The lack of interest of Americans in cash flow had been hypothesized; the lower interest of Europeans in sales was not expected. Whether this outcome reflects cultural bias or educational efforts is uncertain. One hesitates to make judgments about the significantly lower interest in the "socially responsible" project by the Commonwealth participants.

Seventh, when group comparisons are included, the major difference seems to be that *there are more "complex" goals listed, and groups considered more goals in total.* The data supported the hypothesis that groups will state more goals as part of their objectives as a means of avoiding conflict within the organization. Presumably, accepting a goal can be done easily on the assumption that either a conflict over a project will or will not occur. If it does not occur, accepting the goal cost nothing. If a conflict later occurs, a participant may assume that it would occur whether or not the goal were initially listed by the group; the person holding that goal would still retain it whether or not the group initially accepted it.

All of these observations are tempered by the nature of the testing procedure and the data. However, they do tend to provide evidence to accept or reject behavioral characteristics which have been observed or speculated upon by other researchers. Further, the evidence of risk evaluation given the information and means to evaluate it is compelling. Such evidence is important to management scientists, businessmen, and business educators. One must note that this form of risk evaluation was in a businesslike setting. It was *not* restricted to gambling choices or games within the realm of more mathematical models. Those experiments are important; the merit of this approach is to stress the applicability of risk evaluation *in* a business setting *by* executives.

A summary of the particular hypotheses suggested here is presented in Table 7-14. In Chapter 8, we will analyze the issue of implementing a model such as SIFT in a firm.

8

Potential Use of SIFT in the Firm

If you want to understand something, try to change it.

Kurt Lewin

Previous chapters have shown the construction of the SIFT model and given some behavioral results of its usage by executives in a "solo" management game situation. Of greater interest to some readers may be the applicability of the model in a firm. This issue will be approached in this chapter.

The previous descriptions of risk analysis, the models used by some firms, the SIFT model, and the approach to SIFT by the executives in the experiments may have suggested the multiplicity of potential applications of SIFT. Any application is critically linked to the economic and behavioral factors central to the management of the firm which uses the model. Some of these factors were examined in Chapter 3 in which the limitations of risk analysis were investigated.

Among the factors to be considered are:

1. The *nature* of the capital budgeting operation. Is there a capital budgeting problem (i.e., are there opportunities and/or requirements for capital project analysis)? Does the firm need to evaluate projects with sufficient frequency to justify a relatively formalized analysis? Are the projects of sufficient magnitude in cash outlay to make a SIFT sort of analysis "a difference which makes a difference"?

2. The *background* of management. Are they sufficiently oriented toward computers and basic quantitative analysis to accommodate the SIFT system? If not, can a training program be justified in terms of costs and benefits [in turn, related to (1), the nature of the operation]?

3. The *attitude* of the managers in a *stratified* organization. Whatever the nature of the operation and the background of management, an inherent hostility to a system perceived as a threat to existing fiefdom authority must be considered initially. Again, one must include the potential cost of alleviating such attitudinal reaction into the analysis of SIFT's operational impact.

The remainder of this chapter will outline a possible implementation format for SIFT. The discussion will trace the process by which a project might be created and analyzed at successively higher levels of the corporation.

In the use of the interactive model SIFT, a *project sponsor* would first develop forecasts for a proposal. Following his appraisal, a *middle manager*

Portions of this chapter are based on Carter (1971), © The Regents of the University of California.

would evaluate the project individually and in relation to other projects which are proposed in the division. If the project is approved at this level, it goes to *top management* for a two-stage appraisal. Initially, top management might evaluate the project on an individual basis and make a preliminary appraisal. The projects passing this test would next be evaluated using the interactive computer system in conjunction with simulation of the projects in portfolio. At each of the four decision steps, the executive may (1) *accept* the project, (2) *reject* the project, or (3) *reappraise* the project by sending it back to a lower level of management or by reanalyzing it himself.

Project Sponsor's Appraisal

The first step in the decision process involves the development of individual project forecasts by the sponsor. Initially, the sponsor needs to develop expected values for sales, operating costs, etc., for an investment. Proceeding from these figures, a financial advisor can indicate the firm's depreciation and amortization policies for tax purposes and for financial reporting purposes. The actual form for obtaining the projections might be similar to that shown in Table 8-1. This form requires estimates of itemized revenues and expenditures by month (quarter or year) for the life of the project. Once these figures are determined by the sponsor, then a routine "pro forma" computer program could quickly compute many of the results required for analysis, such as period-by-period cash flow, earnings per share contributions, and so forth.

In terms of a system by which one can derive the tradeoffs a person prefers with multiple objective criteria, among many references is the study by Feinberg (1972). He presents the results of a variety of experiments in which individuals were asked to specify multidimensional tradeoffs at various levels, with a range of techniques used to derive their specification. He suggests, based upon the results of Dyer (1972), that an excellent way to derive these tradeoffs is the use of an interactive computer program. Although the SIFT approach shown here does not have the rigor derived in the Feinberg or Dyer proposals, it does parallel their conclusions that the use of an interactive computer system can aid the derivation of the manager's preferences.

Although this analysis can begin at this relatively low level of the firm, the major impact should be at higher levels. If used by the project sponsor at a lower level, the difficulty is that top management insures that the goals and tradeoffs found by that manager and used in the analysis parallel the values of the top management.

The financial planner might then screen the output from the pro forma computer program to decide if the project is worth pursuing. If the advisor and sponsor decide to continue the study, risk analysis simulation should be undertaken.

Table 8-1
Sample Check List for Project Revenue/Expense Estimates

	Monthly Forecasts
	1 2 3 .... N

Development Outlays

Staff
Facilities
Equipment
Inventory
Hiring Costs
Etc.

Sales

Revenues
    Cash Sales
    Credit Sales
Receipts/Time Sales

Operating Costs

Salaries
Shipment Costs
Cost of Goods Sold
Service
Inventory
Etc.

Manufacturing Costs

Inventory Charges
Goods in Process Started
Goods in Process Completed
Capital Equipment Expenditures

Termination Charges

Cancellation Penalties
Salvage Value

Other

General Salaries
Legal Fees
Special Administration Charges
Rent
Etc.

In developing estimates of risk for a project, a general technique involves a question-answer sequence between the sponsor and the planner, as suggested in previous chapters. Estimates of (1) the distribution of the accounting estimates, and (2) the causes of the various outcomes need to be ascertained. This task is difficult and time-consuming. However, the existence of risk estimation in practice in some firms indicates that there are realistic solutions to this problem, as noted in Appendix 2B and Chapters 3 and 4.

The actual computer simulation trials may be executed once the relationships among variables and the estimation of ranges of values are made. These simulations can be run on a batch processing basis. With these results in hand, a recycling stage should be entered. In this stage, the sponsor verifies his projections, carefully checks his assumptions, and makes whatever resimulation trials or sensitivity studies are desired.

In summary, each of the initial proposals can be evaluated in some detail by the sponsor and the firm's financial planner. With the latter's decision on depreciation schedules, inventory allowances, and so forth as input, another computer program can prepare monthly, quarterly, and yearly earnings, sales, and cash flow figures for the proposal. After further detailed analysis and reappraisal by the sponsor, a simulation model of the proposal can be made. This simulation can present sales, earnings, cash flow, and rate of change each period for these variables. After studying these figures, the sponsor can present the project in detail to the division manager for approval or rejection. Table 8-2 indicates the form of report which could be presented to the division manager prior to a decision on a new project.

Table 8-2
Sample Single Project Output

	Period (month, quarter, or year)		
	1	2 ...	N
Sales	X^*	X	X
Profits per share	X	X	X
Cash Flow per share			
Cumulative Sales	·	·	·
Cumulative Profits			
Cumulative Cash Flow			
Change in Profits	·	·	·
Change in Sales			
Change in Cash Flow	·	·	·
Net Terminating Cash Flow	X	X ...	X
Goods in Process	X'	X' ...	X'
Capital Equipment Purchased	X'	X' ...	X'
Net Present Value		X	

X^* is of the form: $\begin{array}{c} Z \\ (A, B, C, D) \end{array}$ and X' of the form: Z

where Z is the median outcome of the factor, and A, B, C, D are the .05, .25, .75, and .95 confidence values for the factor, respectively.

The Cost of Capital

One of the calculations computed by the "accounting pro forma" program is the net present value of the project. This computation requires a knowledge of the firm's "cost of capital." Much controversy centers around the determination of the "cost of capital," as noted in Chapter 2. In the opinion of this writer, the initial analysis of a project (when computing net present value, for instance) should be done on the basis of the firm's average cost of capital for raising additional funds. Unless a sponsor can show conclusively why a project could obtain a differential cost of capital, the average (not marginal) cost of capital for a large block of additional financing should be used. The desirability of this use stems not from economic theory but from management reality. Thus, given a current and projected operating level for the firm, any one project from the universe of possibilities could have several different marginal costs depending on what other projects are accepted first. Hence, this higher or lower cost reflects substantial externalities. As one example, it could be that either no other projects of sufficient size were being contemplated and large fixed financing costs would be required for any single project which is added, or perhaps a given volume of projects would be added requiring new financing anyway (and the incremental variable cost of one more related project is low). Using a marginal cost for each project means that any one project sponsor might argue that a project alone has a lower cost than the marginal cost to the firm from a portfolio of projects. Hence, the initial screening of projects assuming a lower marginal cost of capital might well result in an initial list of projects which substantially changed the firm's cost of capital *in toto*.

The above problem could be reduced in part by central decision making and a two- (or multiple) stage decision process. However, the intracompany "gaming" which is implied by this process would negate any economic purity. Thus, the incentive would be for the sponsor of Project A to induce Projects $B, \ldots, X$ to be selected when the incremental costs to the firm were high. This selection allows a delayed submission of Project A until the costs were low. But, Project $B, \ldots, X$'s sponsors might follow the same strategy, and the result would be that each one waits for the other to move. Hence, organizational and behavioral phenomena which would be induced by using a project's marginal cost of capital could involve a loss of projects proposed, delays in presentations, diseconomic intrafirm rivalry, and other dissonance which offsets any economic benefits from a "true" marginal costing, even if the "true" marginal cost could be determined.

The same conclusion (use of the long-run average cost of funds) holds for justifying use of the same rate over each year as argued in Chapter 2. Otherwise, a project sponsor may wait for a year in which debt was raised, arguing that the project can easily meet the nominal after-tax debt cost (e.g., 4 percent) as a hurdle rate. Then, when equity is issued, top management will find few sponsors willing to subject projects to an all-equity hurdle rate of (say) 10 percent.

This is *not* to say that the firm's historic average cost of capital is the answer. Rather, the argument here is that *each* project should be charged for funds based on the incremental cost of obtaining a large pool of funds. As a simple example, assuming a $100 million asset firm with new capital expenditures which have averaged $10 million per year and $2 million per project, it might be rational to use a hurdle rate based on the firm's average cost of obtaining $20 million over the next two years. Clearly, adjustments can be made at the final decision point for interdependencies in financing among projects. Previously rejected marginal projects might be accepted and other projects might be deferred temporarily. A different cost of capital could be allowed where substantial differences in accessibility of funds exist. Such projects might include a new financing subsidiary, a foreign investment, or a warehouse which could be mortgaged in part. This differential could be allowed *only* in *rare cases* where alternative capital costs are agreed upon initially by the sponsor, the division manager, and the financial manager. However, the point remains that the first analysis for most projects should be based on the firm's average financing cost for a fairly large incremental funding, as noted in Chapter 2.[a]

The Division Manager

The "middle manager" discussion will be brief here because the place of the middle manager in any firm's decision hierarchy is highly flexible. Because of that flexibility, suggestions for behavior vary over a wide range. If (s)he has limited subordinates and limited capital budgeting alternatives, the job involves verification of the sponsor's projections, possible resimulation of the project in conjunction with other projects the division is studying, and a general filtering process before rejecting or forwarding the project. On the other hand, if the corporation is a very large one, there may be several layers of "middle managers" through which a project must pass. Each higher manager has more responsibility, a broader range of competing projects, and an increasing difficulty in juxtaposing the projects in alternative portfolios. Hence, in the latter situation, it seems plausible that the managers at higher levels would find the interactive approach described to be useful. Indeed, the primary basis for arguing that the interactive simulation approach is useful is that it allows a manager who is well supplied with information and criteria to obtain a more complete appraisal of the competing projects than would otherwise be possible. Consequently, in some

---

[a]This argument assumes the incremental cost of capital is based upon a balanced block of financing with debt and equity in proportion to the optimal debt equity ratio. Hence one assumes there is some optimum. For a discussion of this point, see the review of the Modigliani-Miller arguments in Robichek and Myers (1965), for example.

firms the president may consider ten projects totalling $10 million at any one instant. In others, a middle manager might have that many alternatives to consider. As a result of this difference in middle management position from firm to firm, the use of the system depends on the particular manager and the firm. Figure 8-1 shows this decision process and the variability in the middle manager's role.

Top Management

The role of top management in the final decision process will be traced through four stages. First, the individual simulations presented from lower levels will be considered. Second, joint simulations of all proposed projects will be performed, producing a variance/covariance matrix for a number of variables. Third, management will select portfolios of projects based upon (1) the individual simulations, (2) the joint simulations and the variance/covariance matrices, (3) heuristic decision rules, and (4) management's own preferences. Fourth, from the rough sketches of portfolio outcomes produced in the third stage, management may resimulate a subset of portfolios to allow for detailed risk distribution calculations as well as particular financial alterations applicable to individual portfolios.

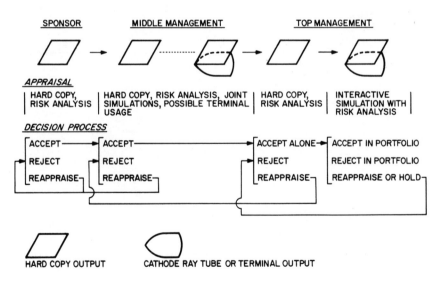

Figure 8-1. Capital Budgeting Analysis by Organizational Levels.

Phase I: Individual Simulations

In discussing the sponsor's project and the middle manager's appraisal, we noted the individual project profiles. From these calculations it is necessary to abstract data for top management. One might argue that a chart such as Table 8-3 should be prepared for each investment alternative. Although monthly figures as shown previously in Table 8-2 would be available, Table 8-3 quickly summarizes the quantitative factors relevant to each decision. In addition, a short summary of other, more qualitative, aspects of the decision should be prepared to aid the top manager in analysis of the projects.

Phase II: Joint Simulation of Projects

Two major batches of data are necessary inputs to this large simulation section. First, the firm needs a simulation model projecting sales, costs, earnings, and the

Table 8-3
Sample Summary of Project Y

Nature of Project: _____

_____

Net Present Value X^*

	Cash Flow	Sales	Profits	Profits per Share
Quarter 1	X	X	X	X
.	.	.	.	.
.	.	.	.	.
.	.	.	.	.
Quarter M	X	X	X	X
Year 1	X	X	X	X
.	.	.	.	.
.	.	.	.	.
.	.	.	.	.
Year N	X	X	X	X

$^*X$ is of the form: $\dfrac{Z}{(A, B, C, D)}$

where Z is the median value of the factor, and A, B, C, D are the .05, .25, .75, and .95 confidence levels for the factor, respectively.

like for the firm with no additional projects. Thus, to detail again the requirements of a simulation model, the firm needs not just raw projections of sales and the like, but also needs a model which shows management's estimate of how sales are related to Gross National Product, industrial production, and so on, for example. Also required are probability estimates for the various contingent relationships. No one can deny that the development of an accurate and complete model is a large task, and the complexity of the model depends on management's time and talent. Then, the second major input to the system is similar simulation models for each of the proposed projects. These models have already been prepared for the preliminary project analysis. Hence, (1) the data are available, and (2) the firm must have demonstrated some skill in model-building. It follows that the development of firm projections, although involving a heavy initial outlay, is neither impossible nor unrealistic given project forecasts.

Once these individual simulation models have been prepared, the firm must perform a simulation of *joint* outcomes. The independent variables which are "forecast" in each simulation trial must be saved in each trial for use in all project calculations which require them. This simulation is required in order to obtain the variance/covariance matrix which is needed for later analysis. As an initial example, consider the criteria of sales, cash flow, earnings per share, and net present value. As in the SIFT examples shown in Chapter 6, one might assume that management requires three-year forecasts for sales and earnings per share. Also, the simulation must include projections for the firm with no change in investments or acquisitions plus several projections for each proposed acquisition to allow for such alternatives as pooling of interest or purchase. Given these values and inputs, a large joint simulation can be run.

From this joint simulation, the firm now has expected values, variances, and covariances of all projects for each of the goals evaluated. The forecast for the firm with no additional acquisitions or investments is considered as Project 1. These data are available for the quantified goals of the firm. It is now possible for the top manager to use SIFT and the interactive simulation system to consider alternative portfolios, just as the executives did in the SIFT model experiments reported in Chapters 6 and 7.

Phase III: Portfolio Selection

In this part of the decision process, the manager is confronted with the following data: expected value, variances, and covariances among projects. These data (for the illustrative SIFT example presented) are computed for sales, earnings per share and cash flow (each year for the initial three years) and the net present value of each project. These results are readily available to the manager at the terminal. Given these data, the manager can quickly compute for any portfolio the expected return and variance along these ten vectors together with a crude estimate of the uncertainty of those outcomes as shown in the SIFT experiments. Phase IV allows a more accurate computation of risk. Since the detailed calculations take management and computer time, it is suggested that this more accurate calculation be used on a smaller subset of portfolios than the number envisioned here. As an example, the manager might have the information presented for Portfolio *A* in Table 8-4. These data are prepared for various portfolios; the manager readily can add or delete projects from a portfolio. These computations can be completed promptly by the manager using the terminal.

Perhaps the most interesting aspect of Phase III is the way in which the manager selects initial portfolios for investigation. There is nothing to prevent the use of a variety of other techniques (such as linear programming, payback period, analysis, and so on) to select starting portfolios. In addition, there are several other heuristic decision rules to aid the manager based on concepts noted in Chapter 2 and Appendix 5B.

The first heuristic is a screening procedure based on yearly data for a particular criterion. From Portfolio *A*, the manager might wish a change which would reduce cash outflow in year 1. Hard copy output from Phase I shows that among the projects in Portfolio *A*, Project 8 has the largest cash outflow in the initial year. (S)he then might have the computer screen the other alternative projects not in Portfolio *A* for those projects which have a lower level of initial cash outflow, using the "Mean Ranking" function in SIFT. From these alternatives, one is able to select projects to substitute in the portfolio and to study changes in return and risk for the various criteria. This screening can be fairly simple or very detailed, depending on management's preference and the

Table 8-4
Sample Output: Interactive Simulation

Portfolio *A*	Projects 1, 8, 19, 25, 26. Period (Quarter or Year)			
	1	2	₀ • •	*N*
Sales (000s)	$10* (2)**	$250 (70)	• • •	$320 (100)
Profits (000s)	−2 (2)	25 (5)	• • •	84 (16)
Profits per share	−.18 (.20)	.25 (.05)	• • •	.84 (.16)
Cash Flow (000s)	−200 (60)	80 (30)	• • •	150 (42)
Net Present Value	$1,675 (423)			

*mean
**standard deviation

number of alternatives. In the complicated case, the threshold levels might be used to eliminate those projects with huge cash outflows, mark with top priority those within the acceptable level, and place the remainder in a reexamination category. For this third category (and the second, if desired) another screening could be made. This screening might rank the remaining projects by declining desirability in terms of net present value. Finally, a third sifting might rank the projects by variance of return and perhaps eliminate those with very large variances. These screenings would take but a few minutes at most for a package of about a hundred projects.

A second heuristic could involve calculation of the "efficient frontier" of Markowitz (1959) described in Appendix 5B using a suitable quadratic programming code. This procedure would use the variance/covariance matrix and expected return from Phase II in conjunction with parametric quadratic programming to generate an "efficient frontier," where the frontier is defined as those portfolios which have *maximum return* for a *given risk* (variance) or, alternatively, *minimum risk* for a *given return*. This procedure sifts through all possible combinations of projects. As shown previously, the "return" to be maximized may be defined to be any variable which one wishes to study, although "return" has traditionally meant the internal rate of return or net present value. For the purposes of this study, it could be third-year cash flow, total sales, second-year earnings per share or whatever. As an example, Portfolio B might be such that management wishes to seek other portfolios with a comparable return in net present value but with a less volatile third-year cash flow. The quadratic programming solution would present output for these criteria. Since the programming algorithm is time-consuming, the following suggestions might be considered. First, this heuristic is recommended for off-line (batch processing) usage either before or during Phase III. Second, some reduction in computation is possible by careful specification; managers may require certain projects to be in a particular portfolio. Other projects could be forced out by redefining some variance or covariance in the matrix to be very large. Third, the heuristic is imprecise in that it computes the risk/return tradeoff for a given criterion; the tradeoff among risk/return optima for different criteria is still the manager's responsibility. As a result, the manager should not expect this calculation to make his decisions, as discussed in Chapter 3.

A third heuristic could start from the assumption of maximizing net present value. By having a screening program ("Mean Rank" order projects in descending net present value) the manager might compose a starting portfolio of the first R projects. If the risk on some criterion is too great (such as too low reported earnings per share in year two), one could search the remaining projects in rank order for more desirable alternatives. One might also search the projects tentatively in the portfolio, eliminating those projects which are contributing to overachievement (or underachievement) on whatever criterion is the focus of attention, subject to constraints on the risk to be tolerated. The point here is the use of a heuristic to compose an initial portfolio.

Several optimization models applied to the sample SIFT data may be reviewed in Appendix 8A. Many heuristics are possible. For example, the Carleton (1970) or Myers and Pogue (1974) mathematical programming formulations would permit any executive to develop a generalized starting point for the portfolio review session. The shadow prices show the cost of various constraints if the executives set minimum sales levels, earnings, or so forth (although none of the models permit restating earnings for additional equity issues during the planning period). From this starting portfolio, the executive might then interact to evaluate the portfolio, observing the more accurate plots of the probable distributions using a version of SIFT which permits access to the original simulation trials. This could be done on a batch process, if desired. Additional heuristics might evolve from the many models proposed in the management science literature, some of which were reviewed earlier in this book. The above suggestions indicate a few of the possibilities.

Phase IV: Detailed Analysis of
Selected Portfolios

Following Phase III, the manager should have a tentative idea of the alternative packages of investments and acquisitions which are to be considered for action. At this point, the executive is forced to consider explicitly the interrelationship between financing and investment decisions. Heuristic decision rules and simulation have aided in finding reasonable alternatives. Now one must evaluate the interrelationship between the particular alternatives and the financing assumptions. Again, the tool for analysis will be heuristics and simulation.[b] Recall that the investments and acquisitions were evaluated on the average cost of substantial additional financing unless there were particular unique factors involved in a project. In Phase IV, it may be useful to reevaluate the portfolios based on the actual amount of funds required by each of the proposed alternatives, the special financing factors which may be caused by the interrelationship among several investments in the portfolios under consideration, and the particular pattern of cash flows under various financing alternatives open to the firm. With these goals in mind, the manager may revert to hard copy, batch process computer simulation using the raw data produced in Phase II above. The manager can estimate interest payments and principal repayments, cash investments, and the like, under the various financing alternatives which are available. Either by resimulation or by adjustment of the figures calculated during the joint

[b]The use of heuristics and simulation to aid in the capital budgeting decision has been discussed in detail by Robichek and Myers (1965), Chapter 8, and Salazar and Sen (1968), among others.

simulation of Phase II, one can prepare pro forma cash flows, balance sheets, and income statements from the data at hand.

In addition, the manager will probably want an accurate distribution of returns along the various criteria, such as the .05-.25-.50-.75-.95 confidence intervals. This distribution can be computed from the previous data, and was not available under Phase III. In Phase III the crude tools used for risk estimates were the variances and covariances. However, two investments with radically different risk characteristics can have the same mean and variance (as shown in Figure 8-2). Hence, once the executive has narrowed the decision to a smaller number of portfolios from the vast number of possibilities, the computer time used to provide detailed risk estimates is justified.

Thus, Phase IV allows the manager (1) to add the special financing considerations and (2) to see the detailed risk estimates of both the projects' and the firm's pro forma statements under various financing strategies. From this analysis, the manager may wish to return to earlier stages. One may seek out new investments (Phase I), simulate different criteria or different models (Phase II), or look at different portfolios (Phase III). The purpose of the interactive system is just such flexibility. The manager is allowed to bring experience to bear on the evaluation at many points where personal talents and values are vital in making the final choice. Figure 8-3 summarizes the top management decision process.

The interactive simulation approach presents the *quantifiable* factors which are deemed important by management. However, the management must also consider many *qualitative* aspects of any decision. Hence, a decision about

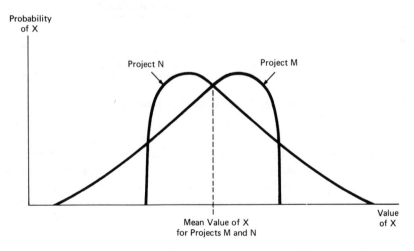

Figure 8-2. Two Projects with Equal Mean and Variance for Criterion "*X*."

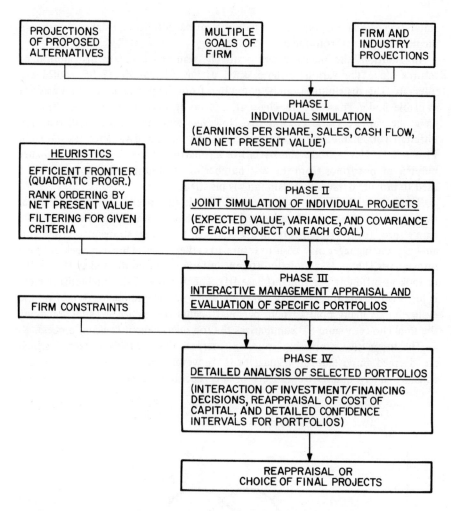

Figure 8-3. Top Management Decision Process.

"risk" can be made both by consideration of variance and confidence intervals and also by consideration of other factors such as technological leadership, general geographic expansion of the firm, and so forth. This mixing of quantitative and qualitative factors would be true for "risk," "uncertainty," "return over time," and other criteria as well. Clearly, a major value of the interactive approach is that it openly allows the manager to blend subjective qualitative judgments with the quantitative process.

SIFT and "Strategic" Capital Budgeting

Sometimes managers may have very ill-defined ideas of the likely profiles of specific projects. Although SIFT has been stressed as applicable to a wide variety of "projects," we may also ask how it could be applied to broad decisions. These decisions might be based on questions such as:

"If we commit $20 million per year for the next five years to plastics, what is our likely earnings base at the end of that period?"

"If we instead spend $10 million on plastics and $10 million on chemicals per year for five years, what will our firm look like?"

"How confident can we be that we will have earnings above last year's after five years if we spend . . . ?"

Clearly, when the estimates for the future are so vague, the impact of SIFT may be minimal. On the other hand, to the extent that historical data are available for these major revenue producing asset groups, then the manager could be more confident of likely returns and variations for the *entire product line* (as a "project") than for a *single project* (i.e., one plant in Oregon). The reason is simply that the product line has certain random elements, but a particular project within that product line has additional variabilities.

Suppose that there are major revenue producing groups, and that management does have a crude idea of the likely earnings contribution per dollar invested in them. Further, from historical data, there may be a good basis for estimating the uncertainties present in those groups, based on Gross National Product, levels of world trade, capital goods spending, etc. Again, because of the fact that the variance of a portfolio is not simply the sum of the individual variances if the projects are not independent, a joint simulation suggested in the SIFT model would be most appropriate.

Before discussing some of the criteria which might be reviewed, consider how projects might be defined. Assume the company is considering major blocks of funds for each of the next five years in three products: plastics, chemicals, and adhesives. The top management may then ask for reasonable guesses as to return and variation for different levels of investment in each asset group. Economies of scale may mean that the return for $20 million may be higher in percentage terms than the return for a $10 million project. Alternatively, saturation of the market or aggressive price cutting by competitors might mean the return would be lower for a larger project. This judgment is reached by management external to SIFT. Management might then prepare an exhibit such as shown in Table 8-5. Some projects are not included at the higher or lower levels of outlays because there are certain minimums or maximums that are practical. There may be

Table 8-5
Projects for Multiple Outlays by Asset Groups

	Outlays per Year			
Asset Group	$10M	$20M	$40M	$60M
Plastics	1	2	3	X
Chemicals	4	5/6	7	8
Adhesives	9	10	X	X
Additional Projects				
	11		$20M plastics, $10M chemicals	
	12		$10M plastics, $10M adhesives	

Budget Constraint: $100M per year or, if projects may be delayed, no more than $400M total in five years.

special economies available if two particular product lines are produced together, and these combinations can be denoted as separate projects as shown. Finally, there may be more than one way of spending a given amount for a product line, reflecting major differences in foreign/domestic outlays, for example. These projects can be labelled jointly in the table, as shown in the category of $20 million in chemicals.

What goals might be used? SIFT and the experiments focused upon earnings per share, cash flow, sales, and rate of return. In addition to levels and growth on these dimensions (which are likely to be very inexact given that this strategic budgeting model emphasizes broad outlays), management might look at:

1. Dollar contribution from domestic and international operations;
2. Product line impact (absolute dollar levels, percentage of industry, or percentage of firm);
3. Asset exposure by major currencies.

Management first decided what product lines and in what dollar amounts the study should be made. After the first pass through the system, they may decide that there is too much exposure in Cruzeiros. The alternative is either to rerun the model, finding a different combination of revenue producing assets, or to reformulate some of the product entries. For example, perhaps the $20 million plastics "project" which depended upon a major selling operation in Latin America could be altered. In either case, management would use the SIFT model on repeated passes to evaluate its decisions on whatever criteria it had selected.

Conclusion

In this chapter, we have explored some of the aspects which surround the application of the SIFT model in the corporation. The variability of the model's use depending on the nature of the firm was emphasized, together with the impact the capital budgeting process offered by SIFT will have on many different levels of management. Finally, a broader suggestion of the possible applicability of SIFT in more policy oriented budgeting decisions was offered.

Chapter 9 will review the book, and will suggest the general impact of models and changing management norms on the corporation of the future.

Appendix 8A:
Mathematical Programming
and the SIFT Portfolio

Information about the mathematical programming approaches to capital budgeting was contained in Appendix 5B. As part of the discussion of the use of SIFT in a corporation, we noted that these mathematical formulations could be employed as a prelude to the interactive analysis of the portfolio. The optimum portfolios under various programming formulations could be taken as a "starting point" for the manager using the SIFT model.

The results of several programming formulations applied to the portfolio of projects in the SIFT test case are presented in Tables 8A-1 through 8A-3.[a] Table 8A-1 shows the result with an objective function of maximizing the net present value of the firm. Table 8A-2 presents the outcome when the objective function is to maximize third year earnings per share, a main goal of many of the executives in the experiments discussed in Chapter 7. Table 8A-3 modifies the earnings per share goal to an objective function which maximizes the sum of three year earnings per share.

Within each of these formulations, the model was funded for two arbitrary budget limitations on the initial outlay, $7,000,000 and $8,000,000. In addition, the application of various constraints on earnings per share resulted in different solutions, and these results are included in the center and right columns of each table.

Finally, each table shows the output from the programming formulation using both a linear programming code and a mixed-integer code. The latter algorithm permits specification of the projects as either being fully in the portfolio (1) or completely out of the portfolio (0). The linear programming code, which is more readily available, does not restrict projects to this 0-1 option, and the result is to include fractional projects in all portfolios. The linear programming solution is shown in parentheses beside the integer solution. The final results of each calculation in terms of the net present value, the yearly earnings per share, and the sum of earnings per share, are noted for the integer solution at the bottom of each table.

A manager could use these alternative formulations to study the cost of pursuing different strategies. One might ask the question, "What sacrifice do we incur in net present value for requiring a 10 percent or 15 percent growth in earnings per share each year?" From Table 8A-1, the answer to this question is:

---

[a]The integer time-sharing algorithm was kindly made available through the efforts of Professor Stephen Bradley and Mr. John Rutherford.

Table 8A-1
Maximum Net Present Value

	1		1A s.t. 10% EPS growth		1B s.t. 15% EPS growth	
Budget: (thousands) Projects	$7000	$8000	$7000	$8000	$7000	$8000
1	1 (1)	1 (1)	1 (1)	1 (1)	1 (1)	1 (1)
2			(.64)	(.63)	1 (.82)	1 (.82)
3						
4	(.5)	(.5)	(.64)	(.63)	1 (.82)	1 (.82)
5	1 (1)	(1)				1
6						
7						
8	(.5)	(.5)	(.36)	(.37)	(.18)	(.18)
9	1 (.5)	1 (.5)	1 (.36)	1 (.37)	(.18)	(.18)
10	(.5)	(.5)				
11			(1)	(1)	1 (1)	1 (1)
12			(1)	(1)	(.38)	(.40)
13	1 (.81)	1 (1)	1 (.65)	1 (1)	1 (1)	1 (1)
14		(.41)		(.23)	1 (.49)	1 (1)
15						
16	1 (1)	1 (1)	1 (1)	1 (1)	1 (1)	1 (1)
17	1 (1)	1 (1)	1 (1)	1 (1)	1 (1)	1 (1)
18	1 (1)	1 (1)	1 (1)	1 (1)	1 (1)	1 (1)
19						
20			1 (.65)	1 (.63)	1 (1)	1 (1)
EPS						
Year 1	$1.58	$1.75	$1.88	$1.95	$4.22	$4.12
Year 2	5.31	5.22	5.25	5.37	5.57	5.78
Year 3	5.70	5.59	6.08	6.19	6.51	6.77
Σ 1-3	12.59	12.56	13.17	13.51	16.30	16.67
NPV (thousands)	$4031	$4041	$3891	$3981	$3289	$3369

Note: 1 denotes project was included. Linear programming solutions are in parentheses, with fractional projects as indicated. 1972 EPS were taken as $3.41.

Table 8A-2
Maximum Third Year Earnings per Share

	2		2A s.t. 10% EPS growth		2B s.t. 15% EPS growth	
Budget: (thousands) Projects	$7000	$8000	$7000	$8000	$7000	$8000
1	1 (1)	1 (1)	1 (1)	1 (1)	1 (1)	1 (1)
2	(.5)	(.5)	1 (.67)	1 (.65)	1 (.83)	1 (.81)
3	(.5)	(.5)	1	1		
4			(.34)	(.31)	1 (.83)	1 (.81)
5	1 (1)	1 (1)	1 (1)	1 (1)	1 (1)	1 (1)
6						
7	1	1 (.79)		1		1
8	1 (.5)	1 (.5)	(.33)	(.35)	(.17)	(.19)
9		(.5)	(.5)	(.33)	(.17)	(.19)
10	1	1	(.33)	(.35)		
11	1 (1)	1 (1)	1 (1)	1 (1)	1 (1)	1 (1)
12	(.59)	1 (1)	1 (1)	1 (1)	(.41)	(.44)
13			1 (.41)	1 (1)	1 (1)	1 (1)
14				(.01)	1 (.34)	1 (.35)
15				1		
16	1 (1)	1 (1)	1 (1)	(1)	1 (1)	1 (1)
17						
18	(1)	(1)	1 (1)	1 (1)	1 (1)	1 (1)
19						
20	1 (1)	1 (1)	1 (1)	1 (1)	1 (1)	1 (1)
EPS						
Year 1	$1.76	$2.66	$4.20	$4.00	$4.17	$3.97
Year 2	6.53	6.93	6.35	6.48	5.77	5.89
Year 3	7.56	7.76	7.10	7.24	6.75	6.88
Σ 1-3	15.85	17.35	17.65	17.22	16.69	16.74
NPV (thousands)	$3304	$3212	$2217	$2111	$3137	$3140

Note: 1 denotes project was included. Linear programming solutions are in parentheses, with fractional projects as indicated. 1972 EPS were taken as $3.41.

Table 8A-3
Maximum Sum of Three-Year Earnings

Budget: (thousands) Projects	3 and 3A (Solutions Are Identical)		3B s.t. 15% EPS growth	
	$7000	$8000	$7000	$8000
1	1 (1)	1 (1)	1 (1)	1 (1)
2	1 (1)	1 (.97)	1 (1)	1 (.86)
3				
4	1 (1)	1 (.95)	1 (1)	1 (.86)
5	1 (1)	1 (1)	1 (1)	1 (1)
6				
7	1			1
8		(.03)		(.14)
9		(.03)		(.14)
10		(.03)		
11	1 (1)	1 (1)	1 (1)	1 (1)
12	1 (1)	1 (1)	(.43)	(.44)
13	1 (1)	1 (1)	1 (1)	1 (1)
14	(.51)	1 (1)	1 (.83)	1 (1)
15				
16	1 (1)	1 (1)	1 (1)	1 (1)
17				
18	1 (1)	1 (1)	1 (1)	1 (1)
19				
20	1 (1)	1 (1)	1 (1)	1 (1)
EPS				
Year 1	$4.80	$5.07	$4.17	$3.97
Year 2	6.17	6.17	5.77	5.89
Year 3	6.93	6.95	6.75	6.88
Σ 1-3	17.90	18.19	16.69	16.74
NPV (thousands)	$2958	$3045	$3137	$3140

Note: 1 denotes project was included. Linear programming solutions are in parenthesis, with fractional projects as indicated. 1972 EPS were taken as $3.41.

Maximize Net Present Value			
	No EPS Constraint	s.t. 10% EPS Growth	s.t. 15% EPS Growth
$7 Million Budget	$4031	$3891	$3289
$8 Million Budget	$4041	$3981	$3369

Another question might be, "What is the difference in net present value if we pursue a policy of maximizing third year earnings per share, or maximizing the sum of three-year earnings?" Drawing upon the bottom lines in all three tables, the answer to this question is:

Net Present Value			
	Max NPV	Max Year 3 EPS	Max Sum of EPS
$7 Million Budget	$4031	$3304	$2958
$8 Million Budget	$4041	$3212	$3045

Suppose the firm decides to accept third year earnings per share or the sum of earnings per share as a goal. Under a budget outlay of $7 million, what is the cost in the achievement of those goals when the requirement for 15 percent earnings per share increase each year is added?

$7 Million Budget		
	No EPS Growth Constraint	s.t. 15% Yearly EPS Growth
Maximum third year EPS	$ 7.56	$ 6.75
Maximum sum of EPS	$17.90	$16.69

As discussed in Appendix 5B, it is also possible to use the dual or shadow values of the constraints in each of the programming formulation results to have an implicit idea of the cost of various projects. Thus, if the budget were to be relaxed, these shadow prices can suggest what projects most usefully would be enlarged. The shadow values also indicate what constraints on earnings per share increases are most costly in terms of the objective function, and so forth. For example, in Table 8A-3, note that the additional constraint in Run 3A requiring 10 percent yearly EPS growth in nonbinding as there is a 10 percent EPS growth in the unconstrained Run 3 solution.

Finally, these tables indicate the costs of using a linear programming solution and then "rounding" the results to include the projects which fit within the budget constraint. As an example, from Table 8A-1, and a budget of $8 million in Run 1B, note that the linear programming solution would imply rounding up Projects 2, 4, and 12 and deleting Projects 8 and 9 in order to be within the budget. This action gives a NPV of $3197 but fails to meet the EPS growth in Year 3. In fact, the integer solution shows that Project 5 should be added and

Projects 8, 9, and 12 dropped completely, which produces a portfolio with a NPV of $3369 which also meets the EPS growth constraints. As an even more dramatic example, note Table 8A-2, Run 2A with an $8 million budget. The integer solution adds Projects 3, 7 and 15 which were never included fractionally in the linear programming solution. Moreover, Project 16, which was included in full in the linear solution (as well as in all the other integer solutions when the goal was to maximize third year earnings per share) is deleted. Similar examples are found in the other tables.

The Impact of Information and the Changing Organization: Implications for SIFT

Pilots will not wear spurs when flying.

U.S. Government flight regulations (1920)

In this chapter, we will discuss the impact of information and organizational change. First, the sharing and manipulation of information is discussed including concerns of the manager and the devices available to assist the analyst. Second, we will discuss the accuracy of information. One of the major causes of "untrue" information in the firm is the nature of the organizational environment. Following a discussion of the current environment, we offer comments on the nature of possible altered organizational environments, linking these changes with the presence of a model such as SIFT. These conclusions will deal with the trend toward more openness in the firm. *Our conclusion will be that if openness does increase, the information systems will be more effective. Similarly, more effective information systems can encourage more openness.* Finally, we will review the book, discussing the implications for management education and management research.

The whole impact of human cognition and information systems is critical in understanding and evaluating the SIFT model. In this book, we have commented on the practical and theoretical issues of capital budgeting. Throughout, however, it should be clear to the reader that the merit of SIFT pivots in large part on the behavioral characteristics of managers, considering the potential influence on those characteristics of information systems, and vice versa.

Information

Of major importance to any specialist who is concerned with the management problem of model implementation is the impact of information. It is quickly apparent that a model's ability to handle arrays of information, the interweaving of multiple dimensions of information in financial theory, and the computer's potential for classification and presentation of informational "bits" has expanded well beyond the realm of current management's usage or awareness of information. Likewise, the importance of "clean" information, of data which are timely and accurate, is noteworthy, for the most elegant theory, the most sophisticated model, and the grandest computer terminal system is severely limited if there is inadequate data input.

191

Many managers cite the importance of a variety of factors as crucial in their decisions, yet the absence of information about those factors coupled with the difficulty of handling what information is available means that the decision is usually based on a fairly simple "model" of the world. This is an ageless problem, not unique to considerations of management decisions. As Kierkegaard wrote, "In relation to their system, most systematizers are like a man who builds an enormous castle and lives in a shack beside it; they do not live in their own enormous buildings. But spiritually that is a decisive objection. Spiritually speaking, a man's thought must be the building in which he lives—otherwise, everything is topsy-turvy." It is in this framework that the output of a model such as SIFT can be seen as allowing the systematizer (manager) to utilize his more elegant models of the world.

From the psychological standpoint, some managers may candidly admit that they would just as soon not know so much about the problem. Whatever the impact on their decision making abilities, they would argue that the additional information breeds more anxiety. A manager with that attitude would do well to ponder this example from psychiatry [Bugenthal (1965)] :

Not infrequently patients will protest my efforts to bring them to greater awareness. They say, in effect, "What's the use of being more aware when I know I'll only be more frightened if I am? What I don't know won't hurt me." Over the years I have used a homely device for dealing with this attitude and have found it a genuine aid. . . .

I say, "I want you to imagine that you are going to cross the street in front of this building at one of two times. You may choose which after I describe the two. In either case you must cross in the middle of the block. Your first choice is to cross it at 5:10 this evening just after the university offices and classes close, the stores begin emptying, and just when traffic is most frantic along the street. The other time will be at 2:00 in the morning when only a very occasional car comes along. However, if you choose 2:00 a.m., you will be thoroughly blindfolded and your ears stopped up completely. Now really imagine yourself crossing at each of those times, and tell me which you choose."

In many, many presentations of the problem, no one has ever seriously chosen the unaware crossing. Moreover, without my elaborating the moral, person after person has recognized the human truth that we are less anxious when we know the hazard than when it is unknown. In this same vein, I have sometimes enjoined a patient, "See your enemy's face. Look at him full on. Don't terrorize yourself with the unknown." In such instances the patient has known clearly that I meant the enemy within, the feared aspect of his own being.

The Sharing of Information

Beyond the development of the basic information, the corporate organization must share central elements of crucial information in order to facilitate decision making. The sharing of key factors of essential information is recognized as a major component of group decision making [see, for example, Varella (1971)]. The process of transmitting information is time-consuming, and thus costly. For example, Mintzberg et al. (1973) found from a study of 25 organizational decisions in nearly as many different firms that a major constraint on the manager was his own cognitive abilities. As a major result, only one fully developed "custom-made" solution to a problem was completed; other alternatives were eliminated at various points in the decision process, partly because of the cost of developing further information and transmitting the expanded data to the participants. In another study of managers, Horne and Lupton (1965) found that the mean proportion of manager's time spent in information transmission was 42 percent, and the next highest proportion of time, 11 percent, was spent in reviewing and coordinating plans. The sharing of information is crucial, for it helps develop a common awareness of a problem: its definition, major aspects, associated criteria for a solution, and probable range of solutions.

One of the fringe benefits of SIFT, common to many data-base manipulative programs, is that information is more easily shared. Once the data are in the system, they can be used by anybody who is permitted to use them, at no extra cost. By having the information present in usable forms, one of the key components of the information transmission chain has been improved. Given the data, the manager must consider how (s)he can use them to solve the problems at hand.

Manipulation of Information

In his paper, "Psychological Study of Human Judgment; Implications for Investment Decision Making," Paul Slovic (1972) considers a variety of psychological elements which affect the investment decision process. He emphasizes, among other points, that

(1) one must seek to aid the "decision maker who is lost in the problem complexity,"
(2) the complexities of data per se, the volume and filtering necessary to derive just those elements important for the decision at hand, cause people not to update their probabilities and expectations as rapidly as they desire, and
(3) there is a substantial problem in integrating the information regarding risk into the decision process itself.

Hence, beyond the powerful computational systems derived for analyzing these problems, there is limited attention given to the cognitive ability of the ultimate user of those systems, the decision maker in business, government, or some other management environment. SIFT is designed to supplement the computationally rigorous mathematical programming "solutions" by reaching the manager with (1) information (s)he can use to gain a feeling for reasonable resolution of the problem complexity and (2) an ability to filter data so as to input probability information into the decision process.

What is emphasized is the importance of providing information in a form which is easy to understand, and which can help him/her reach a conclusion consistent with the acceptance criteria.

Accuracy of Information

Why may the information be "wrong"? Unintentional errors in forecasting or lack of current data are obvious culprits. However, often the problem derives from deliberate bias in the system, from the attempts of managers to protect their position because of the organizational realities. How does one cope with this factor of management?

A metaphorical comparison to the problem of developing a system to provide clean information in the organization is the innovation of color television. Many viewers had black and white systems and were reluctant to convert, for the incremental benefit seemed small and the dollar outlay was high. The economic system then was blocked for many years, and only the patient persistence of a few industry leaders preserved the market (and whether their motivation was a vision of the future or economic self-interest is irrelevant to the case at hand). The economic realities were that consumers would not be swayed to pay the higher outlays for color until there were more color programs, yet advertisers and networks would not broadcast the more expensive color transmissions until there was a market sufficient to offset these costs. Gradually, the tenacity won over the market, and now color transmission and color receiver sales are dominant.

The relationship to the information systems is apparent. One must generate clean data to have an effective information processing/decision system. Likewise, an effective information processing/decision system forces cleaner data.

How does one use data from the system to induce unbiased data in the future? One problem is that it is very difficult to evaluate the deviation of the actual result from the forecasted result. Whereas the sophisticated models nearly always involve a range of possible outcomes, the actual outcome is but one point. There is no repeated trial by which one can judge whether the original estimate of dispersion or risk was accurate. Hence, one cannot determine whether the one-point actual outcome which is far from the "expected value" is the result of accurate modeling and simply the random outcome, or whether the original modelling was wrong. How do we use the control concept in comparing outcome with forecast to monitor the input?

Two alternatives suggested themselves. First, one can verify if the critical input variables which were subject to estimation were consistently biased in one direction. If this is so, it was more than a random error which caused a large number of independent variables consistently above the median value. Similarly, a comparison of outcomes over several projects is a form of control to judge the accuracy of input.

If one finds inaccurate input data, various incentives or threats can be used to improve the data, and their effectiveness depends on the nature of the organizational environment. Ultimately, and most dramatically, one can alter the environment to improve the generation of information.

Organizational Change

The Current Environment

In Chapter 3, we noted that one of the main problems with the implementation of the risk analysis models in several petroleum companies was the impact of certain organizational characteristics. Hence, in appraising SIFT, the impact of the organization on that model and vice versa needs to be considered.

Organization theory is a complex field, and like most social sciences, lacks a large body of relevant empirical work which has consistently replicable results. That is, where hard research data from one environment are cited as having certain implications for management, application of the prescriptions in other environments seem to be ineffective or even counterproductive. In other cases, there is a chicken-egg situation, for the improvement of the environment depends a great deal upon major changes in values, attitudes, and interpersonal skills by all major participants at a common point; evolutionary changes lead to frustration on the part of those with the "new" pattern of behavior and confusion on the part of those operating on the "old" models. [See, e.g., Argyris (1971).]

What are the major elements of the organizational world today? There is no completely accepted version of that environment but perhaps some judgments can be offered on motivation, the organizational environment, and interpersonal relationships.

Motivation is a topic evolving from the ideas of Taylor and Scientific Management through today's social science researcher seeking to understand the values of participants at many different levels in the organization. From the earliest views of economic man, expending effort in order to maximize his income, gradually there appeared more emphasis upon social man, whose work environment became central. This man was willing to trade extra income for a more pleasant/stimulating/satisfactory work environment. How this environment became more satisfactory was a continuing controversy, and initially there was emphasis upon a two factor theory, in which certain characteristics of a job were seen as having positive impact and others having negative impact. The key point of this view was that simply reducing negative factors was not coincident with increasing the positive elements. Then man was viewed as having a hierarchy of needs, in which satisfaction of earlier requirements (safety, food) allowed the person to be concerned with other concepts (self-development, fulfillment, etc.). Hence, money, beyond some level was considered a poor motivator in this schema. However, this hierarchical model has been challenged, and the richer view of this framework is simply that man is complex, in the sense that (s)he naturally may evolve with age from one set of goals and priorities to another set, based on altered values. Hence, the organizational participants's lack of interest in money may not stem so much from a feeling that (s)he has sufficient amounts of it as from a change in the value set so that money is no longer as important as it once was [see Bennis (1966), Hall and Nougaim (1967), Georgopoulos (1957), Schein (1970), Chapter 4, and Turner (1972), Section 15, among other sources]. Whatever the final judgment on the motivation of individuals, one consensus today is that the simple rules for motivating employees are grossly abstracted from the complexities of the situation. At the risk of overstating what current research has shown in this field, it may be fair to say that complex man not only has a personal array of goals, but that the precise ordering of that array may not consciously be present in his/her mind. Furthermore, the ordering of those priorities and the tradeoffs in those goals change with various stages in life. As a result, the motivation of the worker (whether that is a person on the assembly line or in the president's office) is a subtle issue.

Whatever the motivation element, what is the *organizational environment*? Industrialization and mass production have been viewed by many as forcing dependencies and submissiveness to the production line, permitting the worker to use few of his abilities. Thus, the craftsman who completed the product is replaced by the assembly line worker. However, one may also argue that the dependencies, fractionalization of work, and loss of the opportunity to use many of the abilities applies especially to today's well-trained middle and top manager. The necessity of group decision making when there are many professional competences required or great geographical spread of operations require organizational interdependencies that may be most frustrating. Thus, the grey-flannel suit executive of the 1950s, replaced in the popular press by the alienated assembly line worker of the late 1960s may be pushed aside by rising concern for the frustrated middle manager of the 1970s. Many observers have noted the imbalance between the needs of the organization as currently constituted and the needs of the individual. Perhaps the conflict is inevitable to some degree. However, some writers have noted the quiet seething of the frustrated individual, observing that stress is not so much over work as an imbalance between competence, work, and pay. [See Argyris (1957; 1964), Jacques (1970), and Turner (1972), for example.]

Given these aspects of technology and economic growth which have forced the group decision making in the organization, how have individuals in that organization responded? What is the nature of the *interpersonal relationships*, given that such relationships are bound to be of critical importance?

First, the participation of many people in a decision is not a flat answer to "improving" the organizational climate. Neither participation nor job enlargement per se guarantee the quality of effectiveness of a decision, nor the strength of the participants' commitment to the decision [see Argyris (1971), Hulin and Blood (1968)]. Likewise, the general spirit of interpersonal relationships, and the skills of most of us in those relationships, has been commented upon by a variety of organizational interventionists, perhaps most scathingly by Argyris (1971).

It is not stretching the point too much to say that people tend to succeed in the organizational world if they show an acceptable degree of interpersonal incompetence and an equivalent blindness to this incompetence, supported by minimal guilt and a first-rate mind to accomplish the technical tasks or objectives.

As a result, there is a consistent lack of openness, presence of deception, and avoidance of confrontations. Argyris (1969) presents evidence for these conclusions based on the evaluation of 163 meetings in 10 different organizations. He also provides a detailed account of the sharply divergent appraisal of their style of management by top executives at a major corporation when compared with their style as perceived by the subordinates. Jones (1971) confirms this appraisal. If we assume that this environment helps create and foster inaccurate information, then how does one alter it?

Altering the Environment

Earlier, the note was made that participation per se is not a guarantor of an effective organization. Even at the highest levels, more participation may not resolve the imbalance in the executive's mind between the pay, work, and competence. There may be an inevitable imbalance between optimizing life for the executive and optimizing the performance of the corporation. Indeed, one of the major criticisms of the New Left has been the bureaucracy of the corporation and the costs to the individual.[a]

How does one intervene to change the organization? Generally, most practitioners and researchers in this area have emphasized such factors as

---

[a]A cogent description of the New Left's economic values is presented in Lindbeck (1971). As he points out, the more extreme criticism of the corporate bureaucracy's stifling effect often is linked with a damning indictment of the market system. Yet, the most obvious way to reduce the forced interdependence of members within large organizations is to have smaller units, effectively interacting with each other from signals given by prices, i.e., a market system.

openness, a concern with feelings as well as ideas, a desire for valid information, an emphasis on free and informed choice, and a strong commitment to change in the organization. These elements are necessary not just for effective intervention but also in large part to be an effective organization over time. The more effective organization is seen as one which is capable of generating its own change (i.e., intervening in itself).

The literature on effective intervention is vast and the reader is referred to a number of excellent sources.[b] The impact of organizational change and intervention is always difficult to assess although some of the sources cited furnish provocative evidence. Moreover, even if there were no intervention intended, the mere process of studying the organization is likely to change the organization somewhat, an application of the Heisenberg Principle known to scientists.[c]

However, the single key element is probably *choice*. As Bennis (1969) notes:

The basic value underlying all organizational-development theory and practice is that of choice. Through focused attention and through the collection and feedback of relevant data to relevant people, more choices become available and hence better decisions are made. That is essentially what organizational development is: an educational strategy employing the widest possible means of experience-based behavior in order to achieve more and better organizational choices in a highly turbulent world.

Probably, the majority of individuals in this society favor the concept of openness in any organization for reasons of personal fulfillment and general humanistic values. Given such an orientation, from where will the change come?

First, the effectiveness of organizational interventionist as catalyst is considerable. As more managers become aware of the problems generated because of their organizational environment, there probably will be greater interest in using interventionist as a change force.

Second, organizational change may come rapidly (and most economically) from the infusion of junior executives trained in the newer methodology through their normal college or graduate curriculum or (third) from experienced

---

[b]In the field of organizational change, some appropriate readings are:

Argyris (1970), *Intervention Theory and Method.*
Beckhard (1969), *Organization Development: Strategies and Models.*
French and Bell (1973), *Organizational Development.*
Golembiewski (1972), *Renewing Organizations: The Laboratory Approach to Planned Change.*
Lippitt (1960), *The Dynamics of Planned Change.*
Margulies and Raia (1972), editors, *Organizational Development: Values, Process and Technology.*
Schein (1969), *Process Consultation: Its Role in Organization Development.*
Schein and Bennis (1965), *Personal and Organizational Change through Group Methods.*
Zaltman (1972), editor, *Creating Social Change.*
[c]The classic example of the Heisenberg Principle is the man visiting a sick friend, who asks how the friend feels. "Fine" replies the friend, and the effort kills him.

executives "retrained" through management development programs. These people, often a disruptive but effective catalyst, force the firm to change. Exposed to computers, to financial theory, and to models in repeated sequence in their educational experience, they often see the potential and wait for the opportunity to use their new skills. The junior executives are often dismissed as inexperienced or naive, and, as in most social-psychological statements, there is some truth in the charge. However, the pulse is present, and when coupled with the desire of openness as a norm, there is likely to be increasing pressure from these junior people for an "open competition" for corporate funds, for example. In addition, the challenge to educational institutions both for inherent social importance and for their own economic survival is likely to be the continuing training or retraining of managers. Middle managers (which was the group from which the tests of SIFT discussed in this book came) cannot be dismissed as inexperienced or naive, and they clearly have the stature and power to influence the pace of change in the firm.

In addition to interventionists, new managers, and retrained managers, a fourth major force for change should be the researchers in this field of management decision-making. All too often, the descriptive model of what firms are doing becomes the normative model of how firms should behave when viewed through the mindset of a "practical person of affairs." The economic (and moral) dilemma of encouraging the status quo should be considered by those scholars discussing the "real world" while blithely dismissing the ethical implications of that world.

SIFT and the Altered Environment

SIFT and models of its nature can be used for more repressive purposes within the organization. By requiring the data, by helping it on records, and by permitting greater centralization, the model may compound the painful situation faced by many of the executives whose experience was recounted in Chapter 3 as they dealt with risk analysis.

On the other hand, SIFT requires clean, valid information, and the changed environment discussed above would operate to the benefit of SIFT. A more relevant question, however, is whether SIFT would operate to further the interests of participants in that environment.

To the extent that the participants can use more of their skills in evaluating projects, that SIFT stimulates more open discussion of issues, and that valid information is operationally available for the decision making, it would seem that SIFT is not only consistent but a desirable feature of the altered environment suggested earlier. One of its main benefits, in fact, has been the important attribute of enabling an executive to interact directly with the model, and to have groups of executives at various levels in the firm interact with the model. Hence, the model would seem to be a beneficial addition to the changed environment.

Conclusion

In the Introduction, five not-so-mythical Dragons were suggested as contributing to the difficulty in achieving progress in management practice by utilizing new knowledge derived from multiple disciplines. Broadly paraphrased, these Dragons narrowly and overly emphasized the positions of (1) a Financial Theorist, (2) a Management Scientist, (3) a Management Practitioner, (4) a Popular Empiricist, and (5) an Organization Specialist. Characterized and overstated, the concerns of each of these Dragons was noted.

To mix metaphors, these are not straw men. In the first place, they are not easily displaced or mollified. Such failure to vanquish the forces of evil may stem in part from the tenacity of myopia and vested interest which cause each of us to cast away the life buoy of conventional wisdom of our field with great reluctance.

In the second place, and more important, these Dragons are not "bad" in the sense of being completely inaccurate. There is substance to each argument. Among the more tolerant advocates of the positions noted above, each one can acknowledge that the issue is really a degree of emphasis.

The thrust of each chapter and of the book as a whole has been against the Dragons in their most extreme form. Good theory (Dragons 1, 2, and 5) must be concerned with the "real world" (Dragons 3 and 4) at some point in order to be applicable. One intellectual area in isolation is incomplete for assisting the manager, and these theories must thus be integrated, not only with the "real world" but with each other.

Whether we have fully succeeded in integrating the theories with each other and the practitioners' world to a degree sufficient to slay the Dragons is left to the judgment of the reader. It is hoped that at least there is a stimulus to thought generated by this effort.

Review of the Book

To briefly summarize this book, Chapter 2 surveyed capital budgeting techniques as they have evolved, and suggested the impact of risk considerations in the analysis. One popular risk evaluation technique, Risk Analysis Simulation, was reviewed in Chapter 3. The management, technical, and economic problems which have been encountered in the four petroleum firms which attempted to employ it was related. In this chapter and in Chapter 4, we suggested that models can be used effectively and economically, but elements of management sophistication, computer placement and hardware, commitment by participants, and the data availability are central to the success of the project. Given this qualified vote of approval for models in some major financial and strategic planning settings, one could review the mathematics of evaluating risk in a portfolio context in Chapter 5. The emphasis of this chapter was the idea that risk is important, but that portfolio risk, not project risk, was the salient factor. Furthermore, the calculation of the portfolio risk required some judgments beyond the simple adding of project risks. In Chapter 6, we discussed one interactive model SIFT, presenting the rationale for the form in which the model processed data and the need for the interactive component. Chapter 7 contained the evidence from model use by middle management executives. The outcome and the analysis were designed not only to show the form in which they used the model, but also to analyze these managers' values as influenced by their regional and professional background, and their nominal goals for this firm. Finally, in Chapter 8 we discussed the organizational aspects of implementing this model, and suggested the means by which the model could be installed successfully in a firm. In fact, as noted in Chapter 4, the problem of having a "real" management use a sophisticated management tool has been solved in several firms.

The International Utilities example [McSweeney (1972; 1973)] is consistent with many of the proposals presented in the SIFT model. The SIFT model has an explicit incorporation of multiple goals, risk analysis simulation prior to the analysis to permit estimates of final variance of portfolios, and a commitment to use the model at various levels in the organizational hierarchy, and not just at the top level as in the International Utilities example. Furthermore, the SIFT approach suggests a variety of external heuristics which might be used, in addition to the intertemporal mixed integer programming algorithm prepared at International Utilities.

Implications for Management Education

The use of such a model in an educational program has benefits beyond the area of laboratory research. First, it shows managers the potential for analytical techniques used by them to further their own financial goals and values as they reveal them. Second, it indicates the burden of effort on them as executives for searching out information.

Intellectually, the great problem may seem to be the problem of bounded rationality as noted by Herbert Simon. Essentially, masses of data cannot be handled by the limited human mind, yet to deal only with portions of the relevant data may result in suboptimization. This is the classic argument for decentralized management, and also the traditional problem with decentralization. Yet, there are devices available to manage information. Most important, the manipulative ability given to the manager by the program helps in the process of *discovery*.

Most educators agree that self-discovered material is well remembered, probably better remembered than material derived from rote memorization. Much of the emphasis and justification for the case method in business schools is on this same basis: the student who discovers an idea or concept will remember it longer, and the case forces him to seek the problem, i.e., to discover. This discovery has a cost, however, for if mankind were compelled to reinvent the wheel with each generation, civilization would not progress far. Similarly, the most telling criticism of the case method is that the time spent on discovery is not free; if there is a relevant body of knowledge applicable to a field (and calling business a profession requires a presumption of a body of knowledge—or perhaps that is why the term "profession" is applied to business with trepidation by many people), then there is time lost in requiring the student to spend excessive amounts of time in rediscovery.

The analysis derived from a model such as SIFT may permit an executive to define with greater accuracy the feelings (s)he has toward alternative risk positions, fulfillment of various goals at alternative levels, and so forth. As suggested earlier, many mathematical programming formulations can rapidly provide the optimum "answer" given certain formulations of the problem. The difficulty has been in specification of some management tradeoffs and in the restrictions of the optimization technique. A model such as SIFT not only allows the manager to become aware of his/her values, but also encourages the executive to manipulate the data to examine the *cost* of the values, as shown in Appendix 8A.

Finally, an outcome that was quickly apparent in the use of this model with the executives was the "gaming" aspects of the exercise. There were alternative arguments among the group as to what were the "right" goals. Given certain goals, there would then be arguments over who had the "best" portfolio given certain other considerations (risk, etc.). Such discussions not only increased the understanding of the participants of their own values, but also helped them to see in the strongest terms the determination with which others would object to their decisions. This interaction, of course, is one additional benefit of SIFT from the educational standpoint.

Implications for Management Research

Much of this book has dealt with the difficulty of combining financial theory, management science models and devices, and the problems of a general manager. The model has been used to verify the ability of a manager to employ the device to further his goals. The general evidence seemed to be that these managers in this laboratory setting found the model worthwhile. Chapter 8, based upon the survey work reported in Chapter 4, suggested that the model is economically practical. However, there is also a need for increased studies of the work of managers and the information they need, such as the type discussed by Mintzberg (1973) based on his own doctoral research. In addition, the study of how managers trade off goals, what multiple goals they seek, and their general thought processes have only begun to be studied in this book. The nature of the analysis used here is suggestive of the paths which might be most rewarding to future management study. It is also related to the task of management education, for this entire study was carried out within the context of a general financial management course. Clearly, some oversimplifications were made in the model to accommodate this purpose. On the other hand, such a model did have the virtue of suggesting to a number of managers that there were possibilities for using many of the quantitative techniques they had seen, and for working at the computer terminals to resolve some management problems. This discovery, as noted earlier, may be the best form of management education.

No work can possibly present all the relevant materials, arguments and counterarguments, and logical conclusions from so diverse a field as was cited as important in ultimately appraising the complex strategic planning system proposed here. However, one can hope this stimulus to thought can encourage additional models of this genre as well as more detailed tests of this model. To that end, this effort is but the initial step.

Bibliography

Abe, Donald K., "Corporate Model System," in *Corporate Simulation Models*, edited by Albert N. Schrieber, University of Washington Printing Plant, Seattle, Washington, 1970, pp. 71-91.

Alderfer, Clayton T., and Bierman, Harold, Jr., "Choices with Risk: Beyond the Mean and Variance," *Journal of Business*, July 1970, pp. 341-353.

Anderson, C.M., Jr., "The Capital Budgeting Process," *Management Accounting*, September 1972, pp. 30-42.

Applewhite, P.B., *Organizational Behavior*, Prentice-Hall, Englewood Cliffs, New Jersey, 1965.

Archer, Stephen H., and D'Ambrosio, Charles A., *The Theory of Business Finance: A Book of Readings*, The Macmillan Company, New York, 1967.

Argyris, Chris, "The Incompleteness of Social-Psychological Theory: Examples from Small Group, Cognitive Consistency, and Attribution Research," *American Psychologist*, Volume 24, No. 10, October 1969, pp. 893-908.

Argyris, Chris, "The Individual and the Organization: Some Problems of Mutual Adjustment," *Administrative Science Quarterly*, June 1957, pp. 1-24. Reprinted in Turner et al. (1972), pp. 85-96.

Argyris, Chris, *Integrating the Individual and the Organization*, John Wiley and Sons, New York, 1964.

Argyris, Chris, *Intervention Theory and Method*, Addison-Wesley, Reading, Massachusetts, 1970.

Argyris, Chris, *Management and Organizational Development*, McGraw-Hill, New York, 1971.

Argyris, Chris, "On the Effectiveness of Research and Development Organizations," *American Scientist*, Volume 56, November 4, 1969a, pp. 344-355.

Baldwin, W., "The Motives of Managers, Environmental Restraints, and the Theory of Managerial Enterprise," *The Quarterly Journal of Economics*, May 1964, pp. 238-256.

Baumol, W., *Business Behavior, Value, and Growth*, The Macmillan Company, New York, 1954.

Beckhard, Richard, *Organization Development: Strategies and Models*, Addison-Wesley, Reading, Massachusetts, 1969.

Bennis, Warren G., *Changing Organizations*, McGraw-Hill, New York, 1966.

Bennis, Warren G., *Organization Development: Its Nature, Origins, and Prospects*. Addison-Wesley, Reading, Massachusetts, 1969.

Berg, Norman A., *The Allocation of Strategic Funds in a Large, Diversified Industrial Company*, unpublished doctoral dissertation, Graduate School of Business Administration, Harvard University, Boston, Massachusetts, 1963.

Berger, Roger W., "Implementing Decision Analysis on Digital Computers," *Engineering Economist*, Volume 17, No. 4, Summer 1972, pp. 241-248.

206

Bernhard, Richard H., "Mathematical Programming Models for Capital Budgeting—A Survey, Generalization, and Critique," *Journal of Financial and Quantitative Analysis*, June 1969, pp. 111-158.

Bierman, Harold, and Haas, Jerome E., "Capital Budgeting Under Uncertainty: A Reformulation," *Journal of Finance*, March 1973, pp. 119-129.

Bower, Joseph L., *Managing the Resource Allocation Process*, Division of Research, Harvard Business School, Boston, Massachusetts, 1970.

Brown, David E., "Stages in the Cycle of a Corporate Planning Model," in *Corporate Simulation Models*, edited by Albert N. Schrieber, University of Washington Printing Plant, Seattle, Washington, 1970, pp. 92-116.

Brown, David E., "The Xerox Planning Model," American Management Association Seminar on Corporate Financial Models, New York, December 1968.

Bugental, J.F.T., *The Search for Authenticity*. Holt, Rinehart and Winston, Inc., New York, 1965.

Carleton, Willard T., "An Analytical Model for Long-Range Financial Planning," *Journal of Finance*, May 1970, pp. 291-315.

Carleton, Willard T., "Linear Programming and Capital Budgeting Models: A New Interpretation," *The Journal of Finance*, December 1969, pp. 825-833.

Carter, E. Eugene, "The Behavioral Theory of the Firm and Top-Level Corporate Decisions," *Administrative Science Quarterly*, December 1971, pp. 413-428.

Carter, E. Eugene, "An Interactive Simulation Approach to Major Investment and Acquisition Decisions," *California Management Review*, Summer 1971, pp. 18-26.

Carter, E. Eugene, "A Simultaneous Equation Approach to Financial Planning: Comment," *Journal of Finance*, September 1973, pp. 1035-1038.

Carter, E. Eugene, "What are the Risks in Risk Analysis?", *Harvard Business Review*, July-August 1972, pp. 72-82.

Carter, E. Eugene and Cohen, Kalman J., "Portfolio Aspects of Strategic Planning," *Journal of Business Policy*, Summer 1972, pp. 8-30.

Carter, E. Eugene, and Harris, Ralph A., "Time Shared Financial Planning Computer Programs: A Survey and Critique," Working Paper HBS 70-14, Division of Research, Harvard Business School, Boston, Massachusetts, October 1970.

Chamberlain, Neil, *The Firm: Micro-Economic Planning and Action*, McGraw-Hill, New York, 1962.

Chambers, John C.; Mullick, Satinder K.; and Smith, Donald D., "The Use of Simulation Models at Corning Glass Works," in *Corporate Simulation Models*, edited by Albert N. Schrieber, University of Washington Printing Plant, Seattle, Washington, 1970, pp. 138-162.

Cohen, Kalman J., and Cyert, Richard M., "Strategy: Formulation, Implementation, and Monitoring," *Journal of Business*, July 1973, pp. 349-367.

Cohen, Kalman J., and Elton, E., "Inter-Temporal Portfolio Selection Based on Simulation of Joint Returns," *Management Science*, September 1967, pp. B5-B18.

Cohen, Michael D.; March, James G.; and Olsen, Johan P., "A Garbage Can Model of Organizational Choice," *Administrative Science Quarterly*, March 1972, pp. 1-25.

Cole, Edward N., "The Automotive Industry and the Computer Industry: Common Language, Common Future," *Computers and Automation*, October 1973, pp. 8-10.

Conrath, David W., "From Statistical Decision Theory to Practice: Some Problems with the Transition," *Management Science*, April 1973, pp. 873-883.

Cyert, Richard M., and MacCrimmon, Kenneth R., "Organizations," in *Handbook of Social Psychology*, edited by G. Lindzey and E. Aronson, second edition, Addison-Wesley, Reading, Massachusetts, 1967.

Cyert, R.M., and March, J.G., *A Behavioral Theory of the Firm*, Prentice-Hall, Englewood Cliffs, New Jersey, 1963.

Dearborn, D.C., and Simon, H.A., "Selective Perception: A Note on the Departmental Identification of Executives," *Sociometry*, Volume 21, 1958, pp. 140-144.

Dickens, Jared H., "Linear Programming in Corporate Simulation," in *Corporate Simulation Models*, edited by Albert N. Schrieber, University of Washington Printing Plant, Seattle, Washington, 1970, pp. 292-314.

Dickson, Gary W.; Mauriel, John J.; and Anderson, John C., "Computer Assisted Planning Models: A Functional Analysis," in *Corporate Simulation Models*, edited by Albert N. Schrieber, University of Washington Printing Plant, Seattle, Washington, 1970, pp. 43-70.

Doktor, Robert H., and Hamilton, William F., "Cognitive Style and the Acceptance of Management Science Recommendations," *Management Science*, April 1973, pp. 884-894.

Dyer, James S., "Interactive Goal Programming," *Management Science*, Volume 19, No. 1, September 1972, pp. 62-70.

Eiloart, Tim, and Searle, Nigel Dr., "Business Games Off the Shelf," *New Scientist*, September 28, 1972, pp. 575-577, 579.

England, George W., and Lee, Raymond, "Organizational Goals and Expected Behavior Among American, Japanese, and Korean Managers—A Comparative Study," *Academy of Management Journal*, December 1971, pp. 425-438.

Feinberg, A., "Experimental Results with an Interactive Multi-Criterion Optimization Procedure," presented at TIMS XIX International Meeting, Houston, Texas, April 5, 1972.

Finney, D.J. et al., *Tables for Testing Significance in a 2 x 2 Contingency Table*, Cambridge University Press, Cambridge, England, 1963.

Fisher, Irving, *The Rate of Interest*, The Macmillan Company, New York, 1907.

Fisher, R.A., *Statistical Methods for Research Workers*, Oliver and Boyd, Edinburgh, Scotland, 1941.

Fremgen, James M., "Capital Budgeting Practices: A Survey," *Management Accounting*, May 1973, pp. 19-25.

French, Wendell L., and Bell, Cecil H., Jr., *Organizational Development*, Prentice-Hall, Englewood Cliffs, New Jersey, 1973.

Gale, Bradley T., "Market Share and Rate of Return," *Review of Economics and Statistics*, November, 1972, pp. 412-423.

Georgopoulos, Basil S.; Mahoney, Gerald M.; and Jones, Nyle W., Jr., "A Path-Goal Approach to Productivity," *Journal of Applied Psychology*, December 1957, Volume 41, No. 6, pp. 345-353. Reprinted in Turner et al. (1972), pp. 379-386.

Gershefski, George W., "Corporate Models—The State of the Art," *Management Science*, Volume 16, No. 6, February 1970, pp. B303-B312.

Goldie, J. Harry, "Simulation and Irritation," in *Supplement to Corporate Simulation Models*, edited by Albert N. Schrieber, University of Washington Printing Plant, Seattle, 1970.

Golembiewski, Robert T., *Renewing Organizations: The Laboratory Approach to Planned Change*, F.E. Peacock Publishers, Itasca, Illinois, 1972.

Gordon, M.J.; Paradis, G.E.; and Rorke, C.H., "Experimental Evidence on Alternative Portfolio Decision Rules," *American Economic Review*, March 1972.

Grayson, C. Jackson, Jr., "Management Science and Business Practice," *Harvard Business Review*, July-August 1973, pp. 41-48.

Hall, Hall T., and Nougaim, Khalil E., "An Examination of Maslow's Need Hierarchy in an Organizational Setting," *Organizational Behavior and Human Performance*, Volume 3, 1967, pp. 12-35. Reprinted in Turner et al (1972), pp. 366-379.

Hamilton, William F., and Moses, Michael A., *An Analytical System for Corporate Strategic Planning*, Department of Industry, Wharton School of Finance and Commerce, University of Pennsylvania, Philadelphia, Pennsylvania, January 1972.

Hamilton, William F., and Moses, Michael A., *An Optimization Model for Corporate Financial Planning*, Department of Industry, Wharton School of Finance and Commerce, University of Pennsylvania, Philadelphia, Pennsylvania, November 1971.

Hare, Van Court, Jr., *Systems Analysis: A Diagnostic Approach*, Harcourt, Brace and World, New York, 1967.

Hertz, David B., "Risk Analysis in Capital Investment," *Harvard Business Review*, January-February 1964, pp. 95-106.

Hillier, Frederick S., *The Evaluation of Risky Interrelated Investments*, North Holland Publishing Company, Amsterdam, 1969.

Hillier, Frederick S., "The Derivation of Probabilistic Information for the Evaluation of Risky Investments," *Management Science*, April 1963, pp. B443-B457.

Horne, J.H., and Lupton, T., "The Work Activities of 'Middle' Managers," *Journal of Management Studies*, Volume 2, No. 1, February 1965, pp. 14-33.

Hoskold, H.D., *Engineer's Valuing Assistant*, Longmans, Green, and Co., New York, 1905.

Hulin, Charles L., and Blood, Milton R., "Job Enlargement, Individual Differences, and Worker Responses," *Psychological Bulletin*, Volume 69, No. 1, 1968, pp. 41-53. Reprinted in Turner et al. (1972), pp. 210-223.

Ijiri, Yuji, *Management Goals and Accounting for Control*, Rand McNally, Chicago, 1965.

Jacques, Elliott, *Work, Creativity, and Social Justice*, Heinemann, London, and International Universities Press, New York, 1970.

Jean, William H., *The Analytical Theory of Finance*, Holt, Rinehart and Winston, New York, 1970.

Jean, William H., "On Multiple Rates of Return," *Journal of Finance*, March 1968, pp. 187-192.

Jen, Frank, "Investment Decision Under Uncertainty-Theory and Practice: Comment," *Journal of Finance*, May 1969, pp. 343-344.

Jones, Roger, "The Pathology of Success," *Management Decision*, Winter 1971, pp. 224-232.

Katona, G., *Psychological Analysis of Economic Behavior*, McGraw-Hill, New York, 1951.

Keeley, Robert, and Westerfield, Randolph, "A Problem in Probability Distribution Techniques for Capital Budgeting," *Journal of Finance*, June 1972, pp. 703-709.

Kemeny, John G.; Mirkil, Hazelton; Snell, J. Laurie; and Thompson, Gerald W., *Finite Mathematical Structures*, Prentice-Hall, Englewood Cliffs, New Jersey, 1959.

Klammer, Thomas, "Empirical Evidence of the Adoption of Sophisticated Capital Budgeting Techniques," *Journal of Business*, July 1972, pp. 387-397.

Lande, Henry F., "The Use of Computers in Strategic Planning," speech to National Society for Corporate Planning, April 18, 1968.

Lanzillotti, R.F., "Pricing Objectives in Large Companies," *American Economic Review*, December 1958, pp. 921-940.

Ledley, R.S., *Programming and Utilizing Digital Computers*, McGraw-Hill, New York, 1962.

Lindbeck, Oscar, *The Political Economy of the New Left*, Harper and Row, New York, 1971.

Lindzey, G., and Aronson, E., editors, *Handbook of Social Psychology*, second edition, Addison-Wesley Publishing Company, Cambridge, Massachusetts, 1967.

Lipperman, Lawrence L., *Advanced Business Systems*, AMA Research Study No. 86, American Management Association, Inc., New York, 1968.

Lippitt, R.; Watson, J.; and Westley, B., *The Dynamics of Planned Change*, Harcourt, Brace and World, New York, 1960.

Lorie, J., and Savage, L., "Three Problems in Rationing Capital," *Journal of Business*, October 1955, pp. 229-239.

MacCrimmon, Kenneth R., "Elements of Decision Making," paper presented at the Scandinavian-GSIA Joint Faculty Seminar, Aspenasgarden, Lerum, Sweden, August 1969.

Mao, James C.T., "Essentials of Portfolio Diversification Strategy," *Journal of Finance*, December 1970, pp. 1109-1121.

Mao, James C.T., "Survey of Capital Budgeting: Theory and Practice," *Journal of Finance*, Volume 25, No. 2, May 1970, pp. 349-360.

Mao, James C.T., and Helliwell, John F., "Investment Decision Under Uncertainty: Theory and Practice," *Journal of Finance*, May 1969, pp. 323-338. (Also see "Comment" by Frank Jen, pp. 342-344.)

Margulies, Newton, and Raia, Anthony P., editors, *Organizational Development*, McGraw-Hill, New York, 1972.

Markowitz, Harry, *Portfolio Selection: Efficient Diversification of Investments*, Cowles Foundation Monograph No. 16, John Wiley and Sons, New York, 1959.

Marris, Robin, "A Model of the 'Managerial' Enterprise," *Quarterly Journal of Economics*, May 1963, pp. 185-209.

McMillan, Claude, and Gonzalez, Richard F., *Systems Analysis: A Computer Approach to Decision Models*, Richard D. Irwin, Homewood, Illinois, 1965.

McSweeny, James J., "A Strategic Management System—An Operational Concept," Financial Management Association meeting, San Antonio, Texas, October 1972.

McSweeny, James J., "Strategic Management Systems," unpublished paper, International Utilities, January 1973.

Meier, Robert; Newell, William T.; and Pazer, Harold L., *Simulation in Business and Economics*, Prentice-Hall, Englewood Cliffs, New Jersey, 1969.

Meyer, Henry I., and Jennings, Stephen O., "Financial Planning Models at Pennzoil," *Management Review*, December 1972, pp. 22-27.

Miller, Ernest C., *Advanced Techniques for Strategic Planning*, AMA Research Study 104, American Management Association, Inc., New York, 1971.

Miller, George A., "The Magical Number Seven, Plus or Minus Two: Some Limits on Our Capacity for Processing Information," *Psychological Review*, Volume 63, No. 2, 1956, pp. 81-97.

Miller, Irvin M., "Computer Graphics for Decision Making," *Harvard Business Review*, November-December 1969, pp. 121-132.

Mintzberg, Henry, *The Nature of Managerial Work*, Harper and Row, New York, 1973.

Mintzberg, Henry; Ransinghani, Duru; and Theoret, Andre, *The Structure of "Unstructured" Decision Processes*, McGill University, Montreal, 1973.

Mood, Alexander M., and Graybill, Franklin A., *Introduction to the Theory of Statistics*, second edition, McGraw-Hill, New York, 1963.

Morgan, James I.; Lawless, Robert M.; and Yahle, Eugene C., "The Dow Chemical Corporate Financial Planning Model," in *Corporate Simulation Models*, edited by Albert N. Schrieber, University of Washington Printing Plant, Seattle, 1970, pp. 374-395.

Mossin, Jan, *Theory of Financial Markets*, Prentice-Hall, Englewood Cliffs, New Jersey, 1973.

Myers, Stewart C., and Pogue, Gerald A., "A Programming Approach to Corporate Financial Management," *Journal of Finance*, May 1974.

Naslund, B., "A Model of Capital Budgeting Under Risk," *Journal of Business*, April 1966, pp. 257-271.

National Industrial Conference Board, *U.S. Production Abroad and the Balance of Payments*, New York, 1966.

Natrella, Mary Gibbons, *Experimental Statistics*, National Bureau of Standards Handbook Number 91, Department of Commerce, U.S. Government Printing Office, Washington, D.C., 1966.

Naylor, Thomas H., "Corporate Simulation Models and the Economic Theory of the Firm," in *Corporate Simulation Models*, edited by Albert N. Schrieber, University of Washington Printing Plant, Seattle, 1970, pp. 1-25.

Nerlove, Marc, "Factors Affecting Differences Among Rates of Return on Investments in Individual Common Stocks," *Review of Economics and Statistics*, August 1968, pp. 312-331.

Paine, Neil R., "Uncertainty and Capital Budgeting," *The Accounting Review*, April 1964, pp. 330-332.

Pratt, J.W., "Risk Aversion in the Small and the Large," *Econometrica*, January-April 1964, pp. 122-136.

Quirin, G. David, *The Capital Expenditure Decision*, Richard D. Irwin, Homewood, Illinois, 1967.

Raiffa, Howard, *Decision Analysis: Introductory Lectures on Choices Under Uncertainty*, Addison-Wesley, Reading, Massachusetts, 1968.

Raymond, R.C., "Use of the Time-Sharing Computer in Business Planning and Budgeting," *Management Science*, Volume 12, No. 8, April 1966, pp. B363-B381.

Robichek, Alexander A., and Myers, Stewart C., *Optimal Financing Decisions*, Prentice-Hall, Englewood Cliffs, New Jersey, 1965.

Roenfeldt, Rodney L., and Osteryoung, Jerome S., "Analysis of Financial Leases," *Financial Management*, Volume II, No. 1, Spring 1973, pp. 74-87.

Rotch, William, "Return on Investment as a Measure of Performance," unpublished doctoral dissertation, Graduate School of Business Administration, Harvard University, Boston, Massachusetts, 1958.

Rubenstein, Mark E., "A Mean-Variance Synthesis of Corporate Financial Theory," *Journal of Finance*, March 1973, pp. 167-181.

Salazar, Rodolfo C., and Sen, Subrata K., "A Simulation Model of Capital Budgeting Under Uncertainty," *Management Science*, December 1968, pp. B161-B179.

Schein, Edgar H., *Organizational Psychology*, Prentice-Hall, Englewood Cliffs, New Jersey, 1970.

Schein, Edgar, *Process Consultation: Its Role in Organizational Development*, Addison-Wesley, Reading, Massachusetts, 1969.

Schein, Edgar, and Bennis, Warren G., *Personal and Organizational Change Through Group Methods*, John Wiley and Sons, New York, 1965.

Schlarbaum, Gary G., and Racette, George A., "Measuring Risk: Some Theoretical and Empirical Issues," Purdue University, September 1972.

Schrieber, Albert N., editor, *Corporate Simulation Models*, University of Washington Printing Plant, Seattle, 1970.

Seligman, Mrs. Naomi, "Free for All," *Management Sciencee,* Volume 14, No. 41, December 1967, pp. B145-B146.

Shaw, Marvin E., and Penrod, William T., Jr., "Does More Information Available to a Group Always Improve Performance," *Sociometry*, Volume 25, 1962, pp. 377-390.

Shubik, Martin, "Approaches to the Study of Decision-Making Relevant to the Firm," *Journal of Business*, April 1961, 34:101-118.

Simon, Herbert A., *Models of Man*, John Wiley and Sons, New York, 1957.

Simon, H.A., "On the Concept of Organizational Goal," *Administrative Science Quarterly*, June 1964, pp. 1-22.

Slovic, Paul, "Psychological Study of Human Judgment: Implications for Investment Decision Making," *Journal of Finance*, September 1972, pp. 779-799.

Smart, John, *Tables of Interest, Discount, Annuities, etc.*, J. Darby and T. Browne, Bartholomew-Close, London, England, 1726.

Snedecor, George W., and Cochran, William G., *Statistical Methods*, sixth edition, Iowa State University Press, Ames, Iowa, 1967.

Solomon, Ezra, *The Management of Corporate Capital*, The Free Press, New York, 1959.

Spitäller, Erich, "A Survey of Recent Quantitative Studies of Long-Term Capital Movements," *International Monetary Fund Staff Papers*, March, 1971, pp. 189-217.

Terborgh, George, "Some Comments on the Dean-Smith Article on the MAPI Formula," *Journal of Business*, April 1956, pp. 138-140.

Turner, John H.; Filley, Alan C.; and House, Robert J., editors, *Studies in Managerial Processes and Organizational Behavior*, Scott, Foresman, Glenview, Illinois, 1972.

Vancil, Richard F., and Anthony, Robert N., "The Financial Community Looks at Leasing," *Harvard Business Review*, November-December 1959, pp. 2113-140.

VanHorne, James C., "Capital-Budgeting Decisions Involving Combinations of Risky Investments," *Management Science*, October 1966, pp. B84-B92.

VanHorne, James C., *Financial Management and Policy*, Prentice-Hall, Englewood Cliffs, New Jersey, 1974.

Varela, Jacob A., *Psychological Solutions to Social Problems*, Academic Press, New York, 1971.

Vaughn, Donald E.; Norgaard, Richard L.; and Bennet, Hite, *Financial Planning and Management, A Budgetary Approach*, Goodyear Publishing Company, Pacific Palisades, California, 1972.

Wallich, Michael A.; Kogan, Nathan; and Bem, Daryl J., "Group Influence on Individual Risk Taking," *Journal of Abnormal and Social Psychology*, 1962, pp. 75-86.

Ward, John, *Clavis Usurae; or a Key to Interest, Both Simple and Compound*, London, England, 1710.

Webster, William, *Webster's Tables, for Simple Interest Direct, etc.*, third edition, M. Flesher for Nicolas Bourne, London, 1634.

Weingartner, H. Martin, "Capital Budgeting of Interrelated Projects: Survey and Synthesis," *Management Science*, March 1966, pp. A485-A516.

Weingartner, H. Martin, "Criteria for Programming Investment Project Selection," *Journal of Industrial Economics*, Volume 15, No. 1, November 1966, pp. 65-76.

Weingartner, H. Martin, *Mathematical Programming and the Analysis of the Capital Budgeting Problems*, Prentice-Hall, Englewood Cliffs, New Jersey, 1963.

Weingartner, H. Martin, "Some New Views on the Payback Period and Capital Budgeting Decisions," *Management Science*, August 1969, pp. B594-B607.

Weston, J. Fred, "Investment Decisions Using the Capital Asset Pricing Model," *Financial Management*, Volume II, No. 1, Spring 1973, pp. 25-33.

Weston, J. Fred, and Brigham, Eugene F., *Managerial Finance*, Holt, Rinehart and Winston, New York, 1972.

Woods, Donald H., "Decision Making Under Uncertainty in Hierarchical Organizations," unpublished doctoral dissertation, Graduate School of Business Administration, Harvard University, Boston, Massachusetts, 1965.

Zaltman, Gerald; Kotler, Philip; and Kaufman, Ira, *Creating Social Change*, Holt, Rinehart and Winston, New York, 1972.

Indexes

Author and Corporation Index

Subject Index

About the Author

E. Eugene Carter is Visiting Associate Professor of Finance at the Sloan School of Management, Massachusetts Institute of Technology, and an active consultant with several industrial corporations and financial institutions. He has also been an instructor at Carnegie-Mellon University and an assistant professor at the Harvard University Graduate School of Business Administration. Dr. Carter received the B.S. from Northwestern University and the M.S. and the Ph.D. from the Graduate School of Industrial Administration, Carnegie-Mellon University, where he studied under Woodrow Wilson, National Defense Education Act, and Ford Foundation Fellowships. His research interests have involved corporate finance, investment finance, corporate strategy, organizational decision-making, and computer modeling. He has published articles in a variety of academic and management journals.